With a SINGLE BREATH

THE COMPLETE PATH OF MINDFULNESS

MELVIN McLEOD

SHAMBHALA

"This remarkable book is a comprehensive and rich guide to mindfulness for the twenty-first century. It reveals a clear path to living an ethical, caring, and awakened life."

—**Joan Halifax, PhD**, author of *Standing at the Edge*

"In *With a Single Breath*, Melvin McLeod has brought together world-class expertise on mindfulness. This practical guide will be a boon to practitioners at any point on their path."

—**Daniel Goleman, PhD**, author of *Emotional Intelligence*

"This is a masterful guide to a more peaceful, resilient, and contented life. Informed by both modern science and ancient wisdom, Melvin McLeod offers an original, brilliant way of looking at mindfulness as well as deep dives into the insights and experiential practices that can bring us home to our underlying beautiful true nature."

—**Rick Hanson, PhD**, author of *Hardwiring Happiness*

"'Mindfulness is all helpful,' said the Buddha. This skillful book shows how you can directly benefit from the power of mindfulness and use it to bring care to all you touch."

—**Jack Kornfield, PhD**, author of *A Path with Heart*

"In *With a Single Breath*, Melvin McLeod describes mindfulness as a whole life path, one that offers deeper meaning and connection, offering a variety of practices from wisdom teachers around the world."

—**Sharon Salzberg**, author of *Lovingkindness* and *Real Life*

"*With a Single Breath* offers a pioneering vision of mindfulness—not as a technique but as a doorway into who we truly are. Drawing from a treasure trove of teachings and practices, it reveals how presence opens into inner freedom and an intimate belonging with all of life. Here mindfulness becomes a way of living with wisdom, courage, and compassion in our world."

—**Tara Brach, PhD**, author of *Radical Acceptance*

"*With a Single Breath* is both intimate and expansive, weaving together practical guidance with the collective wisdom of many of the world's leading meditation teachers and experts in human well-being. Melvin McLeod serves as a gracious guide, distilling their insights into a clear, heartfelt path that begins with a single breath and unfolds into a deeply compassionate way of living."

—**Dr. Robert Waldinger**, author of *The Good Life and How to Live It*

"Bravo to Melvin McLeod for his foresight and vision to create *With a Single Breath*. He weaves together the disparate strands of the mindfulness movement to create a vision for a comprehensive mindfulness path. He shows us that mindfulness is not merely a stress reduction technique but a new and authentic contemplative tradition much needed in our times."

—**Diana Winston**, director of UCLA Mindful and author of *The Little Book of Being*

"I have been hoping for such a book for years—bringing together mindfulness meditation with relationships, social action, and community. Thank you!"

—**Mirabai Bush**, author of *Almost Home: Dharma, Social Change, and the Power of Love*

"*With a Single Breath* is a beautiful invitation into the transformative power of mindfulness. It presents mindfulness not merely as a helpful meditation technique but as a complete path for living with greater wisdom, compassion, and purpose. What makes this book especially rich is the way it gathers the voices and practices of leading mindfulness teachers, weaving their insights together into a clear and accessible guide for readers. This is an inspiring resource for anyone who wants to cultivate a more peaceful mind, an open heart, and a life that truly benefits others."

—**Kristin Neff, PhD**, author of
Self-Compassion and *Fierce Self-Compassion*

"This wise and eloquent book is medicine for our times. Readers new to mindfulness will find a trustworthy step-by-step guide, and seasoned practitioners will be invigorated by the author's bold, refreshing vision. If you want to reboot your life, or enrich and expand your mindfulness practice, this book is a great place to start."

—**Christopher Germer, PhD**, author of
The Mindful Path to Self-Compassion

"In a time when the word *mindfulness* is everywhere—and often misunderstood—Melvin McLeod brings us back to its true heart. *With a Single Breath* distills this profound practice with rare clarity, wisdom, and authority. A beautiful accomplishment and important contribution to the unfolding of mindfulness in the modern world."

—**Margaret Cullen**, author of *Quiet Strength*

"Melvin McLeod has written the book mindfulness has been waiting for—a brilliantly conceived approach that reveals its depth as a complete path of life while making it genuinely accessible to everyone. Wise, inclusive, written by one of today's most experienced practitioners, this book is a gift."

—**Trudy Goodman, PhD**

Shambhala Publications, Inc.
2129 13th Street
Boulder, Colorado 80302
www.shambhala.com

Cover art: korkeng/Adobe Stock
Cover design: Daniel Urban-Brown
Interior design: Anna Becker

9 8 7 6 5 4 3 2 1

First Edition
Printed in the United States of America

Shambhala Publications makes every effort to print on acid-free, recycled paper. Shambhala Publications is distributed worldwide by Penguin Random House, Inc., and its subsidiaries.

Library of Congress Cataloging-in-Publication Data
Names: McLeod, Melvin author
Title: With a single breath: the complete path of mindfulness / Melvin McLeod. Description: Boulder: Shambhala Publications, 2026. | Includes bibliographical references. |
Identifiers: LCCN 2025052588 | ISBN 9781645474715 trade paperback
Subjects: LCSH: Spiritual life—Buddhism. | Mind and body—Religious aspects—Buddhism. | Breathing exercises.
Classification: LCC BQ4302 .M354 2026
LC record available at https://lccn.loc.gov/2025052588

The authorized representative in the EU for product safety and compliance is eucomply OÜ, Pärnu mnt 139b-14, 11317 Tallinn, Estonia, hello@eucompliancepartner.com.

For Pearl, and all those who are our hope for the future.

CONTENTS

INTRODUCTION

An amazing journey begins with a single breath. With the simple act of paying mindful attention to one breath, you can step onto a complete path that will transform your life.

This book offers a new approach to mindfulness called the Complete Path of Mindfulness. Complete Mindfulness deepens and expands mindfulness practice to benefit every aspect of your life and help you make the world a better place.

You may be someone who is thinking about starting to practice mindfulness because you have heard about the ways it can help you lead a happier, healthier, and more present life. Or you may be among the millions of people today who are already enjoying the benefits of a regular mindfulness practice. You find that it reduces your stress, improves your well-being, increases your resilience, and helps you enjoy life more. These are real and important benefits, but the Complete Path of Mindfulness offers you much more. Whether you've been practicing for years or are just getting started, you can experience mindfulness not merely as a helpful meditation technique but as a complete, transformative path of life.

We all want to lead lives that are happy, meaningful, and beneficial. We want to love and be loved. We want to live in a harmonious and peaceful world. We want these things, and we can have them because of our fundamental human goodness. As human beings, our minds are naturally aware, our hearts are loving, and our world is vivid and beautiful. We don't need to change or improve ourselves. To have the kind of life we want we just need to trust and cultivate who we really are. We have the resources we need and a path that works.

The great strength of mindfulness is that it's about who you already are. Unlike most psychological, spiritual, or meditative systems, mindfulness is not about trying to improve yourself, change yourself, or build some new or better self. Complete Mindfulness works because it draws on your own strengths and positive qualities. It's about cultivating the human nature you already have. It's about training the mind and heart you have now. It's about bringing out the best of who you really are.

In this book you will discover effective meditations that cultivate your natural human wisdom and warmth and benefit your life in many ways. You will learn effective tools to

- develop a calm, stable, and peaceful mind
- increase your happiness and well-being
- learn how to bring the benefits of mindfulness to whatever you are doing
- strengthen your resilience to meet the challenges of life and work with difficult emotions
- experience more confidence and ease the stress of trying to be someone different than who you really are
- develop insight into the true nature of yourself, your mind, and the world you experience
- open your heart and discover your natural compassion toward yourself and others
- live your values and contribute to a more just and harmonious world
- join others in the healing connection of community

This book is your guide to the path of Complete Mindfulness and a resource you can use again and again on your journey. At its heart are practices taught by today's leading mindfulness teachers. Trying these practices as you read this book will immediately help you to start cultivating Complete Mindfulness in your own mind, heart, and life. Then as your mindfulness journey continues you can return to this book again and again to engage with the many mindfulness practices it offers.

But mindfulness is even more than a way for you and me to lead the kind of happy, meaningful, and beneficial life we want. It can help us change the world, maybe even save it.

I believe today's mindfulness movement is of historic importance. It is a new and genuine contemplative tradition that is brilliantly conceived for modern society. It is the answer to an urgent need in the world.

Today the very future of humanity depends on deep transformation—of us as people and of society as a whole. We can't keep going in the direction we are now headed. We need to understand what brings true happiness and what causes suffering, we need more compassion and love, and we need to know in our hearts and bones that we are all connected to each other and to the Earth.

Traditionally people have turned to religion for this kind of deep personal transformation, and over the millennia many have found there what they are seeking. But in the modern world many people are looking for a different approach. They want an effective, evidence-based path to real positive change, one that does not depend on any religious belief system and can be followed by anyone.

As a complete path of life, I believe mindfulness uniquely meets this need. It delivers the positive change we need so badly—the kind of deep transformation traditionally promised by religion—in a framework that is science-based, effective, and can be practiced by everybody. For millions of people today, it is the modern path we need to a better life and world.

This is the promise of Complete Mindfulness. And it all starts with the simple but profound practice of being present. So join me now in taking that one mindful breath together, and let's explore the life-changing journey that is the Complete Path of Mindfulness.

1

THE COMPLETE PATH OF MINDFULNESS

We all want to lead happy, loving, and meaningful lives in a peaceful and caring world. Yet too often we don't get the kind of life and world we long for. We suffer in different ways, in mind and in body, and can't find the happiness we deserve. The world is far from perfect, full of conflict, greed, and selfishness.

Does it have to be this way? The answer is no. The Complete Path of Mindfulness gives us the tools we need to create the kind of life and world we want. Complete Mindfulness addresses four fundamental questions we all ask ourselves that strike at the heart of the human journey. It answers them with a resounding, "Yes, you can have the life you really want!"

Who am I really and what is this world? You and the world you experience are basically good. Your mind is aware, your heart is naturally loving, and this world is beautiful and enjoyable. You don't need to change or improve yourself. You just need to be who you really are, living in the world as it really is.

What is stopping me from leading the kind of life I truly want? There are temporary problems, like confusion, distraction, and misunderstanding, that separate you from your natural happiness and cause suffering for yourself and others. The good news is that when you understand these problems you can do something about them.

Is a life of deep happiness, meaning, and benefit really possible? Because the temporary obstacles can be cleared away and your natural human goodness is always present, the journey is doable, the goal is reachable. By working with your mind, heart, and actions, you can realize your natural goodness and lead the kind of life you want. The awareness and insight that come from mindfulness practice give you the freedom and power to do that.

Is there a proven, effective path to having the kind of life I really want? One effective path to the kind of life and world you want begins with the practice of mindfulness meditation. It gives you powerful tools to become more insightful, loving, ethical, and connected to others. Expanded into a complete path, mindfulness positively impacts all aspects of your life.

I have identified five keys to the Complete Path of Mindfulness. They touch the most important aspects of our lives, and practiced together they deepen and expand the benefits of mindfulness practice. They are the path to a happy, loving, beneficial life and a better world.

The Five Keys of Complete Mindfulness

1. MINDFULNESS MEDITATION: TRAIN YOUR MIND TO TRANSFORM YOUR LIFE

The foundation of the path is our mindfulness meditation practice, through which we train ourselves to rest stably in the present. The rest of the path flows naturally from the calm and awake mind we develop through meditation.

2. INSIGHT: THE POWER OF SEEING REALITY CLEARLY

By applying the natural intelligence of the focused mind we have cultivated in our meditation, we see the true nature of ourselves and our world. We develop insight and eliminate the suffering and stresses caused by misunderstanding the reality of who we are and what we experience.

3. LOVE AND COMPASSION

Mindfulness opens the heart as well as the mind. Connecting us with others, it deepens and expands our natural empathy, kindness, and compassion, which are the secret to a joyful, beneficial life and a more caring world.

4. ETHICS: LIVING YOUR VALUES

Through our insight, we discern what is good and what is harmful so we can live an ethical life that benefits ourselves, others, and society. We live our deepest values in our daily life, our relationships, our livelihood, and our roles as citizens, consumers, and activists.

5. COMMUNITY: THE HEALING POWER OF CONNECTION

It is our heart connection to others that gives our lives happiness, growth, intimacy, and support. From those closest to us to all beings, our connections and communities make life—and the path—complete.

The five keys of Complete Mindfulness are both the path to a good life and essential parts of it. Based on universal human aspirations and capabilities, none of the five keys is dependent on any particular philosophy or belief system. None of them is inherently religious or spiritual. Mindfulness meditators know they are simply training and benefiting from the universal human ability to pay attention. Similarly, our ability to see reality clearly, to be kind and compassionate, to live ethically, and to live in community are simply parts of who we are as human beings.

Of the five keys, the first two—mindfulness meditation and insight—are the foundation of the path. The remaining three keys—compassion, ethics, and community—are how we bring the benefits of our mindfulness practice into our lives and the world.

Of course anything can be done mindfully, so you can define your own path according to your personal interests and needs. But I believe these five keys, which touch essential parts of life, will be a good foundation for your mindfulness journey.

These five keys are not practiced sequentially. They are a holistic path of life in which we practice the five keys simultaneously. Each helps us cultivate the others—our focus unleashes our insight, our insight increases our empathy and compassion, our compassion drives our ethical concern, our sense of community brings us happiness and calms our mind, and so on. They work together in a virtuous cycle in which happiness and benefit grow naturally.

This path improves all aspects of our lives, from our health and well-being to our work and relationships. Yet this complete path of transformation, so broad and so deep, starts with the simple practice of being present and develops naturally from there. So we need to start at the beginning and understand what mindfulness really is.

What Is Mindfulness?

Mindfulness is both a natural power of your mind and a life-changing practice you can do.

The word "mindfulness" is usually used to refer to mindfulness meditation and a whole galaxy of mindful ways to live. In this book when I say "mindfulness" I will usually be referring to mindfulness practice in one of its many forms. But since all mindfulness practices are ultimately ways to cultivate and increase the power of your natural mindfulness, that is where we need to start.

NATURAL MINDFULNESS

Mindfulness is your natural power to focus your attention and use your innate intelligence to understand what you are experiencing. Present in all living beings, it is the foundation of life. It defines what we experience and how we know it.

In its broadest sense, mindfulness can also be called consciousness, awareness, or simply mind itself. In practical terms, it is defined as focus, concentration, or being present with what is happening. At its simplest level, it is simply paying attention.

This is important because what you experience in life depends on what you choose to focus or place your attention on. Things may exist outside your awareness of them—that's for philosophers to decide—but in practical terms your reality consists of what you are mindful or conscious of. So choosing where you place your attention is one of the most important things you can do in life. It defines your reality.

The other important aspect of your natural mindfulness is your mind's power to understand what you are experiencing. Mindfulness is actually a two-part process: focus and insight. First you focus your attention on an experience, whether it is outside of you like a sound or a sight, or inside of you like a thought or feeling. Then, through the natural intelligence of your mind, you have insight into the nature of what you are experiencing.

Using the power of your natural mindfulness is key to success in anything in life. Think of great art, beautiful craftsmanship, productive work, or healthy relationships—they all need the focus, presence, and insight of mindfulness. In sports they call it "being in the zone."

The problem is that generally we are not able to benefit from the full power of our natural mindfulness, and that causes us all kinds of problems. We may not be able to place our attention where we want, or we may focus on the wrong things. Our untamed, unsettled mind cannot focus on things long enough to really understand them, and so we come to all kinds of wrong conclusions about them and make bad choices. We may be lost in thought, fantasy, or distraction and not experience the real life we are living, with all its goodness.

That is why we need to train the mind—so we can benefit from the full power of our natural mindfulness. Reflecting the two aspects of our inherent mindfulness—focus and insight—mindfulness is really a two-part practice.

MINDFULNESS MEDITATION

Calming and stabilizing your mind in the present is the foundation of mindfulness. You do this through mindfulness meditation, which you can do both as a formal practice and spontaneously during the day. The basic practice is amazingly simple (but not easy).

The practice of mindfulness meditation is intentionally resting in nonjudgmental awareness of whatever is happening in the present moment, including your thoughts, feelings, and perceptions of the outside world. You don't judge or analyze yourself or your experience. You simply meet whatever arises with awareness and openness. When your mind inevitably strays into thoughts or distractions, you intentionally return it to the present. You do this gently and without self-criticism.

Through the simple discipline of this practice—returning over and over to what is happening in the moment—you train your mind to rest longer and longer in the present. Because you are not condemning or praising what is happening, but simply seeing things as they are, you experience less stress and struggle. Your mind becomes calmer and more present, but without losing any of its innate intelligence and clarity. Just the opposite.

INSIGHT MEDITATION

Most people associate mindfulness with just the practice of calming and focusing the mind, which of course has many benefits in itself. The insight part is less recognized. Yet developing your insight is the most important part of mindfulness practice. It is the key to mindfulness as a complete path of life.

Our minds have the natural ability to know reality. But how much can we really understand when our minds are always flitting from one thing to the next, never resting anywhere long enough to look clearly and deeply at what we are experiencing?

When our minds are restless, lost in thought, or distracted, our experience of reality—and our understanding of it—is superficial and fleeting. We are prone to all kinds of cognitive errors and misconceptions about ourselves and our world. These cause suffering and distance us from the natural happiness and goodness of life.

Calming and focusing our unstable mind is the essential first step to developing the full power of our insight. Then we give our natural insight a chance to explore in depth the nature of the thoughts and feelings we experience inside and the world we experience outside. We can also cultivate and deepen our insight through specific contemplations and meditation practices such as those we'll learn in this book.

Insight into the true nature of reality sounds pretty abstract, but its benefits are real and significant. So many of our problems stem from misconceptions about the nature of ourselves and the world. We commonly look at things, including ourselves, as solid, fixed, and separate, when in reality they are open, always changing, and interconnected. This mistaken view causes stress and struggle, alienates us from others, and separates us from our true nature and the goodness of this life.

It is insight that makes mindfulness a complete, transformative path. Through insight, we see what is true and what is not. We discern what is helpful in life and what is not, what brings happiness and what does not, what makes the world a better place and what does not. With insight we know how to live ethically, with love, in a good human community. Because so much of our suffering is caused by mistaken views—of reality and of our lives—insight is the key to leading a happy, beneficial, and meaningful life.

How Mindfulness Works

Why does mindfulness make such a difference in your life? How does it work? The power of mindfulness is based on two fundamental truths.

The first is that *mind is an important creator of our happiness and unhappiness, perhaps the most important.* Mind creates many of our problems, and in it are also the seeds of happiness and joy. Therefore, working effectively with your own mind is one of the most beneficial things you can do.

Anxiety, depression, worry, self-criticism, repetitive thought patterns, strong negative emotions, emotional numbness, resentment, despair, irrational thoughts and fears—the list of ways our mind can torture us goes on and on. It might be helpful to take a moment now and catalog the negative thoughts and feelings that make you unhappy and think about how much better life would be without them.

Of course mind doesn't create all our problems. Headed by death and illness, the list of life's real difficulties and conflicts is long. But when problems inevitably arise, it is your mind that determines how you react to them, and that makes all the difference. If you react with despair, hopelessness, and resentment, you will experience an added layer of suffering, making the original difficulty that much worse. If you respond with resilience, equanimity, and self-compassion, you will suffer less and can experience happiness even in the face of life's inevitable difficulties.

If mind is the cause of much unhappiness, it is equally the cause of happiness and joy. You can create your own list of the positive thoughts and feelings that bring you pleasure and joy. Think of the love and happiness you feel when you open your mind to others and this beautiful world. Think of the joy and peace you experience when you feel you are truly you.

The good news is that mindfulness offers you proven, effective ways to work with your mind to help you lead the kind of happy, loving, and meaningful life you want. These reduce your mental suffering, strengthen your ability to face your challenges, and increase your joy in life. They make you better equipped to help others and make the world a better place. The path of working with your mind through mindfulness offers you all this.

The second fundamental truth, and the other big reason mindfulness works so well, is that *it draws on the power and goodness of the present.* Mindfulness is about what really is and who you really are. You don't have to try to manufacture some better self or seek some other reality (even if that were possible). Resting in the present moment you discover that all you need and could ever want is already here in this life, right now. No truth is more powerful and transformative.

Of all the world's systems, mindfulness offers the most effective ways to realize the far-reaching benefits of being in the present. Through your mindfulness practice, you discover the completeness and goodness of yourself and your world. You realize that your mind is naturally open and wise, that your heart is loving and warm, that nature and the universe support you, and that deep down, no matter what happens in life, you are fundamentally okay.

You might find that difficult to believe. After all, how can things be basically good when life is so full of difficulties and pain, when we seem to have so many flaws, and when the world is such a mess? But you don't have to accept the basic goodness of life on faith or try to convince yourself of it. You can always experience the goodness of the present moment, directly and without concepts. You can have a flash of it at any time, especially when your mind is open and there's a break in your usual stream of thoughts. Your mindfulness practice lays the ground for those flashes of goodness to happen and helps you to notice them when they do.

Another way to think of the way mindfulness works is that *practice develops familiarity*. Familiarity is actually one definition of meditation. By returning repeatedly to the present, you become familiar with the true nature of your mind, yourself, and your world. You also become familiar with the ways you stray from the present into mental constructs, and how by doing so you create confusion and suffering. You discover that the real problem is not life itself but your failure to recognize, trust, and experience its goodness.

Complete Mindfulness works because *it is a universal path that cultivates the best of who we are as human beings*. It is a path based on the good qualities and hopes we all share. It brings out our best as human beings and is compatible with any spiritual tradition or philosophy.

Finally, there is a mysterious and magical method that is the key to mindfulness practice and its full, life-transforming power. *The real secret of mindfulness is awareness of your awareness*. When you calm and focus your mind, you expand and deepen your mindfulness of what you are experiencing in each moment, and that has great benefit. But the most helpful thing to be mindful of is awareness itself.

Our awareness is always operating. After all, it is the way we experience things; it is the creator of our reality. But normally all we are mindful of are the objects of our awareness—the things we are *experiencing*—while our awareness operates unconsciously in the background. We are not mindful of our awareness itself, the *experiencer*.

We need to wake up to our own awareness. As the experiencer of life, it is the essence of the mind, of the self, and perhaps of reality altogether. By becoming familiar with your own awareness—and not simply its objects—you fully train your mind and experience the true nature of life.

So when you are doing mindfulness meditation, make it a two-part practice. Cultivate mindfulness of what you are experiencing, certainly, but at the same time, cultivate your mindfulness of the experiencer, awareness itself. This is mindfulness practice at its most complete and transformative.

What Mindfulness Is Not

There are many misconceptions about mindfulness, and these have only increased as it has become more mainstream. Let's correct a few of the myths about what mindfulness is.

MYTH 1: MINDFULNESS IS A GRAB BAG OF SPIRITUAL AND NEW AGE PRACTICES

Everything can be done mindfully. That doesn't mean that everything is mindfulness.

We've all seen that pretty twenty-something woman who symbolizes mindfulness on the cover of mainstream magazines. Sitting cross-legged, wearing a fashionable leotard, she's pretty obviously practicing yoga, not mindfulness.

It is true that yoga can be done mindfully. It's the same for prayer, chanting, gratitude, loving-kindness, and all kinds of other worthwhile practices. They can all be done mindfully, and that only makes them more effective. But they're not mindfulness.

Mindfulness is a specific practice. It includes both formal mindfulness meditation and techniques to help us live mindfully. It's true that there are a lot of different mindfulness practices, and we'll learn many of them in this book, but they all come down to the basic practice of focusing your mind, resting in the present, and cultivating insight into whatever is happening. If you're doing that, it's mindfulness. If you're doing something else, it's not.

MYTH 2: MINDFULNESS IS ABOUT NOT THINKING AND EMPTYING YOUR MIND

Mindfulness is about being aware of whatever is happening in the moment. That includes the thoughts and other things that come up in your mind. It is true that when you get lost in thought the practice is to return to direct experience of the present, and that as your mind quiets you will be less dominated by thoughts. But that doesn't mean you fight against your thoughts or try to stop them. That would be pretty aggressive, and it really doesn't work anyway.

Instead of emptying your mind of thoughts, you just need to understand them. When you see that thoughts are transient and insubstantial, they become less overpowering and controlling. It's true that the clear, direct seeing you cultivate in mindfulness practice is beyond thought and language, but you still need them to function in this world. When you understand their true nature, they are a friend, not a problem, and you don't need to empty your mind of them.

MYTH 3: MINDFULNESS IS NOT CONCERNED ABOUT ETHICS, COMPASSION, OR JUSTICE

Many people associate mindfulness with just the calming and focusing part of the practice, and that leads to this common critique of mindfulness. Because people define mindfulness as purely concentration, they criticize it for not including ethics, compassion, or concern for injustice in the world. They talk about companies that offer their workers mindfulness training purely to improve their productivity. In a famous example, they point to the sniper who focuses his mind in order to kill more effectively.

The criticism that mindfulness is amoral, or at least morally neutral, might be true if it were only concentration, which is merely a technique. But when we add in the second part of the practice—the development of insight—we find that mindfulness makes us not just ethical and compassionate, but profoundly and skillfully so.

If we look at mindfulness as a complete path, we see that it empowers us—impels us, actually—to live compassionately and ethically. Our insight makes us aware of exactly what causes happiness and unhappiness for ourselves and others. Our loving heart inspires us to act ethically, do all we can to reduce the suffering in this world, and tirelessly fight against violence and injustice.

If someone thinks that if people practice mindfulness they will turn off their moral compass, they are in for a surprise. A company may want its employees to practice mindfulness so they take fewer sick days. But since insight always arises as people calm and focus their minds, what they're really going to get are more aware workers who demand better lives and more responsible ethical standards. Anyone who wants to exploit or manipulate people should never encourage them to practice mindfulness. It doesn't put people to sleep. It wakes them up.

MYTH 4: MINDFULNESS IS BUDDHISM

Some people suspect that mindfulness is really covert Buddhism. That's not an unreasonable thing to think. It is true that the Buddha was the world's first great mindfulness teacher and Buddhists are the world's specialists in mindfulness. They have been practicing, studying, and teaching it for 2,600 years. Other contemplative traditions teach about developing a calm, focused, and peaceful mind, but none offers the detailed and effective mindfulness teachings of Buddhism, which have been tested and proven over thousands of years of dedicated practice.

So it is only natural that many of the founders of the modern mindfulness movement draw heavily on Buddhist teachings about mindfulness, or, like me, are Buddhists themselves. But that doesn't make mindfulness Buddhist. How could cultivating a fundamental power of the human mind be the property of any one religion?

Mindfulness meditators know that what they are doing is not Buddhism. They are simply training—and benefiting from—the universal human ability to pay attention. The other keys to the Complete Path of Mindfulness—seeing reality clearly, living ethically, being kind and compassionate, and living in community—are not specially Buddhist either. They are essential parts of who we are as human beings and how we live. They are beyond distinctions of Buddhist or non-Buddhist, of spiritual or secular, altogether. They are simply human.

To those who say that mindfulness is really a covert way to present Buddhism in a secular guise, I would argue the opposite is true—that Buddhism was a covert way to present the mindfulness path in a religious guise. After all, how else could the Buddha have presented his teachings in ancient India except as a religion? After he awakened to his true nature—our true nature—he taught his followers a path of mindfulness, wisdom, and ethical living so they could make the same discoveries he did and ease their suffering.

The Buddha didn't tell us to just accept the truth of what he taught. He said we had to test it ourselves through reason and personal experience. He didn't teach about a god, taking things on faith, sacred texts, or divine revelations. He taught a universal human path without the usual hallmarks of religion, a secular path if you will. But in ancient India the only context in which the Buddha could present his teachings was in the form of a religion, and so he did.

So if there's a bait-and-switch involved, it's not mindfulness presenting religion in a secular guise; it was the Buddha presenting a secular path in a religious guise. If that's the case, today's mainstream mindfulness may be closer to the Buddha's original teachings than the world religion that later developed in his name.

2

MINDFULNESS IN THE MODERN WORLD

An American PhD chemist and a Vietnamese Zen Buddhist monk—two very different people who are largely responsible for the fact that millions of people are practicing mindfulness today.

As different as they are, Jon Kabat-Zinn and Thich Nhat Hanh shared a deep desire to help others and a strategic sense of how to present an ancient contemplative practice to the modern world. Because of their pioneering work, a little-known meditation practice previously associated mostly with Eastern religion today benefits people around the world.

Thich Nhat Hanh: The Father of Mindfulness

Thich Nhat Hanh (1926–2022) was one of the great spiritual teachers of our time. Among his many accomplishments, he made two historic contributions to the modern world.

During his courageous campaign for peace in his native South Vietnam, Thich Nhat Hanh founded the Engaged Buddhism movement. Since the basic vow of Buddhists is to reduce suffering and create happiness wherever they can, he taught that Buddhists need to engage with the world's political, economic, social, and environmental problems and the untold suffering they cause. Today, inspired by Thich Nhat Hanh's teachings and personal example, Engaged Buddhists around the world work for peace, justice, and the environment as an integral part of their spiritual practice.

At the same time that Thich Nhat Hanh profoundly impacted what it means to be a Buddhist, he also offered a gift to the wider world—mindfulness. Through his teachings in classic books like *The Miracle of Mindfulness* and *Being Peace*, he became known as "the father of mindfulness."

Thich Nhat Hanh broke mindfulness out of its Buddhist confines and taught it as a universal human capacity, something all of us can enjoy and benefit from. This revolutionary view of mindfulness, shared by Thich Nhat Hanh and Jon Kabat-Zinn, made the practice available to millions of people and is the basic premise of the mindfulness movement we know today.

Thich Nhat Hanh was not just a great spiritual teacher; he was a master of language. He offered us deep wisdom, cultivated by decades of meditation practice, in the kind of direct, poetic, and relatable language that makes profound truths shine. Take his famous statement that "your true home is in the here and now."[1] So simple, so poetic, so intuitively true. In this one sentence is the essence of mindfulness expressed in a way that touches and inspires us.

For Thich Nhat Hanh, mindfulness is above all a path to happiness, and his teachings were filled with joy and the wonder of life. Take this passage about the miracles we discover when we live with awareness. It evokes the completeness, magic, and goodness we experience when we open ourselves up to the perception of life in this world.

"Around us, life bursts forth with miracles—a glass of water, a ray of sunshine, a leaf, a caterpillar, a flower, laughter, raindrops," he wrote. "If you live in awareness, it is easy to see miracles everywhere. Each human being is a multiplicity of miracles. Eyes that see thousands of colors, shapes, and forms; ears that hear a bee flying or a thunderclap; a brain that ponders a speck of dust as easily as the entire cosmos; a heart that beats in rhythm with the heartbeat of all beings."[2]

While others may describe concentration as just a helpful discipline with various benefits, for Thich Nhat Hanh it is the way to live with joy and happiness in every moment. "Joy and happiness are born of concentration," he wrote. "When you are having a cup of tea, the value of that experience depends on your concentration. You have to drink the tea with 100 percent of your being. The true pleasure is experienced in the concentration. When you walk and you are 100 percent concentrated, the joy you get from the steps you are taking is much greater than the joy you would get without concentration. You have to invest 100 percent of your body and mind in the act of walking. Then you will experience that being alive and taking steps on this planet are miraculous things."[3]

Thich Nhat Hanh often quoted the teaching that "the real miracle is not walking on fire. The real miracle is walking on this Earth."[4] He taught that we don't have to search for joy and happiness in another world. Heaven is right here under our feet. "The Kingdom of God is not a mere notion," he said. "It is a reality that can be touched in everyday life. The Kingdom of God is now or never, and we all have the ability to touch it—not only with our minds, but with our feet. The energy of mindfulness helps you in this. With one mindful step, you touch the Kingdom of God."[5]

Thich Nhat Hanh's emphasis on the living quality of the universe led him to redefine an important philosophical concept, interdependence. This is the insight we develop through our mindfulness practice that nothing exists separately or independently. Everything, including us, is the product of many causes and conditions. We are all interdependent.

But for Thich Nhat Hanh, the concept of interdependence was too abstract. He coined the term "interbeing" to capture the living quality of the relationship among all things. My being, your being, every being—we are all in the mutual relationship known as interbeing. We "inter-are." It is the way we live, the way we exist—because of each other.

He described interbeing this way: "Everything is interacting with every other thing. Interbeing means you don't have a separate existence, you inter-are with everything else."[6] This is not merely a philosophical concept. It is insight into the living nature of interbeing that heals the feelings of isolation and separateness that haunt and depress us. It creates the deep and intimate connection with all things that brings real love and peace into our lives.

But Thich Nhat Hanh was no Pollyanna. He was penetrating in his diagnosis of what holds us back from living the full, happy life that mindfulness offers us. We cannot rest in the present, he says, because we are always running, always struggling. He called this obsessive restlessness our "habit energy of struggling." "The problem is that not many of us know how to allow our body and mind to rest," he pointed out. "We are always struggling; struggling has become a kind of habit. We cannot resist being active, struggling all the time. We struggle even during our sleep. It is very important to realize that we have the habit energy of struggling. . . . Every one of us has the tendency to run," he continued. "We have run all of our lives, and we continue to run into the future where we think that some happiness may be waiting."[7]

Does that sound a bit like you? I know it sounds like me. The good news is that we can calm our relentless habit energy with mindfulness and gentleness. "When we learn to recognize our habit of running," he taught, "we can use mindful breathing, and simply smile at this habit and say, 'Hello, my dear old friend, I know you are there.' And then you are free from this habit energy. You don't have to fight it. There is no fighting in this practice. There is only recognition and awareness of what is going on."[8]

Thich Nhat Hanh taught mindfulness as a complete path that benefits all the important aspects of life. Based on the foundational practices of concentration and insight, he taught us how mindfulness can help us heal our traumas, develop compassion for ourselves and others, live ethically, preserve the Earth, and create a peaceful, just, and sustainable society. As the father of mindfulness, he gave us a guide to its future as a complete path of life.

TEACHING

Healing the Wounded Child Within Us[9]

Thich Nhat Hanh

In each of us there is a young, suffering child. We have all had times of difficulty as children and many of us have experienced trauma. To protect and defend ourselves against future suffering, we often try to forget those painful times. Every time we're in touch with the experience of suffering, we believe we can't bear it and we stuff our feelings and memories deep down in our unconscious mind. It may be that we haven't dared to face this child for many decades.

But just because we may have ignored the child doesn't mean she or he isn't there. The wounded child is always there, trying to get our attention. The child says, "I'm here. I'm here. You can't avoid me. You can't run away from me." We want to end our suffering by sending the child to a deep place inside and staying as far away as possible. But running away doesn't end our suffering, it only prolongs it.

The wounded child asks for care and love, but we do the opposite. We run away because we're afraid of suffering. The block of pain and sorrow in us feels overwhelming. Even if we have time, we don't come home to ourselves. We try to keep ourselves constantly entertained—watching television or movies, socializing, or using alcohol or drugs—because we don't want to experience that suffering all over again.

The wounded child is there, and we don't even know she is there. The wounded child in us is a reality, but we can't see her. That inability to see is a kind of ignorance. This child has been severely wounded. She or he really needs us to return. Instead we turn away.

Ignorance is in each cell of our body and our consciousness. It's like a drop of ink diffused in a glass of water. That ignorance stops us from seeing reality; it pushes us to do foolish things that make us suffer even more and wound again the already wounded child in us.

The wounded child is also in each cell of our body. There is no cell of our body that does not have that wounded child in it. We don't have to look far into the past for that child. We only have to look deeply and we can be in touch with him. The suffering of that wounded child is lying inside us right now in the present moment.

But just as the suffering is present in every cell of our body, so are the seeds of awakened understanding and happiness. We just have to use them. We have a lamp inside us, the lamp of mindfulness, which we can light anytime. The oil of that lamp is our breathing, our steps, and our peaceful smile. We have to light up that lamp of mindfulness so the light will shine out and the darkness will dissipate and cease. Our practice is to light up the lamp.

When we become aware that we've forgotten the wounded child in ourselves, we feel great compassion for that child and we begin to generate the energy of mindfulness. The practices of mindful walking, mindful sitting, and mindful breathing are our foundation. With our mindful breath and mindful steps we can produce the energy of mindfulness and return to the awakened wisdom lying in each cell of our body. That energy will embrace us and heal us, and will heal the wounded child in us.

We suffer because we have not been touched by compassion and understanding. If we generate the energy of mindfulness, understanding, and compassion for our wounded child, we will suffer much less. When we generate mindfulness, compassion and understanding become possible and we can allow people to love us. Before, we may have been suspicious of everything and everyone. Compassion helps us relate to others and restore communication. The people around us, our family and friends, may also have a severely wounded child inside. If we've managed to help ourselves, we can also help them. When we've healed ourselves, our relationships with others become much easier. There's more peace and more love in us.

Go back and take care of yourself. Your body needs you, your feelings need you, your perceptions need you. The wounded child in you needs you. Your suffering needs you to acknowledge it. Go home and be there for all these things. Practice mindful walking and mindful breathing. Do everything in mindfulness so you can really be there, so you can love.

Jon Kabat-Zinn: Mainstreaming Mindfulness

As the creator of the Mindfulness-Based Stress Reduction (MBSR) program, Jon Kabat-Zinn founded what became known as the secular mindfulness movement. Evidence-based, results-oriented, and free of religious belief, it made mindfulness mainstream.

Both Thich Nhat Hanh and Jon Kabat-Zinn described mindfulness as a universal practice that anyone can benefit from. But while Thich Nhat Hanh taught mindfulness in a (lightly held) spiritual context, Jon Kabat-Zinn presented it in a secular, science-based, practical framework that appeals to the modern mind. After all, who doesn't know the value of paying attention? Who wouldn't like to improve their power to focus and be in the present? No leap of faith is required. The benefits are clear. It's common sense.

Based on results you can experience, mainstream or secular mindfulness has made the practice widely accepted in a culture that is often skeptical of religion and claims about things like meditation. With the backing of science and the evidence of their own experience, millions of people now practice mindfulness and enjoy its benefits. This is the historic accomplishment of Jon Kabat-Zinn and the new meditative tradition he founded.

It turns out we know exactly when mainstream mindfulness was born. It happened one afternoon in 1965 when a young grad student in molecular biology at MIT attended a talk by the American Zen teacher Philip Kapleau. Kapleau had been a court reporter at the Nuremberg war-crimes trials, and he described the trauma he experienced listening to stories of Nazi atrocities. His search for answers to the horrors led him to a Zen monastery in Japan, where after six months of intense meditation he had recuperated from the trauma of the trials, and from the ulcers he suffered.

The epiphany Jon Kabat-Zinn had listening to Kapleau's talk that day would change his life and the practice of mindfulness in the modern world. "I realized Kapleau's experience had a universal resonance," says Kabat-Zinn. "I was not interested in religion, but I thought, 'Here's something of intrinsic value that we can offer to people.' I had the thought that the world would be a better place if everybody meditated. There'd probably be a lot less violence and aggression. There'd be greater well-being, greater happiness, a greater sense of agency.

"I thought, 'This is what I've been looking for my whole life.' I started meditating that night and never stopped."[10]

For the next ten years Kabat-Zinn practiced yoga and studied Buddhist meditation. But all this time the idea percolated in his mind that the mindfulness he was now practicing in a Buddhist context could benefit many more people—if only it could be presented in a new way. In 1979 he saw the opportunity to offer mindfulness practice within the medical system. Now he had a strategy to make his vision a reality.

At that point, Kabat-Zinn was doing research in cell biology at the University of Massachusetts Medical School. Talking with doctors in the Pain Clinic and other departments, he realized that they were helping only a small percentage of patients find relief from the pain and stress they suffered. "A lightbulb went off in my head," he remembers. "I asked them, 'Do you think it would be of value if we set up an outpatient stress-reduction clinic based on mobilizing the intrinsic healing capacities of human beings through fairly intensive training in mindfulness meditation and mindful hatha yoga?'"[11]

The clinic heads were happy to refer patients they could no longer help, and Kabat-Zinn found that because these patients had exhausted all their other options, they were open to a new approach based on the practice of mindfulness. The idea was both revolutionary and counterintuitive—they would work not with what they were suffering but with their reaction to it. "They were open to the proposal that, just as an experiment, instead of turning away from or trying to obliterate your pain, we're going to put the welcome mat out for it," Kabat-Zinn remembers. "We're going to investigate the experience of pain by attending to it carefully. Because while you're going to have pain at one point or another in your life, how you are in relationship to it can make an enormous difference in terms of how much you are suffering."[12]

The program would be called Mindfulness-Based Stress Reduction, and with it mainstream or secular mindfulness was born. Right from the beginning, it included all the principles of the worldwide mindfulness movement we know today. It was about solid, provable results—patients reported that they experienced less suffering and more happiness. It was about the importance of mind—patients changed how their minds reacted to the challenges of their condition. It was mainstream—it was based right in the heart of the medical establishment.

MBSR demonstrated the benefits of both aspects of Complete Mindfulness practice: calming the mind and insight. The benefits of calming the mind were already well known, such as more relaxation, contentment, and resilience. The really revolutionary advance of MBSR was to demonstrate the concrete benefits of insight, which transforms how we understand and react to the challenges of life.

To help people dealing with chronic pain, stress, and other suffering, MBSR suggested they look closely at what they were experiencing and see what they discovered about it. When they did that, patients saw that the stress and pain they were suffering was always changing. It was not fixed or solid, and neither was the self that experienced them. These insights helped people find relief, calm, and resilience. They knew that what they were suffering was not as solid or permanent as they thought. They got some distance from their pain and didn't identify with it as much. They discovered the healing power of seeing reality clearly and accurately.

Jon Kabat-Zinn had one more strategy that played a key role in legitimizing and spreading mindfulness. As a scientist, he knew that research and data were key to the acceptance of mindfulness in a society skeptical about the benefits of practices like meditation. So from the beginning of MBSR, he made sure to gather credible evidence that would attract the interest of scientists, doctors, and academics. He recognized that this was the path to legitimacy in the modern world. "I knew from the start that reporting outcomes would be a huge part of the work," he says. "If we didn't document what was going on in the room, it would just be a nice set of stories and anecdotes, no matter how much benefit participants experienced. But if we systematically gathered data and reported our findings in the scientific literature, then if the overall results were medically and psychologically significant, the program might have a much larger impact beyond just what was unfolding in our medical center. It might spread around the world, driven by the compelling nature of the scientific findings and their clinical implications."[13]

And spread it did. The program worked, they had the data to back it up, and interest in mindfulness snowballed. Mindfulness became a legitimate subject of serious study. Mainstream media touted its benefits. Without the complicating factor of religion, governments, companies, and organizations could explore its benefits.

The success of mindfulness as a popular meditation practice is unprecedented in the modern world. It has succeeded for two reasons: because of Jon Kabat-Zinn's brilliant framing of mindfulness for the modern world and because it works. Today people around the world are practicing mindfulness—just as Jon Kabat-Zinn hoped they would—and mindfulness is making valuable contributions in many different fields. Individuals, organizations, and society are discovering proven benefits like these:

- **HEALTH**: Mindfulness lowers blood pressure and improves heart health; strengthens immune systems; helps treat irritable bowel syndrome, colitis, and fibromyalgia; reduces chronic pain; and improves the effectiveness of weight-loss and eating-disorder programs.
- **WELL-BEING AND QUALITY OF LIFE**: Mindfulness reduces anxiety, stress, reactivity, and repetitive negative patterns; increases calm, focus, equanimity, and contentment; improves sleep and memory; and helps develop and maintain healthy habits.
- **EMOTIONAL INTELLIGENCE**: Mindfulness increases compassion, empathy, and understanding of others, and enhances self-care.
- **PSYCHOLOGY**: Professionals who practice mindfulness themselves achieve better outcomes; Mindfulness-Based Cognitive Therapy (MBCT) offers effective treatments for depression, anxiety disorders, bipolar disorder, emotional distress, and addiction.
- **EDUCATION**: Mindfulness improves students' focus, attention, behavior, and academic performance.
- **CAREGIVERS AND FIRST RESPONDERS**: Mindfulness reduces stress and burnout and increases effectiveness.
- **LEADERSHIP**: Mindfulness helps managers become more effective, empathic, and skillful.
- **PRODUCTIVITY**: Mindfulness lowers absenteeism and improves job satisfaction.

These are just a few of the areas in which mindfulness is being applied today. The list goes on and on—recovery, childbirth, parenting, relationships, sexuality, gardening, creativity, crafts, sports—because we are discovering that anything worth doing is done better mindfully. In this book we'll learn ways to bring mindfulness into many different aspects of our life.

We are fortunate to be present at the birth of this authentic new tradition. The mindfulness movement is still in its early stages, and it will be thrilling to see how it evolves and grows in the future. It is already doing so much good and its benefit will only increase.

TEACHING

Mindfulness for All[14]

Jon Kabat-Zinn

Mindfulness for all!

That is a wild thought.

But why not, when you come right down to it? Especially at this moment in time, stressed as we are individually and collectively in so many different ways, both inwardly and outwardly.

And in terms of the wisdom to transform the world, it is not hyperbole. That wisdom is a potential that is wholly distributive, lying with each of us in small but hardly insignificant ways. That wisdom is cultivable through mindfulness in ways both little and big. I have had the privilege of seeing it emerge and flourish in many different domains over the past forty years. Now that incipient wisdom is spreading throughout the world, becoming stronger and evermore an imperative.

The Evolutionary Impact of Meditative Awareness

If it is part of the evolutionary glide path of us humans to progressively know ourselves better, thereby inhabiting a bit more of the sense of the name we gave our species, *Homo sapiens sapiens*; if it is also part of the evolutionary glide path of us humans not to destroy ourselves or create nightmare dystopias beyond those we have already managed to perpetuate, we will need to take a whole new level of responsibility for ourselves, for our own minds, for our societies, and for our planet. Otherwise, if past is any prologue, all of us may unwittingly be contributing, either by omission or commission, in tiny ways that may not be so tiny in the end, to creating a highly unhealthy and majorly toxic world none of us will be happy to inhabit. That is perhaps the understatement of the millennium. The prevailing dis-ease of humanity is playing itself out increasingly before our very eyes. It is also increasingly harder for any of us to ignore, and we do so individually and collectively at our peril.

So mindfulness for all and the cultivation of greater enacted wisdom in how we conduct ourselves and take care of our world is hardly mere hype or wishful thinking. It may be *an*, if not *the*, essential ingredient for short- and long-term survival, health, and ongoing development as a species. But to be up to the enormity of this challenge, the mindfulness I am referring to has to be authentic, nested within a universal framework of nurturing and cultivating wisdom and compassion.

As I am using the term, mindfulness is a way of seeing and a way of being, one that has a long history on this planet. It also has considerable momentum at the moment as it moves increasingly into the mainstream of many different societies and cultures in a variety of ways. Axiomatically, the approach I am advocating has to be and *is* grounded and safeguarded at every level in ethical, embodied, enacted, and ultimately selfless wisdom and action. We might think of mindfulness as one tributary of the human wisdom tradition. While its most articulated roots lie deep within Buddhism, its essence is universal and has been expressed in one way or another in all human cultures and traditions.

As I see it, the increasingly widespread adoption and practice of mindfulness meditation in our individual lives and work, and its intentional application moment by moment and day by day in how we respond to the world we inhabit, could potentially provide the very root of authentic well-being, peacefulness, and clarity within our vast diversity of peoples, cultures, and aspirations on the planet. Mindfulness has something to offer all of us as individuals, and as a global human community I don't think that there is any question that its transformative potential needs to be realized—i.e., made real—in an infinite number of creative ways at this particular juncture in the unfolding of our species, nested within our far-more-fragile-than-we-thought planetary abode.

Complete Mindfulness: The Next Step

The Complete Path of Mindfulness is not just a step forward for you and me as mindfulness practitioners. I believe that defining, teaching, and practicing mindfulness as a complete path of life is the next big step forward in the historic development of the mindfulness movement, one that will dramatically increase its impact on people's lives and our society.

Many leaders in the mindfulness movement are already talking about things like ethics and compassion as a natural extension of their teaching. They are, informally and in their own way, presenting mindfulness as a complete path. Nonetheless, mindfulness is still widely defined as simply a meditation practice, albeit one with a wide range of benefits.

The mainstream mindfulness movement has played a historic role in introducing millions of people to mindfulness meditation. That was the first step in its development as an authentic new meditative tradition in the modern world. Now it is time to take the next step forward and explicitly define mindfulness as a complete path of life. Offering a framework for practicing mindfulness as a comprehensive path will deepen its benefits to people's lives and to society. It will attract many more people who are looking for positive ways to live that can powerfully transform our lives and our world.

With these five keys—mindfulness meditation, insight, love and compassion, ethics, and community—I have described one possible framework for mindfulness as a complete path, but it's not the only one. The important step forward is the basic shift to expand how mindfulness is defined, not the specific path we decide on. My hope is that the framework I am proposing here will inspire a rich and productive discussion about how best to describe mindfulness as a complete path of life and help the mindfulness movement take the next step in its historic development.

That's my hope for the future, but meanwhile you and I can start practicing the Complete Path of Mindfulness right now. In the following chapters, you will learn how to cultivate each of the five keys and discover new ways to bring mindfulness into your life. You will be taught effective meditations, contemplations, and ways to live by leading mindfulness experts, and you will hear from them personally about the challenges and breakthroughs they have experienced on their own mindfulness journeys.

So let's take another mindful breath together and start on the Complete Path of Mindfulness.

3

MINDFULNESS MEDITATION

Tame Your Mind to Transform Your Life

Complete Mindfulness is unique among the world's paths to happiness, well-being, and personal transformation because of its foundation in mindfulness meditation. The rest of the Complete Path of Mindfulness flows naturally from the stable, awake, and discerning mind we develop in mindfulness practice, which gives us powerful tools to become more present, insightful, compassionate, ethical, and connected.

Mindfulness meditation is the simple practice of intentionally resting your attention on whatever's happening in the present moment, without judging it as good or bad, and returning to the present whenever your mind strays into distractions. The Greater Good Science Center at the University of California, Berkeley, defines mindfulness practice as "maintaining a moment-by-moment awareness of our thoughts, feelings, bodily sensations, and surrounding environment through a gentle, nurturing lens."[1]

When you're practicing mindfulness meditation, it helps to have a focal point to place your attention on and anchor you in the present. It's usually recommended that you focus gently on your breathing. As you follow your breath going in and out, your mind will become calmer and clearer and your body will relax. Returning to the breath whenever your attention strays, you will learn to rest more and more comfortably, for longer periods of time, in direct, nonjudgmental experience of whatever's happening inside you and in the world around you.

How can just sitting down and paying attention to your breathing be so transformative? How can something so simple make all the difference in your life? Because it's how to train your untamed mind.

The practical benefits of mindfulness meditation are well known. As your mind becomes calmer and more focused on the present, you experience less stress and mental struggle and more well-being and enjoyment of life. But the benefits of mindfulness go much deeper than that when you consider the profound damage to our lives caused by the untamed mind. When it is wild and uncontrolled, our mind is too often a painful problem rather than our greatest asset.

Reflecting a deep, almost primordial sense of dissatisfaction, our untamed mind is always on the move. Never resting, it is constantly running, struggling, calculating, and striving for something better. We are like cosmic hitchhikers, mentally traveling through the universe, getting lost in thoughts of the past and future, spinning out good and bad scenarios and fantasies. We are too often plagued by repetitive thoughts and feelings we don't know how to stop.

It is an exhausting, unsatisfying, and anxious way to live. Lost much of the time in thought and internal monologue, we lead a kind of insubstantial, ghostlike existence. Grounded only partially in reality, we can't enjoy the full fruits of life.

In Asian cultures, the untamed mind is often called "monkey mind." If you've ever spent time around monkeys, you'll know why. Like the untamed mind, monkeys are clever, restless, and always on the lookout for the next thing to grab. They jump around a lot, squabble, and make a lot of noise. Having an untamed mind is a bit like having a wild monkey living in your head—it's restless, hard to control, and never satisfied. Mindfulness meditation tames your monkey mind.

Mindfulness meditation is sometimes described as uniting or synchronizing your body and mind. When you are lost in thoughts and distractions, your body is in one place and your mind is in another. Mindfulness meditation brings them together. It invites your cosmic hitchhiker home to the real world, which is where your body is.

Thich Nhat Hanh describes it this way: "By taking a mindful breath or a mindful step, you can bring your mind back to your body. In your daily life, your body and mind often go in two different directions. You are in a state of distraction, mind in one place, body in another. Your body is putting on a coat but your mind is preoccupied, caught in the past or the future. But between your mind and your body there is something: your breath. As soon as you go home to your breath and you breathe with awareness, your body and mind come together very quickly. And suddenly you find yourself fully present, fully alive."[2]

To be fully present is to be fully alive: this is both the premise and the promise of mindfulness meditation.

Ideally you can set aside some time every day to practice mindfulness meditation. This is your training time, when you are taming your mind and developing your power to rest stably in the present. Then you can bring mindfulness to the rest of your day. This is when you put your meditation into action, living your daily life as mindfully as you can.

Mindfulness meditation is not just the foundation of the Complete Path of Mindfulness but a lifelong practice we do throughout our entire journey. From the beginning of our path to the end, we can experience again and again the magic of the simple practice that changes everything.

Practices and Teachings

We'll begin by learning the two foundational practices of mindfulness meditation: the seated practice of following the breath, also known as sitting meditation, and walking meditation, which acts as a bridge between formal practice and everyday life.

PRACTICE

Sitting Meditation (Following the Breath)

Melvin McLeod

If you're just starting your mindfulness practice, the first thing to do is set up a good place to meditate. Choose somewhere relatively quiet where you won't be disturbed. Although some noise is inevitable, try to avoid music, television, or other electronic sounds, which are really difficult to ignore. It's nice to meditate in pleasing, harmonious surroundings, so feel free to decorate your mindfulness space in a way that relaxes and inspires you.

You'll want a meditation cushion you can comfortably sit on cross-legged. It should be relatively firm, like the many excellent cushions designed specifically for meditation. It should raise you high enough so your knees are below your hips when you sit. If you find it difficult or uncomfortable to sit cross-legged, it is perfectly acceptable to sit on a straight-back chair instead. There is no need to think of that as second-best.

Once you have your space set up, you take your seat on your cushion or chair. Overall, your posture should be upright but not uptight. You can sit on your cushion cross-legged in whatever way is comfortable—no need to force yourself into a half-lotus or some other strenuous position if that's not easy for you. Place your hands palm down on your thighs or together at your navel, palms up with your right hand cradled in your left and your thumbs touching.

The most important thing is to have a straight but not rigid back. As you are settling into your posture, it can help to imagine that the crown of your head is being pulled gently upward, straightening and slightly stretching your spine. Tuck your chin tucked toward your throat so your head is tilted a bit downward. Your mouth rests slightly open and your gaze is softly focused about eight inches in front of you. You are upright, alert, and relaxed. A good posture feels good.

If you are sitting on a chair, your posture is similar: back straight, head tilted slightly down, soft gaze, hands on thighs or cupping each other. Your feet should rest flat on the floor.

Now that you've arranged your meditation space and settled into your posture, it's time to start meditating. That makes it sound like a big deal, but all you're doing is sitting comfortably, breathing, and paying attention. That's it. It's pretty much doing nothing.

The most common practice is to follow your breath going in and out. You breathe in and experience breathing in. You breathe out and experience breathing out. You can also do a little more advanced practice in which you focus only on the out-breath. You follow your breath going out and dissolving in the space around you. Then you just leave a gap and rest in openness until you focus again on the next out-breath.

You simply focus on your breath as it is. You are not altering your breathing or trying to breathe in any particular way. If your breathing is fast and shallow, that's what you experience. If it's slow and relaxed, that's what you experience. You don't change or judge your breathing. Mindfulness is about nonjudgmental awareness of whatever's happening, and that starts with your breath.

Your focus on your breathing is not too narrow or heavy-handed. While you focus on the feeling of your breath going in and out, you also remain aware of the rest of your experience—the earth below you, the feeling of your body, the space around you, the sights, sounds, and smells you perceive. You could say that 60 percent of your attention is focused on the breath and 40 percent on your environment. After all, the purpose of mindfulness is to live life fully, not to narrow down your experience of it.

We could say there are three main elements in mindfulness meditation: body, breath, and mind. So far we've covered your body and your breath. Now the third makes its appearance—your mind.

It may take only a couple of mindful breaths and—boom!—your mind has strayed into thinking. You're no longer resting in the simple experience of the present moment. You're off somewhere else lost in thought. You could be gone for a minute, you could be gone for half an hour, but sooner or later you're going to wake up and realize, "Oh shoot, I got lost in thoughts." What you do at that moment is very important. It's key to the whole discipline of mindfulness practice.

First, you don't just go back to your train of thought. That can be pretty tempting—you could be enjoying some pleasurable fantasy, or thinking up some great idea that will change the world, or deciding what you're going to do with the rest of your day. It's particularly easy to be sucked back into a train of thought if it's got some emotion attached to it, if it's generating lust or anger or fear or hope that make your internal narrative more energized and sticky. But in the end, it's all just thinking, and where you want to be is in the real world, with your breathing and your body. So you need the discipline to say no to those thoughts, no matter how real and important they seem, and return to the practice.

It helps if you acknowledge what's happening, so it's recommended that you simply note it to yourself as "thinking" or "thoughts" and then return to your breath. You don't criticize yourself for thinking or judge whether your thoughts are good or bad. You just acknowledge them and return to the practice.

Some people think of being nonjudgmental as cool and emotionally neutral. But the nonjudgment you practice in mindfulness is not some dry, clinical observation of yourself. It is real understanding and acceptance, the kind that only comes from a caring and friendly attitude toward yourself. That's why mindfulness requires a warm heart as well as an observant mind. Yes, you see your problematic patterns and the suffering they cause, but you don't blame or criticize yourself. You are the same empathetic and nonjudgmental friend to yourself as you are to others, particularly when they are struggling, as you might be. You just gently note the patterns and return to following your breath.

You do need a lot of patience when you practice mindfulness. Because the habit of thinking is so strong in us, you're going to get lost in thought over and over and over again. It's hard not to get frustrated the millionth time you say "thinking" to yourself, but don't stop to judge yourself—that's just more thinking. Avoid the unnecessary commentary and go back to your breathing.

The good news is that if you stick to the practice you will start to see results. As you gradually tame your wild mind, you will be able to stay longer in simple, direct awareness of the present moment—of your breathing, your posture, and your immediate environment. Your mind and body will relax and you will feel more and more comfortable resting in the moment. You will see that your thoughts are merely thoughts, just energy arising and dissolving. You realize you don't need to believe them, and they begin to lose their power over you.

It's true that mindfulness practice is kind of boring. Just being in the present isn't as entertaining as mentally traveling around the universe, or looking at your phone for that matter. But it is fresh, healthy, and real. Your perceptions are vivid, your body is in balance, and your mind is clear, uncluttered, and awake. You experience your life as it really is—straightforward, wholesome, and good. There is no need to try to manufacture another one.

That discovery is why the simple practice of sitting down, breathing, and paying attention is so transformative. Fully present, you are fully alive, and you experience the goodness of yourself and your world. The secret of mindfulness, unique among the world's life paths, is that doing nothing is the way to discover everything.

Walking meditation, which combines mindfulness and movement, is a transitional practice between sitting meditation and mindfulness in daily life. The mindfulness you cultivate while practicing walking meditation can then be applied to everything you do during your day.

The big difference between sitting meditation and walking meditation is that your focal point is the movement of your legs and feet instead of your breathing. Otherwise, the basic principles remain the same. Your posture is relaxed yet upright, and your body and mind are synchronized. You are mindful of the movement of your feet lifting off the ground, moving forward, and returning to the ground. You gently note when you get caught in thought and return to the experience of your body moving and the environment around you.

You don't need a lot of space to do walking meditation. It's nice to do outdoors, but you can also walk slowly around your house. Many people find it enjoyable and relaxing to make a short session of walking meditation part of their daily practice. You can then take the opportunity to walk mindfully anytime during your day. This is a great way to cultivate mindfulness in all your daily activities.

PRACTICE

Walking Meditation[3]

Leslie Booker

Walking meditation is often described as a meditation in motion.

In this practice, you place your full attention on the process of walking—from the shifting of the weight in your body to the mechanics of placing your foot. Walking meditation is used to offset and shift the energy of sitting practice. It is a bridge to integrate practice into daily life and can be more accessible than a sitting practice for many people.

- Find an unobstructed space where you can walk in a straight line for about ten feet. You can walk for a greater distance if you prefer. Bring your attention down to your feet and slowly shift your weight from side to side and front to back. Being in bare feet can bring more awareness to what needs to happen in the body to create balance.
- Coming into physical stillness, lift the crown of your head up, slide your shoulders down and away from your ears, and lift your chest with dignity and pride. You can clasp your hands behind your back, hold them in front of your body, or let your arms hang loosely to the side.
- Lifting your right leg, notice the weight redistribution in your body. Place your attention on what the left side of your body needs to do to hold your full weight—spreading the toes, engaging the core. Extend the right leg forward, placing the heel on the ground and rolling onto the ball of the foot. As your weight shifts forward, notice how the heel of your left foot begins to lift. Swing the left leg forward and repeat.
- Adding verbal cues is a great way to establish synchronization and rhythm within the body. As the mind begins to wander, use a simple verbal cue like "lifting, moving, placing" as a reminder to bring the mind back to the body. Incorporating a *gatha*, a short verse to support practice, is a common technique used in Thich Nhat Hanh's communities. Here's one that might be used for walking meditation:

(Breathing in) "I have arrived."
(Breathing out) "I am home."
(Breathing in) "In the here."
(Breathing out) "In the now."

- When you get to the end of your walking path, come to a complete stop and take a breath. Turn a quarter of the way, maybe taking another breath, then fully turn all the way around, facing where you just came from. Start over with finding your posture and establishing your balance. Again lift, move, and place the foot.

At the beginning of this practice, you might notice that your steps are very calculated and robotic. See if you can begin to find more fluidity as you connect the breath with movement, perhaps letting go of the phrases and just allowing this to be a fully embodied practice.

When you have come to the end of your practice, stand still, seeing where there is energy in the body and what is still. Notice what has risen to the top and what has been let go of.

Mindfulness meditation requires a gentle, friendly attitude toward yourself. How else could you accept yourself as you are? That's why I love this mindfulness instruction by self-compassion expert Christopher Germer—it engages our heart in the practice. When we meditate with this kind of warmth and affection toward ourselves, the practice is relaxed, natural, enjoyable, and surprisingly easy.

PRACTICE

Affectionate Breathing[4]

Christopher Germer

- Find a posture in which your body is comfortable and will feel supported for the length of the meditation. Then let your eyes gently close, partially or fully. Take a few slow, easy breaths, releasing any unnecessary tension in your body.
- If you like, place a hand over your heart or another soothing place as a reminder that you're bringing not only awareness, but affectionate awareness, to your breathing and to yourself. You can leave your hand there or let it rest at anytime.
- Now begin to notice your breathing in your body, feeling your body breathe in and feeling your body breathe out.
- Just let your body breathe you. There is nothing you need to do. Perhaps notice how your body is nourished on the in-breath and relaxes with the out-breath.
- Now notice the rhythm of your breathing, flowing in and flowing out. Take some time to feel the natural rhythm of your breathing. Feel your whole body subtly moving with the breath, like the movement of the sea.
- Your mind will naturally wander, like a curious child or a little puppy. When that happens, just gently return to the rhythm of your breathing.
- Allow your whole body to be gently rocked and internally caressed by your breathing.
- If you like, give yourself over to your breathing, letting your breathing be all there is. Become the breath. Just breathing. Being breathing.

- Gently release your attention on the breath, sit quietly in your own experience, and allow yourself to feel whatever you're feeling and to be just as you are.
- Slowly and gently open your eyes.

As the founder of the mainstream mindfulness movement, Jon Kabat-Zinn is renowned for his scientific, evidence-based approach to mindfulness that emphasizes its concrete benefits to our lives. This has been the foundation of mainstream mindfulness's popularity. But his understanding of mindfulness has always been much deeper and broader than that. Here he reveals himself not only as an important figure historically but as a great teacher.

TEACHING

How Mindfulness Gives Us Our Life Back[5]

Jon Kabat-Zinn

The art of taking your seat in your own life, which could also be seen as taking a stand of a certain kind, on a regular basis, is in and of itself a profound expression of human intelligence. Ultimately it is a radical act of sanity and love—namely to stop all the doing that carries us *through* our moments without truly inhabiting them, and actually drop into being, even for one fleeting moment. That dropping in is the exceedingly simple, but at the same time, hugely radical act undergirding mindfulness as a meditation practice and as a way of being. It is easy to learn. It is easy to do. But it is also equally easy to forget to practice, even though this kind of dropping in takes literally no time at all, just remembering.

Happily, this intimacy with our own capacity for awareness is increasingly being taken up and nurtured in one form or another by more and more people as it makes its way into various domains of society: from school to elders, from academics to business professionals, from tech engineers to community leaders and social activists, from college students to medical and graduate students, from—believe it or not—politicians, to athletes at all levels of sport. And for the most part mindfulness is being nurtured and cultivated not as a luxury or passing fad but with the growing recognition that it may be an absolute necessity for living life fully and for living life with integrity—in other words ethically—in the face of the starkly looming challenges we are all confronted with every day and with the equally enormous and compelling opportunities and options that are available to us as well in this particular moment in time—that is, if we can see through and transcend at least for a moment our mind's own self-constructed and habitual limitations, the narratives we tell ourselves that are not true enough if they are true at all, and our endemic blindnesses. This enterprise is ultimately one big and extremely vital adventure—full of ups and downs, just as life itself is full of ups and downs. But how we choose to be in relationship to it makes all the difference in how this adventure, the adventure of your life, unfolds. And you have a lot more say in it than you might suspect.

There are many different ways to cultivate mindfulness through both formal meditation practice and in everyday living and working. Formal meditation can be practiced in any number of positions: sitting, lying down, standing, or walking. And what we call *informal meditation practice*, which when all is said and done is the real meditation practice, involves letting life itself become coextensive with your meditation practice and recognizing that everything that unfolds within it, the wanted and the unwanted and the unnoticed, is the real curriculum. When we see meditation in this way, nothing that arises in mind or in our life or in the world is excluded, and any moment is a perfect moment to bring awareness to what is unfolding and thereby learn and grow and heal.

Sometimes being mindful looks like doing something. And sometimes being mindful looks like doing nothing. From the outside, you don't always know. But even when it looks or feels like doing nothing, it isn't. In fact, it isn't a *doing* at all. I know this sounds a little crazy, but mindfulness meditation is much more a matter of non-doing, of simply dropping into *being* in the only moment we ever have—this one—than it is of doing something or getting somewhere. How you are—and wherever you are in any moment—is good enough, at least for now! In fact, it is perfect, if you are willing to hold the moment in awareness while also being gentle with yourself and not forcing things.

The regular practice of mindfulness meditation helps us to access within ourselves the openhearted spaciousness characteristic of pure awareness and to express it in how we act in the world. Mindfulness as a regular practice can literally and figuratively give your life back to you, especially if you are stressed or in pain, or caught up in uncertainty and emotional turmoil—which of course, we all are to one degree or another in some moments or times in our lives.

But in spite of its trendy popularity or notoriety at this moment, mindfulness is above all a *practice*, and at times, an arduous one. For most of us, it requires intentional and ongoing cultivation. And that cultivation is nurtured through the regular disciplined practice of meditation, pure and simple. And simple it is, although not necessarily easy at times. That is one of the reasons that is worth doing. The investment of energy is profoundly beneficial. It is healing. It can be totally transformative. That is one of the reasons people often say that the practice of mindfulness "gave me my life back."

Because your body is what grounds you in the reality of the present moment, awareness of your body is a foundation of mindfulness practice. One effective way to become more aware of your body is with body-scan meditation. In fact, this was one of the first practices used by Jon Kabat-Zinn in the Mindfulness-Based Stress Reduction program that launched the whole mainstream mindfulness movement. Body-scan meditation can be a valuable part of your regular practice, such as this one taught by the Greater Good Science Center that incorporates key principles of mindfulness.

PRACTICE

Mindful Body Scan[6]

The Greater Good Science Center

From your facial muscles down to your toes, body scan meditation can relieve stress and help you discover what your body really needs.

In a body scan, you systematically focus your attention on different parts of your body, from your feet to the muscles in your face. This creates a rare opportunity for you to experience your body as it is, without judging or trying to change it.

This exercise is designed to help you develop a mindful awareness of your bodily sensations, and to relieve tension wherever it is found. Research suggests that this mindfulness practice can help reduce stress, improve well-being, and decrease aches and pains.

This body scan can be performed while lying down, sitting, or in other postures. The steps below are a guided meditation designed to be done while sitting but can be adapted for the posture you choose.

The time required is twenty to forty-five minutes, although evidence suggests that benefit increases the longer you do the exercise.

- Begin by bringing your attention into your body. You can close your eyes if that's comfortable for you. Feel the weight of your body on the chair and on the floor.
- Take a few deep breaths. As you take a deep breath, bring in more oxygen, enlivening the body. As you exhale, have a sense of relaxing more deeply.
- Notice the sensations of your feet touching the floor—the weight, pressure, vibration, heat. Notice your legs against the chair—the pressure, pulsing, heaviness, lightness. Notice your back against the chair.
- Bring your attention into your stomach area. If your stomach is tense or tight, let it soften. Take a breath.
- Notice your hands. Are your hands tense or tight? See if you can allow them to soften. Notice your arms. Feel any sensation in your arms. Let your shoulders be soft.
- Notice your neck and throat. Let them be soft. Relax. Soften your jaw. Let your face and facial muscles be soft.
- Then notice your whole body present. Take one more breath. Be aware of your whole body as best you can. Take a breath. Then when you're ready, you can open your eyes.

According to research, by simply noticing any stress or pain you're experiencing, without trying to change it, you may actually feel some relief. This exercise allows you to notice and release any source of tension you weren't aware of before, such as a hunched back or clenched jaw muscles. Or it may draw your attention to a source of pain and discomfort. Your feelings of resistance and anger toward pain often only serve to increase that pain, and to increase the distress associated with it.

The body scan is designed to counteract these negative feelings toward our bodies. This practice may also increase your general attunement to your physical needs and sensations, which can in turn help you take better care and make healthier decisions about eating, sleep, and exercise.

Evidence shows that time spent engaging in the body scan is associated with greater levels of two components of mindfulness—observing thoughts, feelings, and physical sensations, and non-reacting to stress—and increased psychological well-being.

In addition to your regular mindfulness meditation, there are short mindfulness practices you can do on the spot whenever you need to come back to the present moment. Here are two quick and easy practices you can keep in your back pocket for whenever you want to reestablish your mindfulness. Using practices like these, you'll be amazed how quickly you can reunite your mind and body and return to the present.

PRACTICE

Take Three Conscious Breaths[7]

Pema Chödrön

Pause practice—taking three conscious breaths at any moment when you notice that you are stuck in thought—is a simple but powerful practice you can do at any given moment.

Pause practice can transform each day of your life. If you pause just long enough, you can reconnect with exactly where you are, with the immediacy of your experience.

When you are waking up in the morning, even if you are running late, you could just stop and take three conscious breaths. Just be where you are! Whether you are washing up, or making your coffee or tea, or brushing your teeth, just create a gap in your discursive mind.

Pause and take three conscious breaths. Let it be a contrast to being all caught up. Let it be like popping a bubble. Let it be just a moment in time, and then go on.

Maybe you are on your way to whatever you need to do for the day. You are in your car, or on the bus, or standing in line. But you can still create a pause by taking three conscious breaths and being right there with the immediacy of your experience, right there with whatever you are seeing, with whatever you are doing, with whatever you are feeling.

Another powerful way to do pause practice is simply to listen for a moment. Instead of sight being the predominant sense perception, let sound, hearing, be the predominant sense perception. It's a very powerful way to cut through your conventional way of looking at the world. In any moment, you can just stop and listen intently. It doesn't matter what particular sound you hear; you simply create a gap by listening intently.

When you go out for a walk, pause frequently—stop and listen. Stop and take three conscious breaths.

In any moment, you could put your full attention on the immediacy of your experience. You could look at your hand resting on your leg, or feel your bottom sitting on the cushion or on the chair. You could just be here. Instead of being not here, instead of being absorbed in thinking, planning, and worrying, cut off from your sense perceptions, cut off from the power and magic of the moment, you could be here.

PRACTICE

Three Questions for Coming Back to Now[8]

Leslie Davis

While on a personal retreat, I hiked into Horn Canyon in the east end of Ojai, California. Due to the severe drought, it had been years since water had flowed alongside the trail there, but now I was delighted to cross the creek a few times, jumping from rock to rock.

My mind was clear and focused, taking in the sounds and smells of the trail—glistening poison oak, fragrant sage, infinite wildflowers. With the warm sun on my back, I felt fully alive in the present moment. Such a wonderful gift to be alive! To be awake!

On the way back through the canyon, though, my mind jumped ahead of my body: it was busy planning out what I would do as soon as I got back. First a snack, then another writing session, or maybe both at the same time, then a hot shower. And what would I have for dinner?

Many minutes would pass before I noticed this. How many footsteps did my feet take while my mind carried me away? And how many times in any given day does this occur, or even in just an afternoon?

What can bring us back to the present moment? How can we return to what's at hand—the conversation we're having, the child in front of us, the trail we're walking?

Thich Nhat Hanh has said that "the opposite of forgetfulness is mindfulness. Mindfulness is when you are truly there, mind and body together." In order to wake up from my forgetfulness, I ask myself three questions that prompt me to come back to the present moment:

1. *Where am I?* To find the answer to this, I stop. I physically stop moving, and if I'm sitting, I stand up. I look around, locate myself. Taking a deep breath, I remember that I have a body.

2. *What am I doing?* I take a moment to observe exactly what I'm doing, with no filters, and no judgment. Taking a deep breath, I bring awareness to what I am doing in the present moment.
3. *Who am I with?* I ask myself, am I with someone or am I alone? Who is talking? Am I making eye contact? If I'm alone, I touch my arm or leg, look into my own eyes in a mirror, or close them and breathe. If I'm with someone, I take a deep breath and re-establish our connection.

When I ask myself these questions, I take a few deep breaths and pause to observe what's going on in my mind. To watch and monitor the mind, to see how the mind strays, even when the external circumstances are pristine for being present, is an opportunity for transformation. A quick U-turn back to the breath always gets me headed in the right direction.

Mindfulness meditation can transform your life, but it's only effective if you do it regularly. Taming your wild mind is not easy, and you have to put in the work.

The most effective way to practice mindfulness is to make it part of your daily schedule. Many people prefer to meditate in the morning so they can take a calm and focused mind into the rest of their day, but whatever works for your schedule is fine.

For all of its obvious benefits, it's challenging to stick to a regular meditation schedule in the face of distraction, resistance, and a goal-oriented culture that doesn't value slowing down. Here's mindfulness teacher Diana Winston on all the reasons why we don't meditate regularly, all the reasons why we should, and ten tips to help you maintain a regular mindfulness practice.

TEACHING

Ten Tips for Having a Daily Practice (Even If You Would Rather Be Thrown into a Shark-Infested Ocean)[9]

Diana Winston

Why is it so hard to meditate regularly?

Forget this culture that's devoted to busyness. Forget the fact that Americans report having 16.5 hours of leisure time weekly, once work and household obligations are taken care of, and the time is rapidly shrinking. Forget the fact that we're taught as a culture that busyness is a virtue and God forbid, we should ever take a second for ourselves. Forget that we are bombarded daily with infotainment from television, radio, billboards, internet ads, email, IMs, etc.

Even forgetting all of that, there are still several other reasons it's hard to meditate every day:

1. It's hard because meditation is the opposite of how we've been culturally conditioned.
2. It's hard because it's not necessarily yet a habit. Habits come easily; we just do them. New habits take work.
3. It's hard because sometimes meditation can feel excruciatingly boring. Our lives are far more entertaining than knowing if a breath is long or short.
4. It's hard because there are seemingly far more interesting and necessary things to do. We could watch TV, work out, write poetry, scrub the grout from our showers . . .
5. It's hard because our brains are wired to be stimulated and it takes a tremendous effort to overcome our addiction to stimulation.
6. It's hard because sometimes, we are going through intense emotions that we don't want to feel, and nothing short of restraints are going to make us sit there and feel that grief. No, nothing!

Sometimes the thought of meditating makes us gag. Especially when we're having a difficult time in life. Yet paradoxically, that's the best time to meditate. It's when we need it the most.

If you don't meditate regularly, you have good excuses. You're like most people. It makes you wonder if you should even bother. But you should bother, you definitely should bother, and here's why:

1. In light of the busyness and other cultural factors I've mentioned, *meditation is the ideal antidote*. We should all be meditating in order to give ourselves a break from the incessant speed of our culture. In fact, it's a revolutionary act to sit.
2. *It's good for you*. Study after study demonstrates scientifically (and if science says so it must be true) that meditation reduces stress, lowers blood pressure, boosts the immune system, and creates a general sense of well-being.
3. *Meditation can be quite interesting.* We can gain insight into our mind, hearts, and bodies, the way habits and patterns work, what motivates us, and what we care about.
4. *It can teach us new skills*, like my two personal favorites: equanimity and compassion. As we meditate, sitting through all aspects of experience, the good, bad, and ugly, and we sit there with great calm, letting things come and go, we develop a balanced and non-reactive mind. This skill transfers out into our lives. We also develop a quality of loving acceptance and compassion, as we notice again and again how poignant this human we call ourselves is.
5. The latest rage in neuroscience these days is *neuroplasticity*. It has been assumed that you can't teach an old dog new tricks, but that turns out to be nonsense (although you've never met my mother's dog). The brain, at any age, can create new neural patterns. Brain development isn't just for kids anymore.

The findings are striking—if we practice something, it will rewire our brains, creating a new neural pathway. Forget the old refrain that we'll never change. We can change, absolutely! Therefore, we've got to meditate, preferably on a daily basis in order to cultivate the wholesome states of mind that come through meditation—calm, concentration, wisdom, equanimity, and joy—that eventually become who we are.

6. *What we practice will grow.* If we want to cultivate a busy, anxious mind, practice busy-anxiousness. If we want to cultivate a calm, centered mind, we need to practice it, simple as that. Sure, we can try to practice these virtues throughout the day, but our daily sitting practice is a greenhouse of sorts. It's our daily intensive to focus in on, mold, and remind our mind of states that will benefit it. So who do you want to be? A busy, anxious, obsessed, neurotic, resentful, unhappy cog? Or a relaxed, peaceful, loving, compassionate, wise, happy human? You can choose.

OK, OK, you're saying. She's right. I really should be sitting more regularly. But it still isn't easy. So here are ten tips to help you have a successful daily mindfulness meditation practice.

1. *Be gentle on yourself.* If you think you're a failure and berate yourself for missing a day or a week, meditation then becomes another excuse for self-hatred. Look, meditation training is like swimming upstream, doable, but takes some effort. Be forgiving, yet keep at it.
2. *Allow it to become a habit.* Try to do it at the same time in the same place every day. The way to cultivate a habit is to actually do it. The more consistent you can be, the easier it is for the new grooves to be worn into your brain.
3. *Review your day and pick a time to do it that makes sense.* If you are not a morning person, in fact can't even look at yourself in

the mirror until after you've had your coffee, wait till later in the day. If you come home exhausted every night, try the mornings.

4. *Be willing to be flexible. If you miss your morning session, be creative.* Take a mindful, silent walk at work; sit before you fall asleep. Don't throw in the towel just because your daily routine got upended.
5. *Prioritize.* You need to somehow insert into your brain that meditation is just as important as brushing your teeth, showering, eating, *Friends* reruns, whatever it is. I think it's amazing how much time we find to answer email but how strikingly little time there is to sit daily.
6. *Set your intention.* Ask yourself as you sit down, Why am I meditating today? See what emerges. Then ask yourself, What are my deepest reasons for practice? Return to these motivations when the going gets tough. A liberated mind takes work and reminders.
7. *Pick a doable amount of time.* Don't strive for an hour unless it seems easy to you. Twenty minutes to a half hour can work fine. Up it, if that seems easy and fits in with your schedule. Even five minutes will activate those neural pathways, keep it going. And get a new groove forming.
8. *If all else fails, get your sweet self on your cushion and take three breaths.*
9. *Sometimes sitting truly feels impossible.* Then use your designated time for some kind of spiritually supportive practice: read an inspiring book, listen to a tape, write in your journal.
10. *When you screw up, be gentle on yourself.* I already said this, but I'll say it again, it's key for developing a regular practice.

Complete Mindfulness offers us a broad map of the path, but it is still an individual journey we all take, with the quirks, baggage, traumas, and joys we each bring to it. Leading mindfulness experts and longtime practitioners share the challenges and discoveries they have experienced as they explore the five keys of the path in their own lives. Their stories inspire and support us as we see that we are all on the same journey—even the best-known and most experienced meditators—doing the best we can to bring mindfulness to the challenges of being human.

Journeys on the Complete Path of Mindfulness: Mindfulness Meditation

One night, as I walked home from a yoga class, I experienced that my body and my mind were in the same place at the same time. The evening was very beautiful and conducive to being present. There was the fragrance of the spring flowers and a slight breeze. I felt a sense of complete awakeness, oneness, and open heartedness. I felt the whole world was in my heart, and I knew that real peace and transformation—everything I was going to those rallies for—came from this place.

This was a spontaneous experience, but it happened because of the groundwork I'd laid in my regular mindfulness practice. I had been training my attention to move back into my senses from the thoughts that kept me in kind of a virtual world, and it served me in that moment. The experience was spontaneous, but also on purpose: there was something in me that decided to just stand still, quiet my mind, and take it all in. It was utterly delicious and precious and transporting to step outside of the incessant stream of thoughts and realize the vastness and aliveness of this reality we're a part of.

—Tara Brach

I'd lost both my parents in my teens and I had not been able to deal with the grief. In just the first months of meditation, the spaciousness of mindful awareness practice, just being present with what was arising, allowed the grief to become available to me in a way it never had before.

I could allow the old, trapped sorrow that had been in my body since I was a teenager to finally move through me. It was like a natural process of arising and passing away, and I was able to sit with it until it dissipated. You know, everything in our experience arises and passes away, and I was able to allow that to happen through my mindfulness practice.

Something shifted and, after all the suffering I had been through, finding presence with my breath and body was like a home to me. I could just sit and really appreciate being present. It felt just like balm to my heart.

—Lisa Ernst

If we're not developing mindfulness, we're just in the trance of believing all our thoughts, identifying with all our emotions, operating largely on habit energy, doing the same things we've done again and again, expecting different results.

I think this is actually the fundamental project of mindfulness meditation—to have enough presence of mind to see how habits are operating, to identify the places where we're stuck. Anytime you notice a moment of stress, a moment of difficulty, a moment of reactivity, you can drop a question into the mind: What am I clinging to in this moment? There's almost always an answer, and usually you can name a dozen things that you're clinging to.

—Gullu Singh

My mind is so different than it was in my twenties, when I first started practicing mindfulness. It took me a long time, but my levels of anxiety and self-doubt and all of those things have shifted so significantly over a lifetime of practice. I can't even tell you the bad places I would go into with anxiety, but it just doesn't happen anymore. Of course I'm still anxious about this or that, but the levels of anxiety, the fear, the worry, it's just not that way anymore.

—Diana Winston

There's a contemplative practice researchers call "focused attention." That's where you are deliberately and somewhat effortfully sustaining your attention on one particular object in order to strengthen your capacities for concentration.

I'd say to myself, "Okay, I'm going to pick a focus of attention—like a candle flickering, or a word in my mind, or the sensations of breathing in my chest—and I'm going to stay with it for the next ten minutes. And if I get distracted—and I will—I'm going to come right back."

Notice what happens when you practice that. Neurologically, things start happening in your brain when lots of other activities get quieter and quieter. Developing our capacity for focus, our concentration muscle, liberates our insight, whether it's into our neurotic psychology or into the nature of existence.

That's when things started really exploding for me in my practice. That's when I began to experience a kind of inner peace that was unshakable, that was deeper than all the shake, rattle, and roll in the mind above it.

—Rick Hanson

4

INSIGHT

The Power of Seeing Reality Clearly

By starting your practice of mindfulness meditation, you have taken the first step on the Complete Path of Mindfulness. As you've calmed and tamed your mind, you have experienced less stress and anxiety and more well-being, peace, and enjoyment of life. But that's just the start of what Complete Mindfulness can do for you. The development of insight is the next—and most important—step.

As we've noted, mindfulness practice actually has two parts. The first, and better known, is the mindfulness meditation you've just learned that calms and focuses the mind in the present. The other part of mindfulness practice is the cultivation of insight. This is the second of the five keys of Complete Mindfulness, and it is what makes the path of mindfulness so transformative. It is because of the insight we develop that the power of mindfulness is truly life-changing.

In this stage of mindfulness practice, you use the stable and undistracted mind you have cultivated in the first stage to look at reality clearly and accurately. You develop insight into the true nature of yourself, your mind, and the world you experience, and when you see reality clearly you can live with wisdom and skillfulness.

Insight relieves the deep and pervasive suffering caused by the many ways we misunderstand our reality and who we really are. It is insight that makes the mindful approach to compassion, ethics, community, and all of life uniquely effective and beneficial. Together, the two parts of mindfulness practice—focus and insight—harness the full power of your natural intelligence and awareness.

The concept of insight, of seeing reality clearly, might seem kind of abstract or philosophical, but in fact it is the secret to the full power of mindfulness. As mindfulness researcher Shauna Shapiro succinctly says, "When we see clearly, we can respond effectively."[1]

Why is insight a natural product of mindfulness, perhaps its most important? The problem is that our normal, untrained mind has a hard time seeing reality clearly. Like a restless monkey, we move rapidly from perception to perception, thought to thought, feeling to feeling. Unstable and distracted, we can't focus our mind on anything long enough to really understand it. Our grasp on reality is superficial and often mistaken. Our perceptions are clouded by our opinions, biases, and preconceptions. We make basic cognitive errors in how we see ourselves and our reality.

The great power of the trained mind you develop in mindfulness meditation is that you can look in a sustained and undistracted way into how things really exist. Because your mind is stable, awake, and unbiased, you can examine and understand the true nature of what arises in your mind and in the world around you.

Generally we don't recognize how deeply we misunderstand our reality and the problems that creates for us. In that sense, the most damaging form of ignorance is ignorance of our own ignorance. It means we don't realize how important insight is and what a profound difference it can make in our lives.

Insight corrects the fundamental cognitive errors that distort our experience of ourselves and our world. It also helps us to understand—and ultimately free ourselves from—the deep conditioning we have been subjected to by our family and culture that impede our ability to see reality accurately.

"Seeing clearly is difficult because the lens through which we view the world is blurred by our parents, teachers, relationships, and society," writes Shapiro. "All of these influence our perceptions on conscious and subconscious levels. We come to see ourselves in a certain way, others in a certain way, life in a certain way. Rather than engage the fluidity of the present moment, our views become frozen and static, like a photograph rather than a motion picture. Often, they operate unconsciously. Even at times when we are aware of our conditioned responses, we can't seem to shift them, try as we might.

"Mindfulness has the potential to free us from these conditioned responses," she continues. "It helps us remove the filters, biases, and preconceived ideas that shape our perceptions and cloud our consciousness. Mindfulness helps us choreograph our life through awareness of the way things are, rather than through generationally and culturally conditioned responses."[2]

There are two broad areas in which the insight you cultivate through mindfulness can profoundly benefit your life: insight into the basic nature of yourself and the reality you experience, and insight into what really brings you happiness and unhappiness.

Insight into the True Nature of Reality

We habitually perceive things as solid, fixed, and separate. That includes ourselves and phenomena in the world. We may know intellectually that things are not this way, but it is how we experience them moment to moment. Our insight into how things really exist cuts through this fundamental cognitive error.

With insight we see that everything is always changing. Some things change quickly, others very slowly, but they're all changing all the time. When we look deeply at the world with a focused, aware mind, we also see that things have no solid core, identity, or essence. They are made of many parts, and we cannot find anything in them we could call a single, unchanging self. We also see that things are not separate from each other, that all beings and phenomena are interdependent in a great web of causation. Everything is caused by other things, and in turn is the cause of other things. Nothing exists independently or creates itself. Things are interdependent, or as Thich Nhat Hanh says, they "inter-are." The universe is a beautiful, living, ever-changing interplay of cause and effect.

When you look inside yourself—at your thoughts, feelings, sense of self, opinions, memories, and hopes and fears about the future—you find the same realities. You see that these mental events are transient, interdependent, and, like the apparent self that experiences them, without a solid core or essence. Thoughts and feelings arise, stay for a while, and then disappear. All they really lead to are more thoughts and feelings. Their power depends on how much you believe in them, and you are freed from their hold over you when you see their transient, insubstantial nature. All you really need to do is let them go. With insight into the workings of your mind, you may even glimpse a more open and deeper level of mind, one whose fundamental awareness and well-being are untouched by thoughts, feelings, and the external circumstances of life.

All this might seem kind of abstract, but in fact our misunderstanding of the way things are creates struggle, stress, and unhappiness at the very core of our lives. Insight relieves this suffering. Because we mistakenly believe that things are solid, separate, and independent, we are locked in an exhausting and pointless struggle against the true nature of ourselves and our world. Resistance against reality is futile—and painful.

To maintain the illusion of a solid, unchanging self, we must constantly struggle to tend, defend, and satisfy it. We must deny the basic truths of change and impermanence, including the greatest change of all, death. We pointlessly try to hold on to what can't be held onto and to avoid what can't be avoided. We place our hopes in circumstances that are unreliable because they will inevitably change. Even our apparent triumphs—the times when we successfully gratify or glorify ourselves—are temporary and ultimately unsatisfying.

Seeing ourselves as separate from others, we feel lonely and alienated. In an us-against-the-world struggle, we experience the self as a fixed "me" that must be constantly privileged and protected against threats. As mindfulness teacher Gullu Singh writes, "The most elusive and yet most profound insight comes from observing how our usual sense of self creates suffering and struggle. We can see this in the way we constantly compare ourselves to others, in our desperate need to be seen in a particular way (smart, funny, athletic, etc.), and the fierce defense we mount when our identity feels threatened, like needing to be 'right' in arguments."[3]

Insight relaxes this painful and exhausting struggle to feed and protect the fictitious self, which you now see as pointless and self-defeating. But it doesn't just ease your suffering; it brings you deep happiness.

With insight you understand that you are intimately connected with all people and things. They are part of you, and you of them. There is balance and harmony in your life and your relationships with others are mutually beneficial. No longer fighting to maintain some separate self, you stop your me-against-them struggle with the world and experience it as enjoyable, supportive, and good. Resting simply in reality, you find that things are okay just as they are.

The surprising news is that this healing insight arises naturally from your mindfulness practice, even if that isn't your conscious intention. Once your mind stabilizes and focuses through mindfulness meditation, you naturally look at yourself and the world through the lens of insight because you have automatically engaged your natural intelligence and awareness.

Although insight is a natural outcome of mindfulness meditation, you can accelerate the process with practices that are designed to help you see reality clearly. Some of these are meditations to experience reality directly and nonconceptually; others are contemplative practices in which you use your intellect to analyze the true nature of yourself and the world. Both these types of practices help you overcome your false views of reality and enjoy the real happiness of real life in the real world.

Insight into the True Causes of Happiness and Unhappiness

As we've seen, looking deeply into the true nature of things, including yourself, makes a fundamental contribution to your happiness. But there is another very practical way that insight can contribute to your happiness. It helps you to understand what really brings happiness and unhappiness to yourself and others and what doesn't.

As the Dalai Lama has said, we all want to be happy. This common desire is what defines and unites all beings. This is not a problem. In spite of what we are told by many religions and philosophies, there is nothing wrong with self-interest, nothing wrong with wanting to be happy. The challenge is defining what is truly in our best interest, what will actually make us happy. What we need is enlightened self-interest, an approach to life based on insight into the real causes of happiness and suffering.

Misunderstanding what really brings us happiness is one of our biggest problems. Our search for happiness in the wrong places shapes our lives and our society in damaging ways and it diverts us from the things that would actually give us a life of lasting and deep happiness. This is where insight helps.

There are a couple of standards I'd like to suggest to differentiate what brings real happiness from what doesn't.

If we look at the things that bring us deep and lasting happiness, like a calm mind, love, healing, good relationships, meaningful work, and a good and caring community, we see they always benefit others as well as ourselves. What really brings happiness is always win-win. Conversely, anything that is win-lose will not bring real happiness, even to ourselves.

If my pleasure results in your pain, it's not something that will ultimately benefit either of us. If what benefits me also benefits you, it will bring real happiness to us both.

So much suffering in this world is caused by the belief that happiness is a zero-sum game. It turns our own lives into a competition for happiness. It creates a society driven by short-term selfishness and a winner-take-all mentality in which extreme inequality is built in. But even the winners don't find real happiness in a world like that.

So if you are asking yourself whether or not something will really bring you happiness, this is a good test: Is it win-win? Will it also bring others happiness? Because what is really beneficial benefits everyone.

So there is no self-sacrifice or renunciation required in our search for happiness. We don't need to be "selfless" or martyrs. Understanding the real causes of happiness and unhappiness, all we have to sacrifice are the false causes of happiness that actually bring unhappiness to everyone. We are right to want happiness—real happiness. All we need to renounce is our suffering.

There is something else that tells us whether something truly brings us happiness. Does the happiness last, or is it a passing pleasure or enjoyment that just makes us want more? If something doesn't make us happy in a lasting and meaningful way, it will leave a void in us, an empty and unsatisfied feeling that makes us only want more.

There's nothing wrong with pleasure and enjoyment, with things that feel good. The problem is not pleasurable things themselves, but our compulsive consumption of them because we want them to do something they can't—make us really happy. If you pursue something in the hope it will make you happy, but it only leaves you feeling unfilled and wanting more, that's a sign you are looking for happiness in the wrong place.

This dissatisfaction and the endless search for more it creates has terrible effects on our lives, the lives of others, and society itself. It causes people to accumulate wealth compulsively—far more than they actually need—leaving other people with too little. If you consume obsessively, trying to fill a void that material pleasures, success, or prestige can never satisfy, that's a sign you are looking for happiness in the wrong place.

With these conditions in mind, here's an investigation you can do into what will really bring you happiness and what won't.

Inquiry: What Will Really Make Me Happy?

Here is a series of questions you can ask yourself about what you really want in life, how you are currently looking for happiness, and what you can do in the future to have the real and lasting happiness you seek. Of course, this is just one possible series of inquiries, and I hope it will inspire your personal exploration of what will really bring you happiness and what won't.

- Complete the sentence: I want a life that is . . .
- What kind of person do I want to be?
- What are the things I value most in life?
- What is my current level of happiness and enjoyment of life?
- Where am I currently looking for happiness? What's working and what's not?
- To what extent do I measure my happiness through success, wealth, praise, prestige, or other external factors?
- How much does my happiness depend on my relationships with other people? What qualities in my relationships bring me happiness and what don't?
- Does my happiness depend on how I feel about myself? By what standards do I judge myself?
- How important is what other people think about me?
- To what extent do I look for happiness in short-term enjoyment or pleasure? Do these satisfy me or only leave me wanting more? How do I feel when their enjoyment ends?

- Are there ways I seek happiness that come at others' expense? To what extent do I feel happiness is a zero-sum game?
- What are the things in my life that bring me deep and sustainable happiness? Are they things that also bring others happiness?
- Do I feel guilty about being happy, feel it is somehow wrong or that I don't deserve happiness?
- What are some ways I need to redefine my happiness?
- Do I need to make changes in the external circumstances of my life and the choices I make? What would some of those be?
- What are the qualities I need to cultivate in my heart and mind so I can lead a life of real happiness and meaning?
- Finally, looking back at my answer to the first question, what do I need to do now and in the future to have the kind of life and happiness I really want?

As I said, this is a very personal investigation, and you will certainly have your own questions and issues to contemplate about what will bring you the happiness you want. There is no right answer—except one. If the question is, Can I really be happy? the answer is yes. If this exercise shows you anything, I hope it is this: You have all the resources you need and a real path forward to the kind of life you want. If you know what really leads to it, happiness can be yours.

Practices

Insight practice combines the direct experience of reality with the analytic power of your natural intelligence. Between the two, you can gain an accurate understanding of how things really are, including yourself. By doing the kind of investigation taught here by the psychologist Rick

Hanson, you can free yourself from the cognitive errors about reality that cause so much suffering and enjoy a more open, relaxed, and playful relationship with life.

PRACTICE

Discover the Basic Nature of All Experiences[4]

Rick Hanson

Mindfulness brings many benefits, and perhaps the greatest of all is insight. Insight is knowing what is happening around us and inside us, why it is happening, and how to make it better.

These insights help us let go of the confusions and misunderstandings that make us tense and stressed and create conflicts with others. We increasingly recognize the changing, insubstantial nature of our experiences, which are more like clouds than bricks. Then we hold them more lightly, with less resistance or attachment. We feel more at home inside ourselves, more at peace and stronger, and more able to deal with personal issues or injustice in the wider world.

While insight is a natural function of our mind, it can be cultivated with practice. Through formal meditation as well as mindfulness in the flow of daily life, we become more stably present, with an increasingly penetrating awareness that fosters insights. They may begin conceptually, but gradually become a *felt knowing*. They move beyond words and become the truths you live in and that live through you.

As insight deepens with practice, the nature of all thoughts and things becomes increasingly clear. This is not some sort of philosophy. Insight provides a direct knowing that immediately brings you into a greater ease with the world inside you and around you.

With mindfulness, you can see that any experience consists of multiple aspects or elements. For example, feeling frustrated while stuck in traffic involves body sensations, emotions, thoughts, memories, images, desires, and more.

Second, you see that whatever you are experiencing depends on its causes and conditions: perhaps the phone rang or something moved in your stomach or a background worry about your health has pushed forward into awareness.

Third, you see again and again that your experiences are impermanent. Even the ones that seem regrettably stable—such as that pain in your knee or that ache in your heart—have a shifting, dynamic quality to them.

In sum, as these insights deepen, you realize that *all experiences are made of parts that are connected and changing.* This applies to everything passing through awareness, all of the contents of consciousness. Much as a room can be empty of furniture, every experience is empty of essence, independence, and permanence.

For a sense of this, take a few minutes and try this brief practice. You can do it over the course of just a few breaths, or longer. You just let your mind run for a bit, and then pause to recognize three things about it.

1. Establishing mindfulness, become aware of the experience of breathing, in your chest as a whole or even at a single point on your upper lip. Notice that the experience of breathing has many aspects to it. Perhaps qualities of warmth or coolness, of pressure and release, and more.

   Can you recognize that the experience of breathing is made of parts? Can you know that *every experience* is made of parts?
2. Now return to simply being mindful of the sensations of breathing. Can you recognize that these sensations are occurring due to various causes and conditions, such as the movement of air flowing in and out, and the physical structure of your nose and chest and lungs?

Can you know that *no experience* appears on its own? Can you know that *every experience* is connected to its causes?

3. Now return one last time to simply being mindful of the sensations of breathing—air flowing in and flowing out, chest rising and falling.

   Can you notice that every sensation of breathing is *impermanent* as it appears in awareness and then passes away? Can you know that *every experience* is impermanent and constantly changing?

   Rest as long as you like in this knowing.

These insights into the nature of thoughts and things can be hard-won, as they push against the tendencies of our own biology. Evolving over millions of years, the nervous system attempts to unify what is made of parts, to separate what is connected, and to hold on to what is continually changing. Those sort of delusions helped our ancestors live to see the sunrise, and that passed on the genes that have made our human bodies. But today, with insight, we can become disenchanted in a good sense, and wake up from Mother Nature's well-intended spell.

Recognizing the compounded, "spread out," mosaic-like nature of any experience helps you deal with it not as a tight knot but as something you can unpack, and disentangle, and open up, and air out, and let in some light. Seeing the interconnected nature of your experiences—including important ones such as chronic anxiety or inner peace—draws you naturally into exploring their underlying causes, and what you can do about them.

When you see that all experiences are impermanent, so that no single experience can ever provide lasting happiness, you realize that happiness comes from letting go rather than holding on. Knowing that no experience lasts forever helps you bear the painful ones and hold the enjoyable ones more lightly.

These insights may begin as mere ideas, but they feel increasingly true with regular mindfulness practice. We develop more conviction about them and trust in them. They become the frame in which we receive the next moment arising. Starting in simple, concrete, specific ways, our insights spread out and deepen and become increasingly profound. They free us up and bring us home. They offer the good news that we can influence our relationships and who we are becoming, that we can cling less and love more, and that our deep nature is wakeful and peaceful.

We can also use our insight to understand the patterns of thoughts, feelings, and ways of acting that cause problems for ourselves and those close to us. When we combine our insight into their nature with compassion for ourselves, we can reset our relationship with the world from one of reactivity and trauma to love and wisdom.

PRACTICE

How Insight Frees You from Habitual Patterns[5]

Trudy Goodman

The habitual patterns that arise in us seem to have a life of their own, shaping our behavior into contours of isolation, anxiety, self-criticism, addiction, or other self-destructive habits. These patterns make us unhappy. They are obstacles to what we long for in our lives and might even cause us to give up our goals and dreams in despair.

The good news is that we can become aware of how we get caught in these patterns and learn to move through experience with more love and wisdom. The process of getting stuck in patterned thoughts and feelings happens quite mechanically. The gateway to freedom is to understand this compassionately. In this, meditation is our best friend, allowing us space to relax and receive other dimensions of our being.

The most fundamental pattern that we all have is ignoring impermanence—denying the fact that everything is always changing and can't bring us lasting happiness. We humans imagine that the self is continuous and permanent, even though it isn't and we aren't!

Intellectually we know this, but it just doesn't feel true. This is where our mindfulness practice helps. Practicing meditation with loving awareness, we begin to see change as a constant. We see that we can't breathe in forever—we have to breathe out. This inevitable rhythm is independent of what I want or who I am or what pattern has me in its grip. With mindful awareness, the ebb and flow of breath, the birth and death of experience, become clear. This is wisdom—seeing the way life unfolds so lovingly in us, as us.

Meditation: Loving Connection

Mindfulness meditation is the backward step into simply being here together. We step back from our patterned approaches to experience so we can fully appreciate this life and share it with each other. We can simply create moments of loving connection with ourselves, each other, and our world. Miraculously, this is the way to free our hearts from unhelpful habits of perception. How wonderful!

Sense the space all around you and the thoughts and feelings flowing through your mind and heart. Relax into the fullness of being.

Be 100 percent present with what is seen, heard, and felt. Then step back into the simple fact of this existence, this reality, right now. You can literally shift your body back just an inch, relaxing into a posture of receptivity, poise, and balance.

You can do this whenever you notice your attention has wandered into the past or future. Just be with this particular moment in all of eternity. And be with this next one, too.

To understand the truth of what he called "interbeing," or interdependence as it is more generally known, Thich Nhat Hanh suggested we look deeply into the nature of a single flower. This investigation undercuts our mistaken view that things are solid, separate, and independent. It's amazing how such a simple and straightforward contemplation can change your whole perception of what things are and how they exist.

PRACTICE

The Whole Universe in a Single Flower

A contemplative practice inspired by the teachings of Thich Nhat Hanh

Place a flower in front of you. If you don't have a flower, it's fine to visualize one.

On the face of it, this flower appears to have its own identity and separate existence. But is that really true? It clearly exists, but what is the real nature of its existence?

To answer that question, Thich Nhat Hanh suggests you investigate the causes and conditions that created this flower. If you look deeply into the nature of this flower you will find the whole universe manifesting in it.

You could start with the soil in which the seed of the flower grew, including all the previous generations of plants and beings that made the soil fertile. In this flower you can also see the clouds, lakes, rivers, and oceans that water it, the bees and insects that spread its pollen, the Earth's atmosphere that brings it oxygen, and the sun that gives it light.

In fact, the list of causes and conditions that brought this flower into existence is infinite. Ultimately they encompass everything in the realms of physics, chemistry, biology, and geology. They include the animate and the inanimate. The causes of this flower go from single atoms out to the whole universe. They are all present in this flower; it is their creation.

This is the living truth of interbeing, the infinite web that brings everything into existence. Nothing exists on its own. Nothing creates itself. Everything is created by everything else. Things appear individually, but that is merely the beautiful and magical manifestation of interbeing, the interplay of one and many.

You can think of endless causes that are present in this flower. There is one thing, however, that you cannot find. As Thich Nhat Hanh points out, the whole universe is present in this single flower, but you will never find in it an independent, separate self, no matter how hard you try. It is worth taking a moment now to see if you can find anything in this flower that is independent of the outside causes and conditions that made it exist.

If things don't exist independently, but are merely the products of outside causes and conditions, does that in any way diminish them? Just the opposite. When we see everything as manifestations of interbeing, we experience the universe as a living unity that manifests in a display of infinite variety that is beautiful, vivid, and life-sustaining. Nothing is seen anymore as fixed, alone, or static. All is alive, connected, and in harmony.

You too are a manifestation of interbeing, the creation of infinite causes and conditions. When you turn the light of insight on yourself, you find that, like the flower, the whole universe is present in you. This discovery dispels feelings of alienation and aloneness and brings you a deep, joyful sense of unity and harmony. There is no longer any separation between you and all things.

PRACTICE

The Whole Universe in a Single Person

Melvin McLeod

You are a manifestation of interbeing. Like a flower, the whole universe is present in you.

Like the flower, you too are created by soil, water, air, and light. The whole physical universe supports your life and makes it possible. Take a minute now and look at all the things in the physical world you are inseparable from, all the things that sustain you and manifest in your life.

Now let's turn to the more complex and challenging question of how other people have helped make you who you are. Other people, and society as a whole, are present within you too.

Of course, that starts with your parents. Without them you would not even exist, and in your childhood they shaped how you see yourself, the world, and your role in life. And since your parents got their values and attitudes from their parents, you are also the product of your grandparents, and so on through all the generations of humanity that have led to who you are today.

Take some time now to contemplate the ways in which your parents are causes of who you are. What values and attitudes did you inherit from them? What prejudices and misconceptions? What skills and abilities? How did they shape how you think about yourself? To what extent were your needs, hopes, and fears created by your relationship with them? Are there childhood traumas that still shape who you are? Of all the things in the universe that live in you, your parents are the most important link in the chain of causation that has made you who you are.

Now expand your investigation to include all the people, systems, and institutions you are interdependent with and that every day sustain and enrich your life. All the people who produce the food you eat. The people around the world who create the products you use. The educators who teach you and the health care professionals who heal you. The scientists and scholars who advance the state of human knowledge you benefit from. The culture that, for better or worse, shapes your values, needs, ambitions, and views.

What role has your privilege or lack of privilege played in who you are and how your life has gone? What role has your gender played, and your ethnicity and class? You inter-are with all of human society, the good and the bad. All humanity lives in you, making you who you are.

This simple but powerful contemplation shows you who you really are and how you really exist—as part of the great web of cause and effect known as interbeing. Where before life was marked by isolation and alienation, there is now connection and identification with everything.

I cannot think of another meditation that is so straightforward and rational, and yet so transformative. Do it for even a few minutes every day—contemplating a flower, yourself, or anything else—and you can touch the magic of interbeing.

So far we have applied our insight to the objects of our awareness—the things in the outside world we perceive and the thoughts, feelings, and self we experience in our minds. We have seen that they are impermanent, always changing, and made of many parts. We have not found any fixed and separate identity in them. We have discovered the whole universe within all things—from a single flower to us—through the infinite causes and conditions that create them.

Now we turn from the things that appear to our awareness to the nature of our awareness itself. Does awareness exist in the same way as the things, thoughts, and feelings it experiences? If the real secret of mindfulness is awareness of our awareness, then it is vital to shine our insight on the nature of awareness itself.

PRACTICE

Experience Your Natural Awareness[6]

Diana Winston

Natural awareness is a way of practicing mindfulness in which your focus is on awareness itself, rather than on the things you are aware of. It is generally relaxed, effortless, and spacious, and it can elicit a profound sense of well-being. The term *natural awareness* invites you to notice or rediscover the awareness that already exists and is available to you at any moment.

Because natural awareness is hard to define, it is primarily recognized experientially. Let me give you some markers for it. Experiencing natural awareness can feel like:

- Your mind is completely aware and undistracted, without doing anything in particular to make yourself aware.
- Your mind is like wide open space, and everything in it is just passing by.

- You are aware, but not identified with the part of you that is aware.
- Your mind feels at rest.
- You are noticing that you are noticing, and you are abiding in that awareness.
- Everything just seems to be happening on its own.
- You feel a sense of contentment not connected to external conditions.
- You are simply being, without agenda, and this beingness creates a feeling of timelessness and ease.

How to Shift into Natural Awareness

If you have an existing mindfulness practice, let's look at three deliberate shifts you can make during your classical mindfulness meditation that point you toward natural awareness. Once you have evoked natural awareness, you can then try natural awareness meditations to prolong and deepen your experience.

1. RELAXING EFFORT

Effort in classical mindfulness meditation typically means you rigorously and faithfully return your attention to your main focus, typically your breathing. Relaxing your effort to shift into natural awareness is a little different. It means you rein in the tendency to put your attention on your breath or other objects and just *be* with the objects as they arise.

Many meditators fear that if they stop trying, nothing will happen. Or their mind will wander all over the place if they're not making any effort to do something with it. But just sitting down and not doing anything wouldn't be natural awareness practice—it would be sitting down and doing nothing. Dropping or relaxing effort is very different because we are tuning into the awareness that is already present, and so we don't have to try hard to get there.

Also, you won't necessarily have a wandering mind because you relax your effort after having worked hard to pay attention. Think of shifting into natural awareness like riding a bicycle. You pedal really hard, but then at a certain point you can stop pedaling and coast. The bike stays upright, you're still heading where you want to go, but you're not working so hard. In fact, it's quite exhilarating.

So what does relaxing your effort feel like when you're meditating? It feels like stopping the attempt to wrestle with your unruly mind, fighting to bring it back to the present. Instead, you are resting, relaxing, and exploring the awareness that is already present. It feels immensely joyful to stop the struggle.

2. BROADEN YOUR ATTENTION

In meditation, as in life, your attention can be narrowly or broadly focused. You can think of attention as like a camera. Sometimes you use a telescopic lens to focus on something quite narrow, and sometimes you use a panoramic lens to take a wide landscape view.

When you meditate, you can apply narrow or panoramic attention. An example of narrow focus would be attending primarily to a single object, like your breath. Panoramic attention is wide open—you notice many things at play or just have a general wide view.

Broad, panoramic attention tends to be the type of attention present when we do natural awareness practice. It doesn't equal natural awareness, but it does point us in the direction of natural awareness. Because most of us gravitate toward focused attention in both meditation and daily life, opening up panoramically can invite in natural awareness. It counteracts our usual forward-focus tendencies and allows our minds to rest and reset, kind of like a brain vacation.

3. DROP OBJECTS

As a practitioner of classical mindfulness, probably the most important shift you can make to invite in natural awareness is to move your attention from an object to objectlessness.

Objects of meditation are, simply put, the things you focus on, such as the breath, body sensations, emotions, thoughts, or sounds. Focusing on objects and attending to them is generally how we live our life as well.

Objectless awareness is when you focus less on the *objects* of awareness and instead focus on the *awareness itself*. Objects will arise in your meditation—thoughts, emotions, sensations—but your focus is on the awareness itself.

Experiencing Objectless Awareness

When people tune into objectless awareness, they tend to experience it in three different ways.

IT IS THAT IN WHICH EVERYTHING IS CONTAINED

"Our mind is like the sky," it is sometimes said, "and everything in it is like clouds floating by." When you turn your attention to the sky-like nature of your mind, noticing the boundless space around things, you experience a field of vast awareness in which everything is contained. Some people experience objectless awareness in this way.

IT IS THAT WHICH KNOWS

Most of us are used to focusing on objects when we meditate. But what happens when you make the shift to noticing that which is aware—to seeking the knower? If you start searching for the knower, what do you find?

As you notice things, you can also notice the thing that notices things. You can take your attention from an outward focus on objects and turn it inward, as if you were reversing your attention. You move from that which you are aware of to that which is aware of what you are aware of.

IT IS THAT WHICH JUST IS

Sometimes in objectless awareness you experience a deep felt sense that you are aware. You are here, fully present, and everything seems to be happening on its own. It may feel like this awareness is unshakable, that it is spontaneously present, and that there is nothing you can do to stop being aware. No matter what is happening, including thoughts, you are fully and uncompromisingly aware.

Experience Your Natural Awareness

I invite you to give natural awareness meditation a try. Bring to it a spirit of experimentation and curiosity. Enjoy the process. And trust yourself—if you think you are entering the territory, you probably are.

Here are a few "glimpse" practices that you can insert into your classical mindfulness meditation. I recommend concentrating your mind for a while by noticing your breathing and then shifting over to one of these three practices:

1. RECOLLECTION

One of the simplest ways to access natural awareness is through memory. Let yourself remember a time when you felt awake, connected, peaceful, and expansive—in a state of beingness. Don't try too hard. Let it come to you in a simple way.

Now remember how you felt at the time. What did your body feel like? How about your heart? See if you can invite in a full-bodied experience of the memory. Recall details: sights, scents, sounds, and any other sensory experiences.

Now notice what is happening in the present moment. See if a sense of beingness is present for you just by your imagining a past experience. What does that beingness feel like? Connectedness, ease, presence, relaxation? Let yourself rest here.

2. EXPAND YOUR FIELD OF AWARENESS

Begin with expanded listening—listening out to the far reaches of your hearing. Once you've expanded your listening, open your eyes and broaden your vision. Let your field of vision be expansive, noticing the space between things and viewing peripherally. Then expand your body awareness. First notice your back. Then begin to expand further out, sensing the field around, above, and below you in 360 degrees.

At this point, your senses of hearing, sight, and feeling should all be expanded. From here, you can begin to play with that expansion. Can you stay expanded but also feel embodied? Can you have simultaneous inner and outer awareness? What predominates?

When you notice yourself tensing, just relax your body. It might be possible to stay connected to only one field (sight, sound, feeling), or perhaps you can feel them all simultaneously. Rest in this awareness for as long as you wish.

3. MIND LIKE AN OCEAN

Imagine your mind is like an ocean. On the surface are choppy waves and turbulence. These are the dramas you get caught in: thoughts, fears, emotions, and stories. Imagine sinking below the surface into the infinite depth. Deep in the ocean is a boundless stillness that is completely undisturbed by the turbulence above. Can you connect with this deep tranquility? Once you can sense it, see if you can rest there for a while.

Looking directly at awareness or consciousness itself has been called "taking the backward step," or "shining the light inward." It's a bit like watching a movie. Normally your attention is completely focused on what's happening on the screen in front of you. Now you look at what's happening behind the images. You might find that your awareness is like the screen, the place where your perceptions, thoughts, feelings, and sense of self appear. Or maybe your awareness is like the projector, the very creator of the things it is aware of. (They don't call them projections for nothing.) Once you can look beyond the objects of awareness and directly at awareness itself, you can investigate its nature by asking yourself a series of questions about it.

PRACTICE

Investigate the Nature of Awareness

Melvin McLeod

First, sit in a good meditation posture and take some time to identify your awareness, consciousness itself. If you want, you can use some of the techniques to discover your natural awareness that you have just learned from Diana Winston.

The meditation now is to look not at *experiences* but at the *experiencer*—at consciousness itself, not the things you are conscious of. Let go of the objects of awareness and rest in the knower itself. This is not easy to do because we are addicted to the objects of awareness, the infinite things appearing on our mental screen.

Having done that for a few minutes, ask yourself if you are in fact still stuck on the objects of awareness instead of experiencing the awareness itself. Are you looking at your perceptions and calling them awareness? Or are you creating a thought of awareness and calling that awareness?

Now, to the extent you can separate awareness from the things you are aware of, ask yourself some questions about the nature of your awareness.

- Does my awareness have a shape, size, or color? Does it have parts or is it one thing?
- Does my awareness have a location, such as in my brain or body or somewhere outside?
- Does awareness have a center? Does it have a sense of self or identity?
- Does awareness change according to what it is aware of?
- Does awareness have an owner? Is it my awareness? Is it part of me or am I part of it?
- Is awareness the observer of objects or their creator?
- Is awareness born and can it die? Does it stop and start?
- Is my awareness a material thing, and if not, what is it?
- To conclude the exercise, answer this question:
  What—if anything—can I definitely say about the nature of awareness and my relationship to it?

Journeys on the Complete Path of Mindfulness: Insight

I think of two levels of insight. From the point of view of a practitioner, there's an initial period that lasts forever. And there's a deeper layer that also lasts forever, or at least it seems to!

The initial layer is insight into your own stuff. You realize you've been operating through a set of specific patterns, convictions, and certainties. When you see that, it feels like you have come out of a dream. What you thought was true was just one arbitrary way of looking at things that came about because of cause and effect and your conditioning.

The experience of liberation from that, the feeling of those beliefs and patterns suddenly falling away, is the deeper insight. Sometimes it feels like your whole self is falling away. You see how operating in a more generous or selfless way is more optimal for happiness and functioning. In the end, it's the same insight. There's only one flavor of insight—it's to see what's true.

Those experiences of insight can be quite mundane or they can be very dramatic. Like there's this "wow," and suddenly you're less likely to go into the same old patterns because you have a little bit more space. Now of course most of your patterns come back, sometimes in sneaky ways, and so you have to see them again and again. You have to get completely sick of yourself. You have to get sick of all your shit.

—Jeff Warren

At some point I had insight into what was serving me in my life and what wasn't serving me. What wasn't serving me was upset. What wasn't serving me was a constant sense of vigilance. What did serve me was being whole and competent and human and confident.

What wasn't serving me was withering. I was actually shrinking myself—not in the eyes of others, but in my own eyes. I had to stand as tall as I could—all four foot, eleven of me—and stand in that place of knowing. Mindfulness helped me do that because I got to intimately know the nature of my mind.

—Noliwe Alexander

As my practice deepened, it became clear that moment to moment nothing's holding still, that there's no way to hold on to anything. The quieter the mind gets, the clearer it is that everything's happening on its own. There's nobody there it's happening to. It's just happening. When there's an openness to that changing flow, there's also experience of the open space it's all happening in. So I have found that opening to impermanence also opens to vast, formless awareness itself.

—Tara Brach

It was always clear to me to that self-compassion is needed to provide the safety and acceptance we need to see through the illusion of separate self. When we're scared and feel inadequate, we look for security by trying to improve ourselves, or maybe improve our standing in the world. We get trapped in the drama of the thinking mind and the sense of a separate self it creates. But when we turn the lens of compassion inward, warmth and love will naturally arise and we will feel our connection to the larger whole.

Ironically, even though self-compassion is aimed at suffering, it also frees us from the sense of separation that causes the suffering. That's why self-compassion is as strongly linked positively to happiness as it is linked negatively to things like sadness or depression.

—Kristin Neff

Insight helped me to experience joy for the first time in my life. It was a joy that came out of being with my life as it was, as opposed to thinking that I had to do something to fix myself. I had insight that I wasn't broken in the way I thought I was, and that joy was available to me in this moment.

Mindfulness really showed me how joy is right here. It isn't a project or something I have to keep pursuing and pursuing. One of the great experiences of joy I had—and I'm getting emotional when I talk about this—was when my sense of personal identity or separateness fell away and I just sat with the sound of a bird. When the bird sang, it was as if in my very heart I couldn't distinguish between me and the bird. It was just the bird and the song. It was so joyful, I felt so free.

—Lisa Ernst

5

LOVE AND COMPASSION

Whether we call it love, compassion, kindness, caring, or loving-kindness, it's the heart that makes our lives worth living and our society good.

Throughout human history we've been told that love is the most important thing in life. All the world's great religions and philosophies, and everyone from Jesus to Ann Landers to the Beatles, have extolled the value of love. It's the eternal theme of culture. (Interestingly, when asked to comment on the Beatles' claim that "All you need is love," the poet Allen Ginsberg said, "All you need is awareness. Then love will follow naturally.")

But how do we actually develop more love and compassion? Mostly the advice we get is some version of "Just do it." But that's not very helpful. What we need are effective ways that we can intentionally deepen and expand our love and compassion.

Mindfulness offers us the practical tools we need to have more love and compassion in our lives, ways to become kinder and more caring people. As a complete path, mindfulness opens the heart as well as the mind. It deepens and expands our natural empathy, kindness, and compassion, which are the secret to a happy, beneficial life and a more just world.

So far on the Complete Path of Mindfulness we have worked with our mind. Through our practice of mindfulness meditation, we have started to tame and focus the mind. Through our cultivation of insight, we have started to see reality more clearly and to understand what really brings us happiness and what doesn't. Now we turn from our mind to our heart.

We usually see mind and heart as separate, but they're not. They're just different sides of our basic nature—our awareness and insight on one hand, and our love and compassion on the other. Together they describe who we really are—we are made of awareness and love. Heart and mind are one in us.

Heart and mind are also not separate in the practice of mindfulness. As we've seen, self-compassion is built into mindfulness meditation from the start, allowing us to look clearly at ourselves in a friendly, nonjudgmental way. The late spiritual teacher Ram Dass talked about the practice of "loving awareness." We could equally describe it as the practice of "aware loving." Only if we have love and compassion will our awareness benefit ourselves and others. Only if we have awareness is our love and compassion skillful. Awareness and compassion only work when they work together.

The Power of Self-Compassion

If love is the secret to life, there is a secret to love: it starts with ourselves.

The advice the world generally gives us is the opposite of what we really need to do to develop more compassion and love. The conventional wisdom is that love and compassion mean we have to sacrifice our own happiness in favor of others. Love in that sense is described as "selfless." The problem is that this emphasis on self-sacrifice stops us from following a path to more love and compassion that actually works. Because that path starts with love and compassion for ourselves.

Real compassion embraces everyone, including us. Like all beings, we suffer and long for happiness. We are as deserving of compassion as anyone else. In the eyes of love, there is no separation between ourselves and others. Is it really compassion if we are excluded?

The old saying that "love starts at home" is usually taken to mean "in our own family." But love actually starts in our ultimate home—our own being.

By healing ourselves first, we equip ourselves to benefit others effectively. How can we love others when we can't love ourselves? How can we relieve others' suffering when we don't know how to relieve our own? When we learn how to bring ourselves real happiness, we can help others find it too. Far from being selfish, being happy ourselves is actually one of the best things we can do for others. Finding love and happiness ourselves, we give others hope and show them the way.

Love You Can Trust

Caring for and loving ourselves, often called self-compassion, can help us with a pervasive psychological problem that starts in childhood and affects many of us for our whole lives. It's called "insecure attachment." It makes it hard for us to trust, feel, and give love.

"Insecure attachment" sounds kind of technical, but it's just a fancy term for an experience that's pretty universal. It simply means that when we were young we felt we couldn't really trust our parents' love. Their affection and caring for us seemed to come and go, and we could not be sure they would always be there for us when we really needed them. Our attachment to our parents, our bond with the most important people in our lives, felt insecure and unreliable. It may not have even been their fault. Life itself is not secure, after all, and fears of abandonment and loss through separation, divorce, sickness, or death may have added to our insecurity.

Many if not most of us suffer from insecure attachment to some degree. Not having experienced enough safe, dependable love as children, we now find it hard to fully trust others' love and to experience the universe as a fundamentally loving place. We may have deep feelings of isolation, self-doubt, and anxiety that we are not fully aware of that limit our ability to trust and feel love.

To some degree we all have broken hearts, but we can heal them. There are different ways to help ourselves receive and feel love, and one of them is to give ourselves the love and compassion we need. As Thich Nhat Hanh said in the teaching we read earlier, the wounded child who didn't get the secure love they wanted is still within us, and we now have the chance to give them the compassion and caring they need. By practicing mindful self-compassion, we offer ourselves the kind of nonjudgmental, unconditional love we want so badly and deserve. We can prove to ourselves that love is real and can be trusted.

It is true that developing self-compassion can be difficult. Many of us are plagued by guilt, shame, and self-criticism and feel we are not worthy of love. We may believe the conventional morality that loving and caring for ourselves is somehow wrong or selfish. Based on our childhood experiences, we may not trust love, even our own.

If that's true for you, as it is for so many of us, it may be better to start your compassion practice aimed at others, perhaps those closest to you. Then you can start to practice self-compassion when you're ready.

On the other hand, you could make your obstacles to self-compassion a focal point of your practice. After all, who deserves love and compassion more than people who don't feel they are worthy of love and can't experience it fully? Who deserves love and compassion more than you? Among the practices that follow is a teaching by Diana Winston on ways to apply self-compassion specifically to the obstacles of blame, guilt, and self-criticism. For many of us, this is a good place to start practicing compassion—for our suffering selves.

The Mindful Path to More Love and Compassion

One thing that's unique about the Complete Path of Mindfulness is that it offers us a step-by-step path we can follow to bring more love into our lives and the world. It goes like this: taming the mind leads to insight, insight leads to understanding and empathy, and empathy leads to love and compassion. This simple but effective process works for compassion both for ourselves and for others.

We have already started on this path with our practice of the first two keys of Complete Mindfulness. Our practice of mindfulness meditation has given us a calm and focused mind. We can look clearly at the lives of others and have the strength not to turn away from their suffering.

Looking clearly gives us insight into what people are experiencing, and we develop deep empathy for them. With insight, we see their inner struggles and suffering and understand the causes that have made their lives what they are. We empathize with what they are going through and our heart opens. People are made fun of for saying "I feel your pain," but there's little in life that's more important. Feeling people's pain is the secret to compassion and a better world.

You can apply the same process to yourself. With a mind that is at least somewhat tamed, you look clearly and without turning away at your own suffering. You have insight into the nature of your problems and what causes them. Your heart opens and you feel real empathy for yourself and what you have gone through in life. Feeling your own pain may be difficult, but it is the first step to transforming your life.

Having started on this journey with your mindfulness and insight practices, you can embark on the next part of the path, the intentional cultivation of more love and compassion. Two of the practices that follow are derived from Buddhist meditations that have become widely known and practiced in the modern world. These are *metta*, or "loving-kindness practice" as it is often called, and the compassion practice of "taking in and sending out," also known by the Tibetan term *tonglen*. Neither of these is inherently or exclusively Buddhist. They don't require any particular belief system and can benefit everyone. They are simply effective meditations that any of us can do to cultivate the love, kindness, and compassion we and the world so badly need.

In the practices that follow, we start first with some meditations to cultivate compassion and loving-kindness toward ourselves. They are followed by ways to apply self-compassion to specific challenges in our life, particularly the negative thoughts and emotional states that cause us so much pain. These include meditations specially designed to relax and ground us in our body and ease the stress and trauma stored there.

Then we take the love and compassion we have developed for ourselves and expand it outward. We start with loving-kindness for those closest to us, with family and loved ones. Then we widen our circle of love more and more until it ultimately encompasses all living beings, even our enemies. Finally, we learn the powerful compassion meditation technique of taking in and sending out (*tonglen*) that reverses the self-obsessed way we often approach life and creates a deep bond of love between us and others.

There is probably already someone in your life you feel perfect love and compassion toward. It could be your child or someone else who is close to you. They are someone you would gladly give all your happiness to, someone whose suffering you would happily take on yourself. When you remember that, you see that love and compassion—in fact, perfect love and compassion—are a natural part of who you are and guide your life more than you may know.

With faith in that as your starting place, you can strengthen, deepen, and widen your love and compassion through these practices. They start with someone who really deserves love and happiness—you.

Practices and Teachings

We begin with three different meditations to offer loving-kindness to yourself. These meditations suggest some different phrases that you can say to yourself, or you can find your own words that touch you deeply and intimately. You can do any or all of these variations. The important thing is to give yourself the understanding, warmth, and comfort you deserve and need.

We start with the basic self-compassion meditation as taught by leading mindful self-compassion expert Kristin Neff.

PRACTICE

Mindful Self-Compassion[1]

Kristin Neff

1. Put both hands on your heart, pause, and feel their warmth. You can also put your hand anyplace on your body that feels soothing and comforting, like your belly or face.
2. Breathe deeply in and out.
3. Speak these words to yourself, out loud or silently, in a warm and caring tone:

This is a moment of suffering.
Suffering is a part of life.
May I be kind to myself in this moment.
May I give myself the compassion I need.

The first phrase, *This is a moment of suffering*, is designed to bring mindfulness to the fact that you're in pain. Other possible wordings are *I'm having a really tough time right now*, *This hurts*, or anything that describes the suffering you are experiencing.

The second phrase, *Suffering is a part of life*, reminds you that imperfection is part of the shared human experience. Other possible wordings are *Everyone feels this way sometimes*, *This is part of being human*, etc.

The third phrase, *May I be kind to myself in this moment*, helps bring a sense of caring concern to your present-moment experience. Other possible wordings are *May I love and support myself right now*, *May I accept myself as I am*, etc.

The final phrase, *May I give myself the compassion I need*, firmly sets your intention to be self-compassionate. You might use other words such as *May I remember that I am worthy of compassion*, *May I give myself the same compassion I would give to a good friend*, etc.

Find the wordings for these four phrases that are the most comfortable for you and memorize them. Then, the next time you judge yourself or have a difficult experience, you can use these phrases as a way of reminding yourself to be self-compassionate. This practice is a handy tool to soothe and calm troubled states of mind.

PRACTICE

Kind Words[2]

Christopher Germer

- Please find a comfortable position, sitting or lying down. Let your eyes close, fully or partially. Take a few deep breaths to settle into your body and into the present moment.
- Put your hand over your heart, or wherever it is comforting and soothing, as a reminder that you are bringing not only awareness, but loving awareness, to your experience and to yourself.
- After a while, feel your breath where you notice it most easily. Feel your body breathe in and out, and when your attention wanders, notice the gentle movement of your breath once again.
- Then gently release your focus on the breath, or continue to have

a background awareness of your breathing, as you begin offering yourself words of kindness and compassion, over and over, words that you need to hear, words you can savor. If you already have phrases that are meaningful to you, please use these.

- If you are new to meditating with words and phrases, open your heart and mind to what you need to hear—words of wisdom and compassion that speak to you in the deepest way.
- Open your heart to these words, whispering them gently into your own ear, again and again. Perhaps hearing the words from the inside, allow them to resonate within you. Allow the words to take up space and fill your being, if only for this one moment.
- Whenever you notice that your mind has wandered, refresh your aim by feeling the sensations in your body. Coming home to your own body, feel the importance of your words. Come home to kindness.
- Finally, release the words and rest quietly in your own body. Gently open your eyes.

PRACTICE

Give Yourself Loving-Kindness[3]

Lisa Ernst

First, settle into your posture. Notice how your body feels on the floor, chair, or cushion. Let your attention settle into the body.

Next, focus on your breathing. Notice the sensations of inhaling and exhaling wherever you feel them most strongly. For a few moments just rest with the breath, perhaps feeling a sense of ease, equanimity, and restfulness.

Now locate any emotions you feel in this moment as sensations in the body. Perhaps there's tightness in the throat, a heaviness in the heart, tension in the shoulders, or perhaps you feel at ease.

Whatever you find, just allow your feelings to be as they are. If you find it difficult to stay present, widen your attention to include the entire body. If you'd like, place your hand at your heart and feel the care and kindness you can offer yourself in this moment.

Now, silently repeat phrases that evoke feelings of loving-kindness toward yourself. Here are a few suggested phrases. You can choose all or any that speak to you:

May I be safe.
May I be peaceful.
May I be kind to myself.
May I accept myself as I am in this moment.
May I be held in compassion.
May I be filled with loving-kindness.
May I find joy and equanimity in this moment, just as it is.

Get in touch with the intention of the words—to offer kindness, compassion, and acceptance. But don't force it. As your mind wanders, gently refresh the phrases in your heart.

Do your best to offer yourself the same kindness, support, and acceptance you'd give a friend who's struggling. Can you meet all parts of yourself with kindness, nothing left out? If you're not yet ready, just hold this as an intention and do your best within your capacity, without judgment.

To close the practice, if you like, extend the compassion outward to all beings by repeating these phrases:

May we all be free of pain and sorrow.
May we all be held in compassion.
May we all be safe and at peace.

These three self-compassion practices will help you to develop a general attitude of warmth and caring toward yourself. They lay the foundation for bringing self-compassion to specific things in life you need help with.

Much of our suffering is caused by painful emotions and negative thought patterns. Just because these are happening in your mind doesn't make it easy to free yourself from them—far from it. It is hard to know where they come from and what sustains them, and we can't seem to control them no matter how hard we try.

Mindfulness doesn't change the basic fact that life is full of challenges, but it can change how you react to them. When painful thoughts and emotions arise in the face of difficulties and trauma, either past or present, you can look at them with awareness and self-compassion. Here are three mindfulness-based ways to liberate yourself from their power over you. We start with the renowned four-part self-compassion meditation called RAIN, which can help you deal with any problematic thought, feeling, or pattern you suffer from.

PRACTICE

RAIN: Recognize, Allow, Investigate, Nurture[4]

Tara Brach

RAIN is a practice of radical self-compassion. The acronym is an easy-to-remember tool for bringing mindfulness and compassion to emotional difficulty. RAIN stands for:

Recognize what is going on.

Allow the experience to be there, just as it is.

Investigate with interest and care.

Nurture with self-compassion.

You can take your time and explore RAIN as a stand-alone meditation or move through the steps whenever challenging feelings arise.

1. **RECOGNIZE WHAT'S GOING ON**

   Recognizing means consciously acknowledging, in any given moment, the thoughts, feelings, and behaviors that are affecting you. This can be done with a simple mental whisper, noting what you are most aware of.

2. **ALLOW THE EXPERIENCE TO BE THERE, JUST AS IT IS**

   Allowing means letting the thoughts, emotions, feelings, or sensations you have recognized simply be there, without trying to fix or avoid anything. You might recognize fear, and allow by mentally whispering, "It's OK," or "This belongs," or "Yes." Allowing creates a pause that makes it possible to deepen attention.

3. **INVESTIGATE WITH INTEREST AND CARE**

   To investigate, call on your natural curiosity—the desire to know truth—and direct a more focused attention to your present experience. You might ask yourself: What most wants attention? How am I experiencing this in my body? What am I believing? What does this vulnerable place want from me? What does it most need? Whatever the inquiry, your investigation will be most transformational if you step away from conceptualizing and bring your primary attention to the felt sense in the body.

4. **NURTURE WITH SELF-COMPASSION**

   Self-compassion begins to naturally arise in the moments that you recognize you are suffering. It comes into fullness as you intentionally nurture your inner life with self-care. To do this, try to sense what the wounded, frightened, or hurting place inside you most needs, and then offer some gesture of active care that might address this need.

Does it need a message of reassurance? Of forgiveness? Of companionship? Of love? Experiment and see which intentional gesture of kindness most helps to comfort, soften, or open your heart. It might be the mental whisper: *I'm here with you. I'm sorry, and I love you. I love you, and I'm listening. It's not your fault. Trust in your goodness.*

In addition to a whispered message of care, many people find healing by gently placing a hand on the heart or cheek; or by envisioning being bathed in or embraced by warm, radiant light. If it feels difficult to offer yourself love, bring to mind a loving being—spiritual figure, family member, friend, or pet—and imagine that being's love and wisdom flowing into you.

After the RAIN

When you've completed the active steps of RAIN, it's important to notice the quality of your own presence and rest in that wakeful, tender space of awareness. The fruit of RAIN is realizing that you are no longer imprisoned in or identified with any limiting sense of self. Give yourself the gift of becoming familiar with the truth and natural freedom of your being; it is mysterious and precious!

Mindfulness offers you a whole range of methods to work with painful things happening in your mind and heart. Diana Winston calls this your "mindfulness toolbox," and she opens it up to help you work with the negative feelings about yourself that so many of us suffer from.

PRACTICE

Free Yourself from Guilt, Shame, and Self-Criticism[5]

Diana Winston

My nine-year-old had saved up her money for roller blades. When we were at the sporting goods store, I got inspired too and purchased a pair of old-school white roller skates with pink wheels.

I was thrilled to share this new pastime with her, and we spent the afternoon in blissful mommy-daughter union. We were learning together, it was outdoors, and we were away from screens.

It was all great until the next day, when I caught my toe in a crack, fell, and torqued my knee in an awful direction. Alongside the excruciating knee pain, I was filled with equally painful self-recriminations.

What was I thinking, what a stupid idea, I can't believe I screwed this up. Summer's ruined! I got hurt, what's going to happen to her? I'm such a terrible mom. On and on it went.

Until I remembered to be mindful.

Then I saw I was caught in a painful cycle of self-blame, guilt, and judgment, all intensifying the physical pain and making me even more miserable. I paused and brought compassionate attention to my breath and body. Noticing the thoughts and emotions that were arising, I calmed myself down and found my center. I remembered I was human, definitely fallible, and I would get through this. And I did (although my knee still hasn't fully recovered).

I, like everyone else, suffer from a challenging complex of thoughts and emotions that show up from time to time: self-judgment, self-criticism, guilt, shame. These emotions seem to be at epidemic levels in society today.

Because I've been meditating now for thirty years, I have tools at my disposal that I can deploy to work with these emotions and thoughts. When they pop up, as they did in my roller-skating misadventure, mindfulness tools are there for me. To help you work with your own painful thoughts and emotions when they arise, here is the approach I use, one that has kept me sane (most of the time) and self-compassionate for decades.

How to Get Off the Train of Thoughts

The simple mindfulness practice of returning your wandering mind to the present moment is the foundation. When we get submerged in shame, self-hatred, and guilt, we can train ourselves to come back to the present moment and find relief. It's helpful to develop a regular, daily-ish meditation practice so that we have some understanding and experience with mindfulness in advance. Then we have the tools to apply it on the spot when the going gets rough.

The critical voices inside us take on a myriad of disguises, and mindfulness excels here. We learn to see those thoughts merely *as* thoughts—not to be taken as reality. One of my favorite bumper stickers is "Don't believe everything you think."

Thoughts, while potentially amazing, profound, and brilliant, are also the source of enormous suffering. We all have our top-ten suffering thoughts—worry, judging, comparing, and for most of us, guilt, shame, and self-criticism. We can learn to bring a mindful approach to these thoughts.

I find a couple of analogies helpful.

Thoughts are like snowballs. We start out with a tiny bit of snow and if we're not mindful, it can grow into a giant snowball that overwhelms us. It's important to catch the thoughts when they're tiny to not let them escalate.

Thoughts are like trains. We get on a train ("I blew it today at work") and it leaves the station. The next thing we know we're twenty miles down the track—twenty minutes into disturbing, predictive, globalizing, or catastrophic ruminations ("so I'll probably be fired").

With mindfulness we have some choices. When we realize we're on the train, we can get off—it doesn't matter how long we've been ruminating. Or we can never get on the train in the first place—a thought arises, we see it as a thought, and we stay on the platform while the train passes.

How do we do this? Sometimes simply the power of noticing our thoughts in the moment is enough to help relieve them. Often we harangue ourselves without really noticing we are doing it, so this recognition is key.

One more analogy: You know those thought bubbles that cartoon characters have over their heads? Imagine your critical thought is in a thought bubble. Now you can take the pin of mindfulness and pop it. Ah, sweet relief.

When meditators catch a thought with their awareness, the thought may just dissolve in that moment—they've "popped it" or "got off the train." This is wonderful when it happens, but it may be best-case scenario. So I recommend that people also "note" thoughts: put soft mental labels on them like "self-criticism," "judgment," "worrying," "blaming," etc. Sometimes naming the thought can allow it to "pop." This strategy is often called "name it to tame it."

Now let's say that just labeling thought doesn't do much—we find ourselves still ruminating, acting like a dog with a bone. Then it's time to bring our attention into our body to notice if there is an emotion fueling the repetitive thought pattern.

How to Mindfully Hold Challenging Emotions

Study after study shows the benefit of using mindfulness to regulate challenging emotions. We can be mindful of thoughts and emotions together, or we can focus on a strong emotion alone.

Mindfully holding our emotions starts with recognition—labeling and recognizing what has taken you down: fear, grief, shame, guilt, and so on. We can label emotions in the same way we label thoughts. Often just recognizing, naming, and letting them be there without trying to alter them may be enough.

Or we can shift to investigating the emotion in real time, in our body. What's happening in this moment? *My stomach is clenched, my jaw is tight, my chest feels constricted.* We sit with these sensations and hold them as a compassionate witness, just as I try to do with my daughter when she's upset.

One skillful approach is not to force ourselves to stay solely with the emotion, especially when it feels big and painful. It's helpful to have a pleasant or neutral part of our body that we can move our attention to, and then return to the challenging emotion/sensations in our body when we're ready. (If you don't have an easeful area in your body, you can imagine a nurturing time or place.) Moving our attention back and forth allows for a bit of rest, prevents us from getting overwhelmed, and helps to integrate the challenging emotion. It helps build up our mindfulness capacity to hold the difficult emotion.

As we attend to our emotions mindfully, we track them as they ebb and flow, move and shift, intensify or dissipate. There are very specific sensations we can attend to: pulsing, pounding, contracting, vibrating, tightness, and so on. Sometimes, mindfully being with them allows them to pass through, like weather patterns. Sometimes they don't pass through, but we can hold them in our awareness and we are not disturbed by them. Sometimes they don't pass, and we feel overwhelmed, but a little voice inside us knows we're okay, even in the midst of strong, challenging feelings.

The key to the mindful approach is what's typically called "disidentification." This is the moment of recognition that we are not our thoughts or emotions. We go from "This is my thought or emotion that I'm entirely caught in," to "This thought is moving through me." "My thought" becomes "the thought." "Being the thought" is now "being *with* the thought."

This way we become disentangled from our painful thoughts and feelings, but we still have them. We're not trying to use mindfulness to become mindful zombies with no affect. With disidentification we are present with and fully embodying our experience. Yet we have some space, some witnessing, and I daresay, some freedom.

When we *get* disidentification, so much freedom arises.

Use Your Mindfulness Toolbox

We can work with all of the mindfulness-based tools I have described, one by one, or in combination. Some of them will work for you at different times. Some you will feel more drawn to; some will feel less useful. You can use them in meditation, or on the spot in daily life. Together, they form a comprehensive approach to mindfully holding challenging emotions. But remember to be gentle and kind to yourself in the process.

Will these techniques free you entirely from self-criticism, shame, and guilt? Probably not, but sustained practice will give you significantly more freedom from them, especially when supplemented with self-compassion practices and a recognition of your inner goodness.

Personally, I have found that much of my core suffering has been transformed over time. I have significantly less self-hatred than I used to. I attribute that to my mindfulness practice (and other modalities like therapy). And when shame, guilt, and judgment do arise, like in the roller-skating fiasco, when you cultivate mindfulness and wisdom, you will find your (yup, I'm going here) footing, stay stable in the midst of reactivity, and experience (sorry) way smoother skating!

So many of us feel at some deep level that we are unloved, perhaps not even worthy of love. As we talked about earlier, this is often the result of insecure attachment, of not getting the reliable love from our parents that we needed. In spite of that, there have undoubtedly been times in life when someone loved us, and Stephen Murphy-Shigematsu invites us to remember what they felt like. That will help us trust that we were loved, we are loved, and we've always been worthy of love.

PRACTICE

Remember Someone Who Loved You

Stephen Murphy-Shigematsu

When I was a child the nuns and priests in my Catholic school told me that Jesus loved me and protected me. And there was a guardian angel who was there to wrestle with the devil should he come near. It gave me a sense of safety and belonging to believe that God loves us unconditionally and that we are each of infinite worth.

Years later, I felt the same sense of being cared for when I experienced loving-kindness meditation practice. Now I saw that God's love comes to us through people. I found that remembering a loving person's voice and face brought love down to the human level, grounding it in acts of kindness.

In my twenties I spent several years as a teacher in day care, kindergarten, and elementary schools. There I found the opportunity to practice what I was learning about love.

At the time, *Mr. Rogers' Neighborhood* was very popular among young children. On his program Fred Rogers constantly gave children the message that he liked them just the way they are, that he believed in them, just as they are. When he asked people at the Emmy Awards ceremony in 1997 to remember someone who cared for them, I realized that he was inviting them into the sacred space I had experienced in loving-kindness practice.

In the classroom, I found that when I loved my students, or reminded them they were loved by others, it helped them to feel worthwhile and lovable. Knowing that someone loved them, they felt safe, worthy, and connected. They learned to listen to the gentle messages around them that they were loved.

As a psychotherapist, I meet people who are in pain because they have forgotten how they have been loved in their lives. They judge themselves and develop a narrative that they are unlovable and don't deserve love.

Remembering the love they have received in life helps them create a new narrative that soothes feelings of unworthiness, quiets the harsh voice of self-criticism, and muffles the fear of imposter syndrome. They are released from the grip of their crippling victim consciousness, realizing that if someone loved them before, someone can love them again. Their new narrative tells them that if they were worthy of love once, they still are.

I've found that even if someone didn't receive much love early in life, emotional reflection on times they were loved in the past can change them, one warm memory at a time. Remembering times we were loved re-teaches us that love and trust are possible and feel reassuringly familiar.

In my classes on the practice of heartfulness, I do an exercise on remembering someone who has loved us. This isn't just nostalgia—it's healing. I introduce the exercise with Mr. Rogers's instructions: "All of us have special ones who have loved us into being. Would you just take, along with me, thirty seconds to think of the people who have helped you become who you are? Those who have cared about you and wanted what is best for you in life."

I invite people to say softly to themselves, "I am loved."

Then say to a loving person they remember: "Thank you for loving me."

And if they feel like it, they can add, "Thank you for letting me love you."

This is usually all we do, but sometimes a short guided reflection may be useful for those who have difficulty, due to trauma, neglect, or emotional loss, remembering a caring person. A trauma-informed approach requires gentleness, creativity, and safety for people who may not have clear memories of being loved, but did experience some moments of kindness and deserve now to feel held and worthy.

Guided Reflection: You Are Loved

I invite you to think of someone who has loved you.

If no one comes to mind, that's okay. Many of us have not had the love we needed and deserved. The love you did receive may not have been perfect, but at some moments in your life somebody treated you with kindness. Someone listened to you. Someone believed in you.

Try to remember how someone cared for you in gentle, subtle ways—through a smile, a warm touch, or a small act of kindness. If still no one comes to mind, perhaps there is a pet who gave you love.

Let them come to you, and remember what it was like to be in their presence. Know that their love lives inside you. You have been loved. You are not alone.

When you're ready, come back gently. And carry that love with you.

Anxiety, fear, and stress—these have always been part of the human condition. But they seem even worse in the modern world, which is so full of things to worry about and fear. Here is a four-part practice based on mindful breathing you can do when anxiety and fear limit what you're able to do and reduce your enjoyment of life.

PRACTICE

Mindful Breathing to Calm Anxiety and Fear[6]

Melvin Escobar

When I was twelve years old, I experienced a near drowning at a public swimming pool. I'd been to the pool many times, but since I'd never had swimming lessons, I always stayed in the shallow end. One bright and sunny day, my best friend convinced me that he could teach me to swim. I'd just need to jump off the diving board into the deep end of the pool, and he'd instruct me from there. He swore he'd catch me somehow. Needless to say, he didn't catch me, and I found myself suddenly over my head in the most terrifyingly literal way. Naturally, I panicked. Gasping for air, I inhaled gulps of water before the lifeguard jumped in to drag my water- and trauma-logged body out of the pool.

I avoided all bodies of water for the next twenty years. Until one day, sitting on the shores of a beautiful mountain lake, I resolved that when I got back to the city, I would learn to swim. I went home and enrolled in swimming classes through my local community college. Equipped with several years of mindfulness practice, I was finally going to face my fear.

I wanted to be able to be in the water without being flooded by anxiety or experiencing agonizing flashbacks from that fateful day. It was an excruciating three semesters. I'd get home from class, and my husband would ask, "How'd it go?" My pat response was, "I survived."

Mindful breathing was my lifeline. There were days when I was so overwhelmed I had to get out of the pool before class was over. But just as often, my practice enabled me to stay connected to my body and the present moment. Over time my anxiety began to abate.

Now I'm happy to report that, when it's safe enough, it's nearly impossible to keep me out of the water! Even though I still get overwhelmed at times, I bow to my body-mind and acknowledge that it's simply trying to protect me from harm.

The path of mindfulness is about learning how to navigate the unpredictable waters of life with awareness, insight, and compassion. In these anxious times, there are plenty of stressors affecting our breathing. Moment to moment, we may be unconsciously anticipating the next ping of our phone or the next horror in our feed. The looming chaos in our political and planetary atmospheres weighs on us constantly, along with the ever-present demands of work and family.

Amid all the challenges of life, one thing we have agency over is our breath. The practice of mindful breathing not only reveals that respiration is both automatic and voluntary, it empowers us to choose the quality of breath appropriate to each moment.

In times of intensity, as when literally or metaphorically drowning, our breath becomes short and shallow; its purpose is to create the energy we need to get ourselves out of danger. But energy from a fight-or-flight reaction that isn't discharged can manifest as toxic stress. Practicing mindful breathing can help us metabolize excess energy or pre-empt the reactivity that produces it. In fact, a growing body of research is revealing substantial benefits for the body and mind when we breathe diaphragmatically or engage in other mindful breathing practices.

When entering into any mindfulness practice, it's important to let go of the idea that there's one right way to be mindful. You can be sitting, standing, moving, or lying down. Your eyes can be opened or closed. You can be in your home or a cubicle (or a swimming pool). What matters most is the quality of your attention and intention.

While a variety of mindful breathing practices have been handed down over time, I will be offering an approach that's based on focusing your attention on body, feeling, mind, and mental objects while following the breath. Let's dive into the four parts of this practice.

1. **MINDFULNESS OF BODY**

   Begin by noticing that the body is already breathing. Take long, smooth breaths into your entire body, from the tips of your toes and fingers all the way to the top of your head. Allow your breath to expand into your belly. Observe the sensation of your breath as it enters into and passes out of your nose or mouth.

2. **MINDFULNESS OF FEELING**

   Next, gently notice where the body may be holding excess tension. Can you find ease or even joy via your breath? Bring kind awareness to whatever sensations are present; label them as pleasant, unpleasant, or neutral. Focus your attention on the pleasant aspects of breathing. You might try on a slight smile, vocalizing as you exhale, or imagine a warm and protective light surrounding you as you breathe.

3. **MINDFULNESS OF MIND AND MENTAL OBJECTS**

   Now, contemplate the mind. The mind can be conceived of as a flow of nonstatic sensations: thoughts, feelings, and physical perceptions that float around in the field of awareness. As you take this moment to meditate, allow these sensations to arise and pass away along with the breath. Instead of overidentifying with them, cultivate a sense of nonjudgment and gratitude. Breathe with whatever is present, for it's merely the flotsam and jetsam carried along by the currents of consciousness.

4. **CONTINUING YOUR PRACTICE IN DAILY LIFE**

   As you draw your practice to a close, relish any moments when you experienced clarity of mind. Appreciate the stillness that was made possible amid the ebbs and flows of sensation inherent in the aliveness of your body.

Consider these questions as guidance for bringing the practice into your daily life: How can a daily practice of mindful breathing buoy me in times of distress? How can I stay mindful of my breath when I feel at risk of going under? How can mindful breathing help me more skillfully navigate the choppy waters of my community and society as a whole?

So much of our trauma and stress is held in our body. But our body is also the source of deep relaxation, healing, and connection to the Earth. It is a good friend we can get to know better. By bringing our mind and body together, meditations like these two ease the suffering we hold in our body and connect us to the natural goodness and well-being of embodiment.

PRACTICE

Grounding Touch[7]

Cyndi Lee

My beagle, Little Bit, can sense a storm gathering. The reason I know this is because Little Bit uses the language of her body to communicate her fear. From just the slightest shift in air pressure, her chunky little body starts quivering. Then, at the first clap of thunder, she springs off her stubby legs and torpedoes herself through the air, taking aim for the familiar protection of my arms. I am her port in a storm.

When we humans feel an emotional storm brewing, the adrenaline rush of powerful feelings often renders us unable to control our body, speech, or mind. Holding our breath and quivering, we might find ourselves meeting [emotional] heat with anger, anger with angry words. Or we keep our afflictive emotions inside where they fester. Grief in our chest, anger in our jaw, fear in our knees—all eventually reveal themselves via pain in our joints or reduced movement capacity.

Instead of trying to deny these feelings, taking refuge in the body means that we begin to make friends with our body. We listen to our body and treat it the way we would treat someone we care about. Instead of pushing it too hard or being afraid to move it at all, we can walk the middle path of intuiting what is appropriate for our body, which means what is appropriate for us.

Get More Friendly

We have so many goals for our bodies: lose weight, get sculpted, be healthier, more attractive, keep that youthful glow! Like a dysfunctional romantic relationship where we expect our partner to meet our every need, we don't relate to our body as our friend, but as the agent for achieving all of our hopes and fears.

To begin thinking of our body as the place where we feel good helps to shift our goal from wanting to jump higher and run faster to feeling better and living a more engaged, vibrant life. Do this in small bites I call "exercise snacks." Get up and move around for ten minutes here and there. Circumambulate the house or office, do three sun salutations, walk your dog, turn on music and play.

Instead of unrealistic goals that almost make failure a given, this is just about feeling good more often. This is how you can slowly redefine your relationship with your body, from something outside of yourself that needs to be different, to a refuge that is always there to provide you an experience of integration and well-being.

Get Curious

We can take a lesson from the physical practice of yoga. The Sanskrit word for "pose" is *asana*, which translates as "to sit with what comes up." Whether you are sitting, walking, or jumping rope, notice what is coming up: joy, resistance, old memories, insights. Include it all. When your mind strays, re-anchor it via the feelings of your body, your emotions, or your breathing.

These sensations occur only in the present, so the body works as a perfect home base for the wandering mind. Notice not just what your body is feeling, but how you feel about what you are feeling. You will discover that while your body has been changing all the time, your ideas about your body, and what it can or cannot do, have become frozen. That's an interesting insight too.

Maintaining continuous awareness in this way is called "mindfulness of body"—an effective practice for learning to be bigger than we think we are, for expanding our comfort zone, and for lightening up a little bit through the recognition of impermanence.

How to Practice Grounding Touch

Grounding touch is a simple micro-practice for taking refuge in your body when you feel stressed and need a time out. It's a method for connecting to your emotional state through your body, using the warmth of your hands and the calmness of your breath to ground and stabilize your nervous system.

- Stand or sit upright with your feet firmly planted. Place one hand on your chest and one at the base of your spine. You can also place hands on your heart, belly, forehead, or thighs.
- Inhale through your nose for four counts, exhale through your nose for four counts, and repeat. Feel the movement of your breath beneath your hands. Let your mind ride on the breath, like a raft on the ocean.

- You can do this practice anywhere—sitting on a park bench, walking from the elevator to your desk, in the stairwell at work, and even in the bathroom. You can do it anywhere and anytime you need to be grounded in the refuge of your body.

PRACTICE

Deep Relaxation[8]

Sister Chan Khong

Body and mind are two faces of one reality and they support each other. Because of the way we live and consume, stress accumulates in our body and erodes our sense of well-being. By taking care of your body and incorporating moments of deep relaxation into daily life, you can reduce stress, anxiety, and irritation, and help balance body and mind.

Sometimes our body needs to rest, but our mind still wants to do many things. Though we think we can overcome the needs of the body with our mind, this is not something we can continue doing forever. From time to time we need to stop, bring our awareness back to our body, and relax. Otherwise, tension builds up and we can lose our temper very easily and be unkind. When we're disturbed by a strong emotion or we feel we're burning out—that it's all too much and we're going to crack—that's the perfect moment for deep relaxation.

In the same way that we practice being aware of every state of our mind—accepting, understanding, then releasing each state that arises—in deep relaxation we practice this way with our body, visiting every part with awareness, acceptance, care, and without judgment.

A full session of deep relaxation can last from twenty minutes to an hour. We use our mindfulness like a ray of light to scan our body, bringing awareness and relaxation to each part.

1. **AWARENESS OF BREATH AND EARTH**

   Lie down on your back with your arms at your sides. If you prefer, you can sit in a chair. Make yourself comfortable, close your eyes, and relax. Begin to follow your breathing and just be with your in-breath and out-breath. Feel the earth beneath you, supporting you. Bring your awareness to your abdomen rising and falling. If you feel agitated or dispersed, put your hand on your abdomen and feel it rise and fall as the air goes in and out. Say quietly to yourself, "Breathing in, I am with my in-breath. Breathing out, I am with my out-breath."

2. **BODY SCAN AND GRATITUDE**

   Continue to follow your breathing as you bring awareness and relaxation to each part of your body from the top of your head to the tips of your toes. You can begin with the hair on your head, your scalp, brain, forehead, and so on. For each body part, say something like this quietly to yourself: "Breathing in, I am aware of my eyes. Breathing out, I release the tension in all the tiny muscles around my eyes."

   As you bring your attention to each body part in turn, contemplate your gratitude. For example, we often forget our heart, yet it beats night and day. Now we have a chance to pay attention to our heart and show our appreciation to our heart. Say silently to yourself, "Breathing in, I bring my attention to my heart. Breathing out, I am aware of my heart."

3. **LET GO INTO DEEP RELAXATION**

   Bring your awareness back to your abdomen rising and falling. You might enjoy some minutes of quiet or gentle music. If during the session you feel yourself falling asleep, don't resist. The sleep experienced during deep relaxation is brief but it's free from agitation and is nourishing and healing.

Once the session is over, move your arms and legs, then open your eyes. Sit up gently. Do some stretching. Slowly stand up. Take a moment to breathe and be aware of the sensations in your body.

When you're having an intense day at work, school, or with family activities, and you don't have time for a full deep relaxation session, divide your day into segments and relax between each segment or activity. I myself take several short deep relaxation breaks every day. We think we can't take a moment to rest, but just a few minutes of deep relaxation can renew us and bring peace and vitality back to body and mind.

Find a place to lie down where you won't be disturbed. If there's not enough space, pull a chair near the wall, close your eyes, and stretch out your legs. Relax your body and follow your breathing. Bring your attention to just a few of your body parts instead of doing the whole sequence. The shoulders are often a good place to bring our attention: "Breathing in, I'm aware of my shoulders. Breathing out, I relax my shoulders and release the tension." After relaxing like this for a few minutes, you will come to your next activity refreshed and with more physical energy and mental clarity.

Deep relaxation can also help if you have trouble sleeping. Lie down on your bed and become aware of your breathing. Place your hand on your abdomen, feeling it rise and fall with your in-breath and out-breath. You might say quietly to yourself, "Breathing in, I'm aware of the muscles in my face. Breathing out, I release the muscles in my face," or simply, "Breathing in, I smile. Breathing out, I release." A gentle smile will relax the muscles in your face and help calm your nervous system. This is loving-kindness directed to yourself. Even if you don't sleep, resting in this way can be almost as good as sleeping.

Because love truly begins at home—in our own being—these self-compassion practices establish the foundation for developing more love and compassion in our lives. We have generated kindness and warmth toward ourselves and a forgiving and understanding attitude toward our problems and suffering. We have worked with difficult thoughts, emotions, and traumas, and we have relaxed and grounded ourselves in our body. We have done a lot of healing.

Now we can expand our compassion outward so that it embraces more and more beings, from those close to us to people we don't know, and even to our enemies. We can generate love and compassion until eventually they include all beings and things. We are transformed, and with us the whole world.

This is the power of love and compassion, which is harnessed by this unique version of traditional loving-kindness (*metta*) meditation taught by African-American mindfulness teacher Arisika Razak. In it she expands our loving-kindness practice to embrace not merely personal suffering but also the intense and pervasive suffering people experience because of racism, misogyny, and all the other hurts and injustices of society.

PRACTICE

Loving-Kindness (*Metta*) Meditation[9]

Arisika Razak

I have experienced illness, heartbreak, aging, and disability. As a Black, elder, cisgendered woman, I live with the trauma of social oppression on a daily basis. Like many of us, I'm also profoundly disturbed by the current suffering in the world.

In these troubled and troubling times, loving-kindness is my foundational practice. I am truly grateful for loving-kindness meditation. I practice it when I'm afraid, uncertain, or despairing. It helps me stay grounded and keeps my heart open to others. I use it to send affirmations of unconditional love to friends and benefactors, and to affirm the well-being and safety of survivors of climate catastrophe, war, and social injustice.

I believe loving-kindness practice asks that we reject social oppressions, such as racism, classism, homophobia, nativism, transphobia, ableism, antisemitism, and Islamophobia. In practicing loving-kindness, we relinquish feelings of anger, hatred, or superiority—feelings that lead to the "othering" of those different from us. When the troubles of the world seem overwhelming, I use loving-kindness to address the suffering of beings both human and other-than-human. Even when I don't know them by name, I send loving-kindness to individuals and communities experiencing drought, famine, human trafficking, and genocide.

In my personal life, I practice loving-kindness when I'm concerned about my son's welfare, and my husband and I do loving-kindness for each other and the world as part of our New Year's blessing. Sometimes when I've been in deep and seemingly irresolvable conflict with a colleague, I've (privately) offered them loving-kindness to remind myself of our shared humanity.

There are many versions of loving-kindness practice. As I practice it, there are four parts to the meditation.

The first part involves practicing loving-kindness for the self. This is how we begin because we cannot offer loving-kindness to others if we are not well resourced ourselves; we cannot invoke safety for another if we do not, even for a moment, feel safe ourselves.

In a culture where we're often criticized and encouraged to negatively judge our bodies, minds, abilities, and disabilities, the practice of loving-kindness helps us recognize that we have inherent worthiness and that we are deserving of respect, support, and tenderness just as we are. Then I repeat:

May I be safe and protected from inner and outer harm.
May I be strong and healthy in mind and body.
May I care for myself with ease and joy.
May I be happy, truly, truly happy.

In the second part of loving-kindness practice, we bring to mind a benefactor, someone who has helped or supported us. This can be a mentor, teacher, or beloved friend. As you recite the loving-kindness phrases, imagine that the person is standing or seated in front of you:

May you be safe and protected from inner and outer harm.
May you be strong and healthy in mind and body.
May you care for yourself with ease and joy.
May you be happy, truly, truly happy.

The third part of the practice is dedicated to a neutral person, someone we do not know by name and with whom we have neither a negative nor a positive connection. They could be a bus driver, delivery person, or someone we pass in the street. As with the benefactor, we should visualize this person.

If you're doing loving-kindness practice for people that you've never actually seen in real life, you can use images from the media or your own heart. For example, if I'm doing loving-kindness for a particular group of people seeking safety in times of war, I might say, "May all those fleeing war in (name of country or area) be safe and protected from inner and outer harm," while I picture people I've seen in a newspaper or other media. I then repeat these phrases:

May you be safe and protected from inner and outer harm.
May you be strong and healthy in mind and body.
May you care for yourself with ease and joy.
May you be happy, truly, truly happy.

In the fourth and final phase of this meditation, we invoke loving-kindness for a difficult person, someone with whom we are in conflict, or who has acted against us.

Offering loving-kindness to someone who caused us lasting harm is an advanced practice. So, when we first begin offering loving-kindness to difficult people, we should begin with those who have caused us minor annoyance rather than those whose acts have evoked significant trauma. The phrases are the same as for the benefactor and the neutral person:

May you be safe and protected from inner and outer harm.
May you be strong and healthy in mind and body.
May you care for yourself with ease and joy.
May you be happy, truly, truly happy.

At the East Bay Meditation Center, where I teach, I am a member of an affinity group called Every Body, Every Mind, which describes itself as "a weekly practice group for people living with disabilities, limitations, differences, and chronic illnesses." Many in this group do not have strong or healthy bodies and feel it is harmful to affirm a state of being that denies the reality of the body they live in. Some of us require assistance to carry out the activities of daily living, and we cannot always individually care for ourselves with ease and joy.

So I now use these words for loving-kindness meditation so that I may be more inclusive of all beings, regardless of their abilities and disabilities.

May I be safe and protected from inner and outer harm.
May I be strong and healthy in mind and body, and if that's not possible,
may I still find moments of well-being and joy in the body I have.
May I care for myself with ease and joy, and if that's not possible may I find
community who care for me with ease and joy.
May I be happy, truly, truly happy.

May you be safe and protected from inner and outer harm.
May you be strong and healthy in mind and body, and if that's not possible, may you still find moments of well-being and joy in the body you have.
May you care for yourself with ease and joy, and if that's not possible may you still find community who care for you with ease and joy.
May you be happy, truly, truly happy.

Loving-kindness is a practice of great profundity. It embodies the eternal truth that hatred never ends hatred but can only be healed by love. This is truly the medicine needed to heal our sick and ailing world. While we are each part of the world's problems, the practice of loving-kindness invites us to be part of the compassionate solution to these problems by not engaging in feelings of enmity and hatred.

While traditionally metta practice starts with offering loving-kindness to ourselves, many people today find that difficult because of deep-seated feelings of guilt and self-criticism. Because it is hard to give ourselves love when we don't feel we deserve it, it can be easier to offer loving-kindness first to someone close to us. For many people, this is a good place to begin metta practice.

PRACTICE

Loving-Kindness for a Loved One[10]

Christopher Germer

Allow yourself to settle into a comfortable position, either sitting or lying down. If you like, put a hand over your heart or another location that is soothing as a reminder to bring not only awareness, but loving awareness, to your experience and to yourself.

Bring to mind a person or other living being who naturally makes you smile. This could be a child, a grandparent, your cat or dog—whoever naturally brings happiness to your heart.

Let yourself feel what it's like to be in their presence. Create a vivid image of this being in your mind's eye. Allow yourself to enjoy their good company.

Now, recognize how much they wish to be happy and free from suffering, just like you and every other living being. Repeat softly and gently, feeling the importance of your words:

May you be happy.
May you be peaceful.
May you be healthy.
May you live with ease.

You may wish to use your own words to capture your deepest wishes for your loved one, or continue to repeat these phrases.

When you notice that your mind has wandered, return to the words and the image of the loved one you have in mind. Take your time and savor any warm feelings that arise.

Love and compassion create an intimate bond with beings that breaks down all separation between ourselves and others. Sharon Salzberg, the renowned teacher of loving-kindness, says that metta practice changes our whole relationship to life from one of isolation and fear to connection and safety.

TEACHING

Healing Separateness: The Power of Loving-Kindness[11]

Sharon Salzberg

When we practice *metta*, often called loving-kindness practice, we open continuously to the truth of our actual experience, changing our relationship to life. Metta—the sense of love that is not bound to desire, that does not have to pretend that things are other than the way they are—overcomes the illusion of separateness, of not being part of a whole. Thereby metta overcomes all of the states that accompany this fundamental error of separateness—fear, alienation, loneliness, and despair—all of the feelings of fragmentation. In place of these, the genuine realization of connectedness brings unification, confidence, and safety. . . .

What unites us all as human beings is an urge for happiness, which at heart is a yearning for union, for overcoming our feelings of separateness. We want to feel our identity with something larger than our small selves. We long to be one with our own lives and with each other.

If we look at the root of even the most terrible addictions, even the most appalling violence in this world, somewhere we will find this urge to unite, to be happy. In some form it is there, even in the most distorted and odious disguises. We can touch that. We can draw near and open up. We can connect—to the difficult forces within ourselves and to the different experiences in our lives. We can break through the concepts that keep us apart. This is the true nature of love and the source of healing for ourselves and our world.

This is the ground of freedom.

Metta is the ability to embrace all parts of ourselves, as well as all parts of the world. Practicing metta illuminates our inner integrity because it relieves us of the need to deny different aspects of ourselves. We can open to everything with the healing force of love. When we feel love, our mind is expansive and open enough to include the entirety of life in full awareness, both its pleasures and its pains. We feel neither betrayed by pain nor overcome by it, and thus we can contact that which is undamaged within us regardless of the situation. Metta sees truly that our integrity is inviolate, no matter what our life situation may be. We do not need to fear anything. We are whole: our deepest happiness is intrinsic to the nature of our minds, and it is not damaged through uncertainty and change. . . .

Practice: Remembering the Good Within You

Sit comfortably, in a relaxed way, and close your eyes. As much as possible, let go of analysis and expectation. For ten to fifteen minutes, call to mind something you have done or said that you feel was a kind or good action—a time you were generous, or caring, or contributed to someone's well-being.

If something comes to mind, allow the happiness that may come with the remembrance. If nothing comes to mind, gently turn your attention to a quality you like about yourself. Is there an ability or strength within yourself you can recognize? If still nothing comes to mind, reflect on the primal urge toward happiness within you, and the rightness and beauty of that.

In this reflection, even if impatience or annoyance or fear should arise, don't be disheartened or anxious—see if you can return to the contemplation without guilt or judgment.

The heart of skillful meditation is the ability to let go and begin again, over and over again. Even if you have to do that thousands of times during a session, it does not matter. There is no distance to traverse in recollecting our attention; as soon as we realize we have been lost in discursive thought, or have lost touch with our chosen contemplation, right in that very moment we can begin again. Nothing has been ruined, and there is no such thing as failing. There is nowhere the attention can wander to, and no duration of distraction, from which we cannot completely let go, in a moment, and begin again.

The essence of love and compassion is our basic human wish to make all beings happy and relieve their suffering. The amazing thing is that you have the power to do that. In fact, you're already doing it. Think of the times every day when you do your best to take away people's suffering and give them happiness. They could be the people closest to you, they could be strangers, but I'm sure you take every opportunity you can to take a negative experience or encounter and turn it into something positive.

Taking in the bad, sending out the good—this is our magic power as human beings, the true alchemy of life. It is also the reverse of the way we too often operate—hoarding the positive for ourselves and pushing the negative onto others. This is the way to an unhappy life and a dog-eat-dog society.

That's why the practice of sending out and taking in, also known by its Tibetan name *tonglen*, is one of the most powerful and transformative meditations you can do. By reversing our usual self-centered approach to life, it takes our natural power to turn the negative into the positive and makes it a superpower.

PRACTICE

Sending Out and Taking In (*Tonglen*)[12]

Judy Lief

The world today is in chaos, full of suffering, confusion, and greed. It's easy to become overwhelmed and shut down, but closing our hearts isn't helpful to anyone. We practice sending out and taking in, generally known by its Tibetan name *tonglen*, to touch into and strengthen our inherent capacity for compassion and courage—the inner qualities that sustain us as we meet the challenges of engaging with this suffering world.

Tonglen enhances our trust in our ability to be kind and, at the same time, it enhances our understanding of the selfish and negative energies that are also a part of us. It is rooted in our natural tendency to love and connect with one another.

The natural in- and out-breath is the starting point for this compassion practice. Our breathing links us with the world around us: inside out, outside to in. Without willing it or even noticing it, we're always sending our own energy out into the world and taking in whatever energies are coming at us. We're not separate from one another. We're linked. This practice begins with this quality of connection, of linkage—with oneself, with others, with the world.

Although we're engaged in such an exchange all the time, here we're intentional as to what we send out and what we take in. In this compassion practice we visualize sending out things that bring people happiness, such as love, kindness, well wishes, confidence, strength, and support, and taking in things that cause them to suffer, such as fear, doubt, pain, confusion, and sickness. We offer to others what is good and we take in what is bad so that others may be free of it.

The practice of sending out positivity and removing negativity can be a regular part of your daily meditation session. In the midst of your daily life there are also many opportunities to apply this practice in action. You can touch into it in any situation that needs your love and compassion.

Here is how to practice tonglen—sending out and taking in—in five steps:

1. **TOUCH SPACIOUSNESS**

   Sit quietly. Relax and breathe simply and naturally. Let go of restlessness. Let go of the past and the future and of compulsive thinking and planning. Be still. Touch spaciousness. Imagine that you are like a vase. Within you, there is vast space. Around you, there is vast space. Between the two, there's a subtle boundary. Breathe in. Breathe out. Let the inhalation dissolve within. Let the exhalation dissolve without. Begin the practice with a brief gap. Take a moment to stop and start fresh.

2. **RELATE TO ENERGIES**

   Evoke positive energy as bright, cool, and refreshing, and send it to all beings on the exhalation. Evoke negative energy as tarry, thick, and claustrophobic. Remove it from all beings as you breathe in. Let your breathing flow.

3. **GET PERSONAL**

   Begin with a situation that evokes real feelings for you. It could involve the person you care about the most. It could involve someone who is sick or suffering, someone you're worried about. Touch into your feeling of love for that person and your concerns about them. As you breathe out, send out love and sincere wishes for their well-being. As you breathe in, take in their pain or confusion in order to free them from such obstacles.

4. **EXTEND**

   Think of the many others—past, present, and future—who suffer in similar ways. Extend your tonglen to these many beings.

5. **DAILY LIFE**

   Return to the simplicity of just resting and breathing. Let the meditation session dissolve. Then carry a tonglen attitude, a light touch of tenderness, into your life.

When we practice tonglen—when we *live* it—we transmute selfishness and suffering into love and connection and lead a life that is meaningful and beneficial. Taking in the negative and sending out the positive—this is the true magic power of life.

TEACHING

The Ultimate Alchemy[13]

Pema Chödrön

In order to have compassion for others, we have to have compassion for ourselves. In particular, to care about other people who are fearful, angry, jealous, overpowered by addictions of all kinds, arrogant, proud, miserly, selfish—you name it—means to not run from the pain of finding these things in ourselves. In fact, one's whole attitude toward pain can change. Instead of fending it off and hiding from it, one can open one's heart and allow oneself to feel that pain, feel it as something that will soften and purify us and make us far more loving and kind.

The tonglen practice of taking in and sending out is a method for connecting with suffering—ours and that which is all around us—everywhere we go. It is a method for overcoming fear of suffering and for dissolving the tightness of our heart. Primarily it is a method for awakening the compassion that is inherent in all of us, no matter how cruel or cold we might seem to be.

As you do this practice over time, your compassion expands naturally.

We begin the practice by taking on the suffering of a person we know to be hurting and whom we wish to help. For instance, if you know of a child who is being hurt, you breathe in the wish to take away all the pain and fear of that child. Then, as you breathe out, you send the child happiness, joy, or whatever would relieve their pain.

This is the core of the practice: breathing in another's pain so they can be well and have more space to relax and open, and breathing out, sending them relaxation or whatever you feel would bring them relief and happiness.

However, we often cannot do this practice because we come face to face with our own fear, our own resistance, anger, or whatever our personal pain, our personal stuckness, happens to be at that moment.

At that point you can change the focus and begin to do tonglen for what you are feeling and for millions of others just like you who at that very moment are feeling exactly the same stuckness and misery. Maybe you are able to name your pain. You recognize it clearly as terror or revulsion or anger or wanting to get revenge.

So you breathe in for all the people who are caught with that same emotion and you send out relief or whatever opens up the space for you and all those countless others. Maybe you can't name what you're feeling. But you can feel it—a tightness in the stomach, a heavy darkness, or whatever. Just contact what you are feeling and breathe, taking it in for all of us and sending out relief to all of us.

People often say this practice goes against the grain of how we usually hold ourselves together. Truthfully, this practice does go against the grain of wanting things on our own terms, of wanting it to work out for ourselves no matter what happens to the others. The practice dissolves the armor of self-protection we've tried so hard to create around ourselves. In Buddhist language one would say that it dissolves the fixation and clinging of ego.

Tonglen reverses the usual logic of avoiding suffering and seeking pleasure, and in the process we become liberated from a very ancient prison of selfishness. We begin to feel love both for ourselves and for others, and we begin to take care of ourselves and others. It awakens our compassion and it also introduces us to a far larger view of reality. By doing the practice, we begin to connect with the open dimension of our being and the unlimited spaciousness of reality.

Tonglen can be done for those who are ill, those who are dying or have just died, or for those who are in pain of any kind. It can be done either as a formal meditation practice or right on the spot at any time. For example, if you are out walking and you see someone in pain—right on the spot you can begin to breathe in their pain and send out relief.

Or, more likely, you might see someone in pain and look away because it brings up your fear or anger, your resistance and confusion. So on the spot you can do tonglen for all the people who are just like you, for everyone who wishes to be compassionate but instead is afraid, for everyone who wishes to be brave but instead is a coward. Rather than beating yourself up, use your own stuckness as a stepping stone to understanding what people are up against all over the world.

Gradually, as you do this practice over time, your compassion expands naturally and so does your realization that things are not as solid as you thought. As you do this practice, gradually, at your own pace, you will be surprised to find yourself more and more able to be there for others even in what used to seem like impossible situations.

It takes courage and strength to open yourself up fully to the suffering of this world. Love and compassion will break your heart, and so as you care for others you must care for yourself too. When the suffering feels overwhelming, as it did for Joan Halifax when she helped care for a burned child, you can use her five-part self-care practice called GRACE.

PRACTICE

GRACE: Help When Your Heart Breaks[14]

Joan Halifax

In the early morning, a weary man dressed in tattered clothes walked into a rural Himalayan mountain hospital with a grimy, reeking bundle in his arms. I was in Nepal serving in one of Upaya Zen Center's Nomads Clinics. The doctor who was heading up our team approached the man, who wordlessly began to unwrap this large knot of rancid rags to reveal inside a young child who was severely burned on her head, arms, back, and chest.

When we examined the little girl, we saw that some of her burns were filled with writhing white maggots and other burn sites were badly infected. The man was a mute, but his eyes conveyed terrible sadness and deep resignation. Our intercultural medical team immediately mobilized, and the child was taken into a small wooden room, where local nurses and our Western team began to tend to her terrible wounds.

From the beginning, I was not only observing the clinicians and child but also my own mental and physical state. I had worked as a consultant in the burn unit at the University of Miami School of Medicine in the 1970s, and I was aware from my past experience of how painful debridement is. This is a process that entails the removal of infected or dead tissue from a wound site, and the clinicians were doing a massive and masterful job on this child.

My heart went out to the little girl as her burns were being cleaned. Her crying was reflected in her father's distressed eyes. In the midst of the procedure, the child seemed to have slipped into my skin. I realized that I was overwhelmed by my perception of her pain—my heart rate had increased, my skin had grown cold and clammy, and my breath had quickened. I realized that my identification with the child's experience had gone out of control, and if I were to stay in the room, I needed to shift from hyperattunement to care, from empathy to compassion.

This was an example of the kind of empathic distress, secondary trauma, and moral suffering that caregivers often experience when interacting with those who are suffering. GRACE is a process I created to move out of such distress and into grounded and principled compassion.

The mnemonic for GRACE is this: *Gathering* attention, *Recalling* intention, *Attuning* to self and other, *Considering* what will serve, and *Engaging* and ending.

Gathering Attention

Gather your attention by pausing, taking an in-breath, and giving yourself time to get grounded. On your exhale, invite yourself to be present in a place of stability in your body. You can also bring your attention to a phrase or an object. Use this moment of gathering your attention to interrupt your assumptions and expectations and to allow yourself to relax and be present.

Recalling Intention

Recall that your intention is to serve others, act with integrity, and preserve the integrity of others. Your motivation keeps you on track, morally grounded, and connected to your highest values.

Attuning to Self and Other

Attune to self by first noticing what's going on in your own body, heart, and mind. Notice whatever biases might be present and shift your perspective accordingly. Then attune to the other person and what they might be experiencing physically, emotionally, and mentally.

Considering What Will Serve

Consider what will really serve by letting assumptions go and insights arise. As the encounter with the other person unfolds, notice what he or she might be offering in this moment. What are you sensing, seeing, learning? Ask yourself, What will really serve here? Draw on your expertise, knowledge, and experience, and at the same time, be open to seeing things in a fresh way. Don't jump to conclusions too quickly.

Engaging and Ending

Engage, enact ethically, and then end the interaction and allow for the emergence of the next step. Compassionate action emerges from the field of openness, connection, and discernment you have co-created with the other person. Draw on your expertise, intuition, and insight and look for common ground consistent with your values and supportive of mutual integrity.

Catching myself in a distressing and fragile situation as I watched the young Nepali girl in pain, I shifted my attention to the simple sensation of my feet on the floor. I took an in-breath and allowed myself to get grounded. I then recalled briefly that I was there to serve, as were all those who were working on the child. I kept my awareness on my situation and stayed grounded. When my heart rate slowed and my head cleared, I lent my attention again to the child. All this occurred in a matter of a few seconds.

I recognized that though this was a very hard thing for this child to go through (and for the clinicians as well), the doctors and nurses and aides were saving the child's life.

As soon as I had this thought, I was flooded with warmth and a deep sense of gratitude that the man had brought his daughter to the clinic and that our team, including these compassionate Nepali nurses, were there to keep this little girl alive. I took in the whole room and sent love and strength to all who were there, including the child.

I was to see her and her father hours later, as he departed the clinic with her in his arms. Her face was bright and relaxed, and her eyes were luminous, as were the eyes of her father. Years had dropped from his face. I lightly hugged them both, bowed, and saw in her father's hands the medicines that would help her to continue to heal.

After I watched him moving carefully down the trail with his daughter held close, I had the thought that if this was the only person who was aided by our work, the months of preparation for Upaya's Nomads Clinic were worth it.

Written by the great religious scholar Karen Armstrong, the Charter for Compassion offers us a vision of a world worth living in, one with hope for the future. At a time when the values of love, kindness, and compassion seem to be in decline and are even devalued and mocked, this is a call we can rally around with confidence that here is the key to human life. If someday there is a world constitution, it could be the Charter for Compassion.

TEACHING

The Charter for Compassion[15]

Karen Armstrong

The principle of compassion lies at the heart of all religious, ethical, and spiritual traditions, calling us always to treat all others as we wish to be treated ourselves. Compassion impels us to work tirelessly to alleviate the suffering of our fellow creatures, to dethrone ourselves from the center of our world and put another there, and to honor the inviolable sanctity of every single human being, treating everybody, without exception, with absolute justice, equity, and respect.

It is also necessary in both public and private life to refrain consistently and empathically from inflicting pain. To act or speak violently out of spite, chauvinism, or self-interest, to impoverish, exploit, or deny basic rights to anybody, and to incite hatred by denigrating others—even our enemies—is a denial of our common humanity. We acknowledge that we have failed to live compassionately and that some have even increased the sum of human misery in the name of religion.

We therefore call upon all men and women to restore compassion to the center of morality and religion, to return to the ancient principle that any interpretation of scripture that breeds violence, hatred, or disdain is illegitimate, to ensure that youth are given accurate and respectful information about other traditions, religions, and cultures, to encourage a positive appreciation of cultural and religious diversity, and to cultivate an informed empathy with the suffering of all human beings—even those regarded as enemies.

We urgently need to make compassion a clear, luminous, and dynamic force in our polarized world. Rooted in a principled determination to transcend selfishness, compassion can break down political, dogmatic, ideological, and religious boundaries. Born of our deep interdependence, compassion is essential to human relationships and to a fulfilled humanity. It is the path to enlightenment and indispensable to the creation of a just economy and a peaceful global community.

Journeys on the Complete Path of Mindfulness: Love and Compassion

I live in East Oakland, California, largely a poor and working-class African-American and LatinX community. Recently I got lost and found myself driving around among homeless encampments and tents and people hanging out at liquor stores. In some ways I am glad that I got lost because I forced myself to look directly at the degradation of our communities caused by society's centuries-long inhumane treatment of Black Americans and people of color. I wanted to turn away, but I forced myself to look squarely into the depth of suffering.

It's painful. There's no doubt about it—it hurts. I came home from my drive and I was weeping, but sometimes there are good tears. They were tears of insight, tears of deep compassion, that came to me. When you see how people's lives are affected so violently and painfully in this world today, it doesn't get any easier. I'm cultivating the importance of not turning away.

—Noliwe Alexander

My son Rowan is autistic, and I learned to regulate his emotions with my self-compassion practice. When I was resistant or reactive or focused on fixing the problem,
his tantrums would get worse. So I would put my hands on my heart and say to myself, "I know this is hard, Kristin. I'm here for you. It's going to be okay." I would focus on calming myself down. Then he would resonate with that and he would calm down.

The biggest gift we can give to others is to show up as a compassionate presence. Whether your child's autistic, or you're dealing with a partner who's upset from work, whatever the situation is, we resonate with each other emotionally. So what you cultivate through your self-compassion immediately impacts the person you're with. It's not theoretical. It happens in real time.

—Kristin Neff

To really help people, you can ask the question that civil-rights activist Ruby Sales suggests: Where does it hurt? That's another way to ask, What is it you really need? We can ask that of ourselves or other people: Where does it hurt?

There's a story about compassion I love. You are walking in the woods and you see a small dog. You go to pet the dog, but it lurches at you and bares its fangs. You go from being friendly toward the dog to being angry. Then you realize the dog is snarling at you because its leg is caught in a trap, and your attitude toward the dog changes to compassion.

This story illustrates a very powerful practice you can do if you want to cultivate compassion—to see behind people's masks to the vulnerability and pain that's there. When you see that people too have their leg in a trap because of the circumstances of life, your heart opens because you see the pain and vulnerability behind their mask. And if you see your own leg is in a trap, you will be forgiving and kind toward yourself too.

—Tara Brach

When you repeat a phrase like "May everyone have happiness," it might cultivate kindness, but it might also bring up things that get in the way of kindness.

Then that becomes your work. Can you have kindness toward the absence of kindness? Can you allow yourself to be exactly as you are with a kind approach?

This can be a practice where people open up to the places they're not feeling love. If you investigate what you're experiencing with curiosity and kindness, you see what obscures your ability to connect with the kindness that is inside all of us. Then a kind of healing happens and we have more capacity to love.

—Diana Winston

The wonderful thing about loving-kindness and compassion is the joy factor. It's the experience of being at home, being at home in one's own skin.

What does it mean to be at home? It means to be accepted as you are, but it also means to be wanted. In other words, you're not just acceptable, you're accepted. There's warmth and joy there. It's not just existence. It's thriving.

—Christopher Germer

6

ETHICS

Living Your Values

Ethics are the way we live our deepest values. They are not some set of externally imposed rules—the ten *shalt nots*, etc. They come from within us and reflect the kind of life we want to live and the kind of person we want to be.

Our ethics are our values in action. They are a concrete expression of our good hearts and our insight into what is beneficial in any situation. They guide how we act—and don't—in our daily life, in our relationships, at work, and in our roles as consumers and citizens. They are our roadmap to life.

So far in our journey on the Complete Path of Mindfulness we have worked on ourselves—on taming our mind, cultivating our insight, and opening our heart to love and compassion. Now we turn to how we act and manifest our values in the world—how we lead a life that is good for ourselves and others with ethics as our guide.

The Mindful Path to Ethical Living

Living ethically is like developing more love—we don't have to "just do it." Our practice of the first three keys of Complete Mindfulness—mindfulness meditation, insight, and love and compassion—gives us a practical, step-by-step path we can follow to lead an ethical life that will benefit other people, the world, and ourselves.

In this case, the three keys are practiced in the reverse order from how we have practiced them so far. First, our intention is set by our love and compassion. Because we love and care for everyone, both others and ourselves, our goal in everything we do is to create happiness and reduce suffering. This is the basic ethical standard that guides all our actions. As it turns out, it is also how we fulfill our own desire to lead a life that is happy, meaningful, and beneficial. A life devoted to creating real happiness for others and reducing their suffering is a life worth living.

Love and compassion give us the *why* of ethics. Our practice of insight gives us the *how*. It helps us achieve our goal of creating happiness and reducing suffering skillfully and effectively.

Our insight into the truth of interdependence or interbeing shows us that our actions matter. Our ethical standards are not merely a personal issue. We are not just the product of outside causes and conditions that make us who we are. We ourselves are a cause and condition that make others who they are. If the whole universe is present in us, we are present in the whole universe. We create the universe every bit as much as it creates us, and we have an ethical responsibility to it. Our actions reverberate farther and longer than we may know, perhaps forever. We matter, and so does how we think, speak, and act.

But it is not so easy to know exactly how to bring more happiness into this world. Too often we mistakenly think something is good when actually it is harmful to ourselves and others. Conversely, we may think of something as negative when in reality it is beneficial. That's particularly a problem when our judgment is based on our perceived self-interest. So often, "what is good" really means "what is good for me."

The good news is that through insight we can understand what really brings people happiness and what doesn't. It makes our ethics accurate and skillful. With insight, we see all the ways that we and others look for happiness in the wrong places and actually cause suffering. We commit to not acting in those ways and not encouraging others to. We develop ethical guidelines that advance our basic goal to reduce suffering, or at least not to create it. Then, knowing what brings deep and lasting happiness, we act to express and encourage things like kindness, openness, joy, and connection. In this way we fulfill our basic ethical commitment to creating happiness in ways that are effective and skillful.

As we've discussed, things that truly bring happiness are good for both ourselves and others. That gives us a helpful ethical guideline. If we can act in a way that makes others *and* us happy, we should do it. Good ethics are always win-win in the long run.

But it's not always easy to know what will make others happy, no matter how close we are to them. There may be some general principles of what creates happiness and what doesn't, but there are a lot of differences and subtleties from person to person. Insight gives us deep empathy for others, and that helps us to understand them deeply—what they want, what they like and don't, where they are on their journey of life, and what their goals are. Only real empathy helps us understand what people are experiencing in life, the conditions and influences that have made them who they are, and the right thing for us to do or say to help them. Equipped with insight and empathy, we can act skillfully to achieve our goal of bringing others happiness.

So far, our love and compassion practice has shown us *why* we want to act ethically, and our insight practice has given us a pretty good idea of *how* to act ethically. But it isn't always easy to do the right thing ethically—to create happiness and not cause suffering—in the heat of the moment. Too often, we act impulsively and counterproductively. We fall under the control of reactive emotions and old patterns and act in ways that we wouldn't if we had a moment to think about it first. In the middle of all the stresses and complexities of life, we find ourselves doing or saying things we know we shouldn't and then regretting it.

Mindfulness meditation gives us the tools to actually follow the ethical standards we have set for ourselves through our insight and compassion. The calm mind we have developed in our meditation practice gives us a chance to pause for a moment before we act, and in the gap before impulse and reactivity take over, we can make a conscious, considered choice about what we want to say and do. This gives us a chance to follow the standards of ethical speech and behavior that we have set for ourselves. It gives the best in us a chance to be in charge rather than the impulsive and reactive.

This may sound like a small thing, but think how much damage is done when we act in impulsive and reactive ways that cause harm, sometimes to those we love most. How much better this world would be if we could all take a little time to reflect before acting, if we could cut, even for a moment, the connection between emotional reaction and action. In my own life, I know that I could reduce the harm and suffering I cause if I could create a little space before I speak or act, and I bet you could too.

Of course it is hard to remember to do that in the heat of the moment, but that's where a regular mindfulness practice is helpful. After all, mindfulness meditation is all about training ourselves to pause, step away from the momentum of the untrained mind's energy, and let our natural wisdom shine. If we can do that on the spot when things get challenging, life would be a lot better for us and those around us.

Beyond "Thou Shalt Not": The Many Dimensions of Ethics

People often think of ethics as kind of one-dimensional, as simply some list of *shalt nots* that governs our personal behavior. But ethics go much further and deeper than that.

First, ethics are not simply about the things we shouldn't do. Of course "first do no harm" is good advice for all of us, not just physicians. If our intention is to reduce suffering, then the first thing we need to do is make sure we aren't creating suffering ourselves. The shalt nots are good because killing, stealing, lying, sexual misconduct, etc., cause other people suffering (and us too). So it's important to follow the traditional ethical injunctions against acting in ways that cause harm. But that's not enough. Our ethics need to have a positive side too. They need to be about the things we should do, not just the things we shouldn't.

So if our intention is not just to reduce suffering but to create happiness, then our ethics must include all the ways we can act to help people be happy. To speak and act with kindness, to be generous and just, to meet people's needs and help them enjoy life—these can all be part of our commitment to living ethically.

Second, our ethics should also address all the ways we live in society—as consumers, citizens, workers, and community members. Modern thought teaches us that so much of the world's suffering is created at the societal level. Economic, political, and social systems that are unjust and uncaring damage people's lives in the billions and threaten the very future of the Earth. Our ethics must include a commitment to alleviating the suffering caused by greed, conflict, and indifference operating on a global scale. This understanding too is a reflection of our mindfulness practice, which both makes us aware of all the causes of suffering in the world and inspires us to change them. This insight is a powerful tool for effective activism.

As author and mindfulness teacher Dan Zigmond writes: "After the killing of George Floyd, I was asked by a reporter whether meditation at a time like that was immoral. It can feel that way—like hiding or turning away—but I said I believed that meditation is the opposite. Mindfulness is the practice of not turning away—of paying complete attention and facing whatever is happening in this moment. That includes not just what's happening in our mind and in our personal life, but what's happening in the wider world. We have an obligation to see the world clearly and to face suffering head-on. Meditation is not only permissible in the face of great suffering, it is a moral obligation."[1]

Societies themselves have ethics that reflect their collective values. Does a society value caring, respect, and community? Or does a society promote an us-against-them, everyone-for-themselves ethos? A society's basic values influence business practices, government policy, and how people treat each other. As citizens, we not only set our own ethical standards but also contribute to the overall ethics of our community and society.

This expansive view of ethics—encompassing the good as well as the bad, society as well as the individual—is reflected in Thich Nhat Hanh's historic statement known as the "Five Mindfulness Trainings." These five commitments hold us as mindfulness practitioners to a high ethical standard. We are enjoined not to cause harm and to create well-being and happiness for ourselves, for those close to us, and for the world as a whole. It is full-spectrum ethics, covering all the ways we impact others through our thoughts, words, and actions.

You might find some of the particulars of the Five Mindfulness Trainings a bit too black and white for your taste—I know I do—but overall they offer us a profound and comprehensive set of ethics based on mindfulness, insight, and love that any of us can aspire to live up to. I hope the practices and teachings that follow will inspire you to contemplate the mindful ethics that you would like to guide your life and how you show up in the world.

Practices and Teachings

PRACTICE

The Five Mindfulness Trainings[2]

Thich Nhat Hanh

1. **REVERENCE FOR LIFE**

   Aware of the suffering caused by the destruction of life, I am committed to cultivating the insight of interbeing and compassion and learning ways to protect the lives of people, animals, plants, and minerals.

   I am determined not to kill, not to let others kill, and not to support any act of killing in the world, in my thinking, or in my way of life.

   Seeing that harmful actions arise from anger, fear, greed, and intolerance, which in turn come from dualistic and discriminative thinking, I will cultivate openness, non-discrimination, and non-attachment to views in order to transform violence, fanaticism, and dogmatism in myself and in the world.

2. **TRUE HAPPINESS**

   Aware of the suffering caused by exploitation, social injustice, stealing, and oppression, I am committed to practicing generosity in my thinking, speaking, and acting. I am determined not to steal and not to possess anything that should belong to others; and I will share my time, energy, and material resources with those who are in need.

   I will practice looking deeply to see that the happiness and suffering of others are not separate from my own happiness and suffering; that true happiness is not possible without understanding and compassion; and that running after wealth, fame, power, and sensual pleasures can bring much suffering and despair.

I am aware that happiness depends on my mental attitude and not on external conditions, and that I can live happily in the present moment simply by remembering that I already have more than enough conditions to be happy. I am committed to practicing right livelihood so that I can help reduce the suffering of living beings on Earth and stop contributing to climate change.

3. **TRUE LOVE**

Aware of the suffering caused by sexual misconduct, I am committed to cultivating responsibility and learning ways to protect the safety and integrity of individuals, couples, families, and society.

Knowing that sexual desire is not love, and that sexual activity motivated by craving always harms myself as well as others, I am determined not to engage in sexual relations without mutual consent, true love, and a deep, long-term commitment.

I resolve to find spiritual support for the integrity of my relationship from family members, friends, and communities with whom there is support and trust.

I will do everything in my power to protect children from sexual abuse and to prevent couples and families from being broken by sexual misconduct. Seeing that body and mind are interrelated, I am committed to learn appropriate ways to take care of my sexual energy and to cultivate the four basic elements of true love—loving-kindness, compassion, joy, and inclusiveness—for the greater happiness of myself and others.

Recognizing the diversity of human experience, I am committed not to discriminate against any form of gender identity or sexual orientation. Practicing true love, we know that we will continue beautifully into the future.

4. **LOVING SPEECH AND DEEP LISTENING**

Aware of the suffering caused by unmindful speech and the inability to listen to others, I am committed to cultivating loving speech and compassionate listening in order to relieve suffering and to promote reconciliation and peace in myself and among other people, ethnic and religious groups, and nations.

Knowing that words can create happiness or suffering, I am committed to speaking truthfully using words that inspire confidence, joy, and hope. When anger is manifesting in me, I am determined not to speak. I will practice mindful breathing and walking in order to recognize and to look deeply into my anger. I know that the roots of anger can be found in my wrong perceptions and lack of understanding of the suffering in myself and in the other person.

I will speak and listen in a way that can help myself and the other person to transform suffering and see the way out of difficult situations. I am determined not to spread news that I do not know to be certain and not to utter words that can cause division or discord. I will nourish my capacity for understanding, love, joy, and inclusiveness, and gradually transform anger, violence, and fear that lie deep in my consciousness.

5. **NOURISHMENT AND HEALING**

Aware of the suffering caused by unmindful consumption, I am committed to cultivating good health, both physical and mental, for myself, my family, and my society by practicing mindful eating, drinking, and consuming. I will practice looking deeply into how I consume the four kinds of nutriments, namely edible foods, sense impressions, volition, and consciousness.

I am determined not to gamble, or to use alcohol, drugs, or any other products which contain toxins, such as certain websites, electronic games, TV programs, films, magazines, books, and conversations. I will practice coming back to the present moment to be in touch with the refreshing, healing, and nourishing elements in me and around me, not letting regrets and sorrow drag me back into the past nor letting anxieties, fear, or craving pull me out of the present moment.

I am determined not to try to cover up loneliness, anxiety, or other suffering by losing myself in consumption. I will contemplate interbeing and consume in a way that preserves peace, joy, and well-being in my body and consciousness, and in the collective body and consciousness of my family, my society, and the Earth.

One of the most important things we can do in life—and something that mindfulness helps a lot with—is to pause before we act. That way we have time to determine whether we're about to do or say something beneficial, or whether we're under the control of impulses, emotions, or reactivity and are about to do something harmful, which is to say unethical.

When we do pause, how do we decide what we're going to do? The practice that follows suggests we ask ourselves some questions that will help us assess the benefit or harm of what we are about to say or do. In this particular practice, the questions are about speech, but they can be applied to anything we're about to do. Pausing to ask ourselves these kinds of questions can ensure that we speak and act beneficially and ethically.

PRACTICE

Mindful Speaking[3]

Gil Fronsdal

Some people find speaking to be one of the most challenging areas in which to be mindful. The interpersonal concerns, wishes, and feelings that come into play when speaking can be so compelling it is easy to lose ourselves in conversations.

By being attentive while speaking it is possible to grow in self-understanding. Speech is an expression of one's inner life. Through mindfulness we can better care for the quality, well-being, and development of our inner life.

One way to do this is to simply ask yourself why you say what you do. What motivations prompt you to speak? What emotions and feelings influence what you say? What are you trying to accomplish in speaking? What are you thinking just before speaking?

Often there is not just one answer to these questions. Continued reflection can reveal how complex and varied the motivations are for what we say. Even something as simple as providing information someone has asked for can have multiple motivations or influences. Most obviously we may want to be helpful. In addition we may wish to make a good impression or, at least, avoid a bad impression of ourselves. We may hope for something in return, even if it is just a bit of appreciation or admiration. We may desire to keep the conversation going or we may be trying to end it. We might speak out of a generous impulse or it may be out of a sense of duty. Because there can be so many simultaneous motivations or concerns operating in even the simplest act of speaking, it is useful to keep inquiring so we can recognize as many intentions as possible.

Being mindful as we speak can reduce tension we may have while speaking. This is especially the case when our mindfulness includes "bodyfulness," i.e., awareness of our body as we speak. When we recognize the physical tensions or strains that build as we speak, we can relax, or at least not continue letting the tension build. We might notice that our physical posture and gestures reinforce psychological tensions as much as express them. The more we are aware of these physical aspects of speaking, the wiser we can be about how we use our body.

The rewards of mindful speaking are great. We are less likely to say things we later regret and more likely to speak wisely and thoughtfully. Remaining mindful while speaking gives us more choice in what we say. By recognizing these choices, speaking can become more deliberate and considered.

Before we speak, it helps to ask ourselves five questions:

1. *Is what I am about to say true?*

   Mindfulness is a practice of honest recognition of what is happening. By speaking only what is true we are speaking in ways that support the clear seeing that mindfulness fosters. As the saying goes, *Lies hide, truth reveals.*

2. *Is it kind?*

   Just because something is true doesn't mean that saying it is kind. In fact it can sometimes be so unkind that speaking the truth is likened to a stick with which to club people.

   The greater good for everyone, including the person who speaks, is better attained by speaking with genuine interest in the welfare of others. How we speak has a powerful effect on the way we affect each other. While speaking harshly with hostility may accomplish what we want in the short term, it is counterproductive in the long term. By speaking in ways that are kind, friendly, and respectful, we are better able to foster ongoing considerate regard for each other.

   By speaking with kindness people are also better able to hear the important things we have to say. Even better, we can aspire to speak so people are uplifted more than depressed by what we say. The saying associated with this is, *Kind speech are words from the heart.*

3. *Is it going to be useful?*

   Even speaking the truth is not always useful or beneficial. It is not useful if the person you are speaking to is unable to hear it or take it into account. It is counterproductive if the person ends the conversation or becomes excessively defensive or offensive.

   Considering how to speak the truth is an aspect of considering what is useful. Speaking respectfully is helpful, as is being careful with the words we use or the tone of voice in which it is spoken. The saying is, *If not beneficial, why say it?*

4. *Is it timely?*

   Sometimes it is only useful to speak if the timing is right. We need to be mindful of the context of the situation and of the person to whom we are talking. Someone may not be in the mood for the conversation, or they may not have the time or energy to attentively listen. They may be too preoccupied or defensive. Or perhaps it is not useful or kind to speak about some things if third parties are listening.

   Even though something is true doesn't mean it is appropriate or helpful for the conversation to be public. It can therefore be useful to wait, sometimes a long time, until the time is right for speaking. The saying is, *Only when the time is right does truth take flight.*

5. *Does it create concord?*

   The final criterion for mindful speech is to consider whether what we are going to say and how we are going to say it is conducive for social concord. Does what we say create more division and separation between others and ourselves, or does it support mutual understanding, healthier relationships, and social harmony? Stated more simply, do we speak so it pushes people apart or brings them closer?

This last question is an encouragement to avoid any rigid separation between self and others, between one's own group and other groups of people, and between one's own welfare and the welfare of others. Instead we search for ways to have mutual understanding and mutual support. This is related to the saying, *Speak so you become each other's companion on the journey.*

These five questions are particularly important when we are having difficult conversations. At those times strong mindfulness can help us avoid saying that which makes things worse, not better. Not only can we stay rooted in the present moment so we can track our own feelings, thoughts, and impulses before we speak, it is also a time to consider if what we are about to say is true, kind, useful, timely, and conducive to concord. If it's not, then it is time to consider other options for how and when to speak.

Mindfulness and ethics are inseparable. Because we want our lives to be positive and beneficial, we are mindful of our impact on others and the world. Is there anything more important to be mindful of?

Living ethically is an essential—and natural—product of our mindfulness practice. That practice includes mindfulness of the ills in society today, so many of which are caused by "othering" people who are different than us. One helpful thing you can do, says mindfulness teacher and law professor Rhonda Magee, the author of *The Inner Work of Racial Justice*, is make a conscious effort to engage with diverse communities. That transforms both our ethics and our mindfulness practice.

TEACHING

How Diversity Transforms Your Ethics—and Your Mindfulness[4]

Rhonda V. Magee

The practice of discerning right from wrong and applying what we learn in everyday life, what we might call ethics-in-action, is seen by many as an inherent aspect of mindfulness. Perhaps for this reason, many assume that mindfulness provides enough of an orientation toward ethics that we don't need to spend much energy focusing on it. We teach interconnection and compassion, many seem to say, and ethical behavior flows naturally from that.

Maybe. But I believe that there is value in emphasizing the ethical underpinnings of mindfulness. Doing so might better enable the kinds of sometimes risky actions—speaking truth to power, courageous storytelling, living and working across lines of difference, organizing against overconsumption, violence, and ignorance, and more—that are often necessary to grow and sustain capacity for living more compassionately together.

In the cultural West, the legacy of the countercultural revolution in the mid-twentieth century (promoting individual freedom for everyone all of the time) set us up to be wary of other people's morality. To this day, we are often allergic to following someone else's rules.

But I do not see mindful ethics as a call to adhere to rules, to gain approval as a "good meditator." I see their value in their practical effect. They remind us to pay close attention to why and how we do these things, and to how they affect others. They help us incline ourselves toward more caring behavior in response. Practicing ethics, we *experience* the principle of not causing harm as a touchstone in daily life. We come to know it not as an "add on," but as the very foundation of mindfulness.

Mindfulness can remind us of what we learned as children about how to tell the difference between right and wrong. This will look a bit different for each of us. For me, for example, the "ethics in a nutshell" coming out of my mindfulness practice is infused with what feels to me like soulfulness. When contemplating whether or not to take any given action, I ask: Will it cause suffering in myself? In the world? And more specifically: Will it cause more harm among those who've already suffered more than their share? Or will it help diminish it?

This deceptively simple inquiry practice won't solve all of our problems. But it will help keep us mindful of the fact that we live in a world with others, a fact replete with moral implications.

Here is the next rub. Even if we are willing to practice for ethical living, we come across the hard truth that doing so is not easy. And figuring out what truly compassionate steps to take in response? Often, this is more difficult still.

For these reasons it is clear that in addition to exploring what ethics is, we need support in discerning how to make good on *applying* ethical insight in our everyday lives.

Does the way we practice and teach mindfulness help us do that? Can it help us do it more, and better?

I think so. To deepen its impact, though, we need more than the teachings and practices. This is where *communities of practice* come in.

Communities in which we can consistently work with real human beings to meet conflict and difference as it arises in and around us give us the organic structures of experience and support that we need to live ethically. They require that we soften our tendencies toward overinvesting in ourselves to the detriment of others. And in these times, when we can see all around us the temptations of tribalism and self-focusing as means of responding to fear and dread, teachings, practices, and experiences which disrupt the temptations of Othering could not be more timely or important.

To support us in softening the temptations of Othering, we need a mindfulness capable to looking at the barriers to caring across lines of real and perceived difference. Cultivating such mindfulness benefits from actually being in diverse communities. Living with social and cultural difference helps attune us to the ways that our cultures make "normal" casual, everyday and systemic harm to vulnerable Others. It suggests that mindfulness, practiced rightly and alongside other people, prepares and inspires us to address it.

Looking back, I can see how my efforts to live ethically in the world have been strengthened by both working and living in multicultural communities. I learn about ethics from the inside out while moving through the negotiations, temporary pauses, intermittent battles, reframing of problems as possibilities—and more—that decades of living in diverse communities demands.

Over the years, I've meditated on how being with difference assists us in minimizing harm as we struggle while changing together. Because when it comes to mindfully discerning what to do about conflicts in the broader world, cultivating the ability to sit with the perspectives of people whose experiences differ from our own is essential.

I take inspiration from those who have gone before. I read about spiritual justice activists whose lives suggest that they practiced like this, and it gives me reason for hope. Studying the very embodiments of ethics, the exemplars of the good, the unselfish, the needlessly kind across a range of religious traditions—people like the Buddha, Jesus, Martin Luther King Jr., Grace Lee Boggs, Thich Nhat Hanh—one sees that they, too, moved between worlds and among those at the margins of their societies. They were as often as not working with those different from their original "tribes." They navigated worlds of different perspectives and values. And the actions they took were tempered by—and elevated by—a capacity to see themselves in the eyes of people who did *not* look like them, and whose lives had taught them different views on questions of right and wrong. This is the ethics of mindfulness in action.

A commitment to such ethics has never been more important than in the multicultural societies in which so many of us live in the modern era. It helps us combat the Othering in our midst, to see through the dehumanizing messages with which we are constantly bombarded. They help us live well, side-by-side with people who are different from ourselves. Cultivating this aspect of mindfulness, then, is critical in these times, when doing the opposite has diminished the communing together that leads to its natural arising and led to increased tribalism and other pathways toward its very opposite.

Our mindfulness can support us in considering where, when, and how to act for justice, and in creating new institutions, policies, and practices that reduce suffering. How, precisely, can this be done? Rather than offer a specific prescription, I suggest that our whole practice, in these times, must be energized by and grounded in questions like this. The answers we need to explore, the ones that reflect the values and insights of mindfulness, will arise when we bring insight to our socially embedded lives—to the particular histories, lingering inequities, power differences, thinly veiled melancholy, deferences and resentments, all while keeping our hearts open.

These answers will be flexibly attuned to the fact that the changing situations in which we find ourselves matter, and that they are not static. Everything is always already changing, in ways we variously experience as good, bad, or neutral. Practicing ethics in diverse communities helps us see, in these changes, that the reality of multiple and conflicting experiences will not break us. Instead, from such experiences, novel possibilities emerge.

Becoming aware of the not-so-obvious but nonetheless harmful consequences of our everyday choices—and practicing, courageously, living differently together as a result—is the true power of mindfulness in the world today.

Because doing so is not always easy, ethical practices invite working toward repairing the harms we—even partly, even unintentionally—cause. When, as a result, we disrupt those everyday habits and conventions—when we choose caring for others, consuming less, telling more of the truth, respecting others' things, respecting others' bodies and sexual integrity, and sobriety—we feel the changes in our hearts, minds, and bodies, in the very seat of our being itself.

Being mindful of not only the obvious but also subtle forms of greed, hatred, and ignorance in our lives and society nurtures the ethical roots of engaged mindfulness. Exposing ourselves regularly to the dimensions of harm that move through conventional social habits and processes of identification can help us when we meet the so-called "Stranger"—whether within ourselves and families; in our communities; in the café down the block; or in the news reel or social media post from the other side of the world. It is being in regular and well-supported contact with the Other that can help show us just *how* to meet the Stranger in the spirit of planetary loving-kindness that is, I believe, the ultimate gift of mindfulness in these times.

Indeed, this is why when I stand for a socially attuned and ethical form of mindfulness. I stand for seeing more clearly what supports its organic arising. I stand for what binds us together as one quilt, strengthened by the warp of conflict and weft of new cultures, unexpected reversals, and beginning again.

The quiet ethical revolution I call for here is, then, so much more than a renewed call to attend to the old rules. It's a way of being and doing, capable of stitching together the patches of our inherent already-belonging. This might better be called "ethics-*ing*." It's a way of seeing our mindfulness practice as the means of cultivating moral imagination. It can help us explore what Beyoncé encouraged millions to practice—*standing together* and *standing for something, even when we can barely stand one another*.

When we find ourselves at untraveled crossroads, may a reconceived mindfulness—enriched by the soulful, creative, and compassionate heart qualities that support making change ethically—ground, uplift, and dance with us there.

The Dalai Lama is more than the world's best-known Buddhist teacher. He is a moral guide for humanity. Starting with his famous statement that "My religion is kindness," he offers the world a vision for society based on the best of what it means to be human. If you want to be a force of good—and that seems to be the point of life—Daniel Goleman, the author of *Emotional Intelligence*, lists six ways the Dalai Lama says you can do it.

TEACHING

Six Ways to Be a Force for Good[5]

Daniel Goleman

The time for a force for good has come.

Each of us can join in that force for a better world, and mindfulness plays a crucial role.

The Dalai Lama has laid out a strategic map for this force, focusing on the good each of us can do. There are three steps: First, gain inner composure. Second, follow an inner rudder toward compassion. Third, act now, in whatever way you can.

Each of us has tools for helping to change the world in a better direction, and science backs that up.

Mindfulness, of course, offers a powerful method for that inner calm and clarity. The best research shows that from the beginning mindfulness strengthens concentration and lessens distractedness, so we can better focus on our goals. And mindfulness also calms the knee-jerk amygdala, that trigger for reactions we regret later. So mindfulness practice gives us that inner foundation of mental strength.

As for compassion, here, too, research bears out the power of loving-kindness meditation—the natural accompaniment to mindfulness—to increase our concern for others, up our generosity, and be more likely to put those feelings into action by helping someone in need. We engage life with compassion as a guide to what we do.

Then from that calm, clear, and caring stance, the Dalai Lama says, act now. Each of us has tools for helping to change the world in a better direction. Each one of us has a personal sphere of influence—some of us have various positions of power, or we may have special skill sets. We can combine those with the particular way we are called to use them for the better.

There are six arenas which the Dalai Lama sees as critical for the future of our world:

1. **OPPOSE US-AND-THEM THINKING**

   In these times this seems a compelling place to put our energy. As the Dalai Lama notes, reaching out across divides can be healing. Decades of research show that friendships between people in the "us" and "them" groups, especially among children, eliminate bias.

2. **THE ENVIRONMENT**

   "The Earth is our home, and our home is on fire," the Dalai Lama says. Global warming has become the poster child, but there are eight global systems that support life on our planet, each of which sustains continual damage from daily human activities. The range of ways to help here range from eliminating petroleum-based plastics from our lives and the supply chain to demanding clean air.

3. **OPPOSE INJUSTICE**
   The very social order creates structural inequities. Working together to eliminate them can create a better future for everyone.

4. **A MORE HUMANE ECONOMICS**
   The growing gap between rich and poor, the Dalai Lama says, seems a "moral crime." A humane economics means finding avenues to lessen the rich-poor gap.

5. **HELP THOSE IN NEED**
   This one seems a no-brainer. But the ways to enact such help include not just giving direct aid—like a handout to a homeless person—but also helping them help themselves, for example, through job training.

6. **EDUCATE THE HEART**
   The world's future is in the hands of our children. An education that includes mindfulness and caring will give the young tools to naturally act toward a better society.

Finally, act now, in whatever way you are called to. Otherwise the toxic forces at loose today will define our time. But each of us acting in our own way can together create a stronger force for good.

The way we live as consumers and citizens is a form of practice. As in meditation, the choices we make require discipline, awareness, concern for others, and clear insight into what causes problems in the world and what brings well-being and sustainability. The economist Clair Brown offers us this advice on the practice of living ethically as if the future depended on it. Because it does.

PRACTICE

Living Mindfully in a Time of Climate Crisis

Clair Brown

When we recognize how deeply connected we are to one another, to our communities, and to the planet itself, we understand that living mindfully and ethically includes reducing the impact of our daily activities on the environment.

Each of us can take steps to reduce our environmental impact by reducing personal greenhouse gas emissions. Many people already make efforts to reduce waste sent to the landfill by recycling glass, plastic, and paper, composting kitchen scraps, and carrying reusable bags. These are great habits, but they only reduce the average American's annual emissions by about 2–5 percent.

Greater reductions come from tackling transportation, which makes up 28–30 percent of a person's emissions, especially from driving gas-powered vehicles and flying. Most households can reduce miles driven by having only one car, and then taking public transit or ride sharing or making short trips by biking or walking. Reducing flights, especially long-haul leisure trips, is especially impactful. One roundtrip transatlantic flight can generate as much CO_2 equivalent per person as a year of driving a hybrid car.

Your choice of foods also has a large impact on your greenhouse gas emissions. Eating locally and seasonally supports nearby farmers and reduces the energy used to transport food. Reducing or eliminating beef from your diet will lower your food-related emissions even more, since beef has an environmental footprint that is about ten times the footprint of poultry and fifty to ninety times the footprint of plant-based proteins like peas and other legumes. You can substitute beans and other plant proteins for meat as your diet becomes more vegetarian.

We don't want to waste food, because about 30 percent of food is wasted globally, and even more is wasted in the US. Ensure your food isn't wasted by taking home doggie bags when dining out, and use the wilted veggies in your refrigerator to make soups and stews. Then compost food scraps during meal prep, and your food waste vanishes.

Water too is precious. You can conserve water by taking shorter showers, using low-flow fixtures, and even collecting water that flows down our sinks and showers for watering plants. In the garden, choose drought-tolerant plants and use mulch to retain soil moisture to conserve garden water. Plus support pollinators and your garden's ecosystem by using natural pest-control methods and avoiding chemical pesticides or overfertilizing.

How we use electricity and gas in our homes matters both for our budgets and for our carbon footprint. Utilities use fossil gas and even coal in many areas to power electricity. By dressing for the season, you can lower the thermostat in the winter and raise it in the summer and reduce your carbon footprint as you save energy and money.

In wealthy societies, overconsumption drives emissions and overflowing landfills. Fast fashion, electronics, and home goods often end up in landfills after little use. Before making a purchase, ask yourself, Do I really need this? Will I use it more than once or twice? Many people find joy in buying less and using what they have more creatively. Many of us are learning that life becomes more fulfilling when we stop centering our time around shopping or acquiring things. Instead, we can spend time outdoors, prepare meals with family, volunteer, or get our hands dirty in the garden.

Actions to reduce personal carbon footprints are helpful, but they are not enough. Unfortunately our individual lifestyle choices do not begin to reduce our personal carbon emissions enough to stop adding to global warming. This is because our choices reflect the current systems: energy provided by local utilities powered from coal and gas; food produced from industrial agriculture; and tax and benefits perpetuating inequality. National policies that create new systems of clean energy, regenerative agriculture, and less wasteful consumption related to inequality are urgently needed if we are to create a livable planet for ourselves and future generations.

The scale of the climate crisis requires national-systems transformation. We need to move rapidly from fossil fuels to renewable energy, and from industrial farming to regenerative agriculture that heals soil and restores biodiversity. We must address the vast inequalities that drive overconsumption and environmental degradation. Our cities need to become sustainable hubs of clean energy, widely used public transit, walking and biking, effective composting and recycling systems, and energy-efficient buildings. We can evaluate economic performance not by how much we produce or consume but by the well-being and quality of life of people and nature.

Living mindfully includes working with others to reduce emissions globally and locally. One person may not have the power to change the world alone, but together we do. Once you decide that you want to work on an environmental project that you care about, you will find the right group for you. People are working on all types of projects, from shutting down coal plants or halting fracking, to restoring local parks or wetlands, to setting up field trips to teach school kids about fossil fuels and greenhouse gas emissions. The experts tell us that there are no quick solutions to reducing global emissions, only that we must do it as quickly as possible.

When we work side by side with others for something bigger than ourselves, it gives us a sense of purpose and reminds us that the health of the environment and our own health are interconnected. It reminds us of our place in this web of life, and Barry Commoner's statement of the law of ecology: "Everything is connected to everything else. There is one ecosphere for all living organisms and what affects one, affects all."

The path is not easy. To care mindfully for the planet takes time and also takes courage. It takes an educated, ethical approach to our personal life choices. It takes the courage to resist the false promises of consumerism, to work with others to end using the fossil fuels that are harming us all, and to work for a healthier, clean-energy world. This is the task of our time. Each of us has a role to play, rooted in love, ethics, and mindfulness, and carried forward by our collective desire for a just and thriving world and sustainable planet.

Facts and science are important guides to living in a way that meets the needs of humanity and the planet. But even deeper, even more inspiring, is our personal connection with the living universe. While facts inform the mind, it is life and poetry that speak to the heart. So as we go through our day trying to live in the most beneficial way, we can recite these short verses by Thich Nhat Hanh that help us touch the living truth of interbeing.

PRACTICE

Earth Gathas: Recitations for a Sustainable Life[6]

Thich Nhat Hanh

Turning on the Water

Water flows from high mountain sources.
Water runs deep in the Earth.
Miraculously, water comes to us
and sustains all life.

Even if we know the source of our water, we often take its appearance for granted. But water is what makes all life on Earth possible. Our bodies are more than 70 percent water. Our food can be grown and raised because of water. Water is a good friend that nourishes the many thousands of species on Earth. Its benefits are infinite.

Reciting this *gatha* before turning on the faucet or drinking a glass of water enables us to see the stream of fresh water in our own hearts so that we feel completely refreshed. To celebrate the gift of water is to cultivate awareness and help sustain our life and the lives of others.

Looking at Your Empty Bowl

My bowl, empty now,
will soon be filled with precious food.
Beings all over the Earth are struggling to live.
How fortunate we are to have enough to eat.

When many people on this Earth look at an empty bowl, they know their bowl will continue to be empty for a long time. So the empty bowl is as important to honor as the full bowl. We are grateful to have food to eat, and with this *gatha*, we can vow to find ways to help those who are hungry.

Serving Food

In this food I see clearly
the entire universe
supporting my existence.

When we look at our plate, filled with fragrant and appetizing food, we should be aware of the bitter pain of people who suffer from hunger and malnutrition. Looking at our plate, we can see Mother Earth, the farmworkers, and the tragedy of the unequal distribution of resources.

We who live in North America and Europe are accustomed to eating foods imported from other countries, whether it is coffee from Colombia, chocolate from Ghana, or fragrant rice from Thailand. Many children in these countries, except those from rich families, never see the fine products that are put aside for export in order to bring in money.

Before a meal, we can join our palms in mindfulness and think about those who do not have enough to eat. Slowly and mindfully, we breathe three times and recite this *gatha*. Doing so will help us maintain mindfulness. May we find ways to live more simply in order to have more time and energy to change the system of injustice that exists in the world.

Touching the Earth

Earth brings us into life
and nourishes us.
Earth takes us back again.
We are born and we die with every breath.

The Earth is our mother. All life arises from her and is nourished by her. Each of us is a child of the Earth and, at some time, the Earth will take us back to her again. In fact, we are continuously coming to life and returning to the bosom of the Earth. We who practice meditation should be able to see birth and death in every breath.

Touching the earth, letting your fingers feel the soil, and gardening are wonderful, restorative activities. If you live in a city, you may not have many opportunities to hoe the earth, plant vegetables, or take care of flowers. But you can still find and appreciate a small patch of grass or earth and care for it. Being in touch with Mother Earth is a wonderful way to preserve your mental health.

Watering the Garden

Water and sun
green these plants.
When the rain of compassion falls,
even the desert becomes a vast fertile plain.

Water is the balm of compassion. It has the capacity to restore us to life. Rain enlivens crops and protects people from hunger. In Buddhism, the Bodhisattva of Compassion is often depicted holding a vase of water in her left hand and a willow branch in her right. She sprinkles down compassion, like drops of nurturing water, to revitalize tired hearts and minds weak from suffering.

Watering the garden, the compassionate rain falls on the plants. When we offer water to plants, we offer it to the whole Earth. When watering plants, if we speak to them, we are also speaking to ourselves. We exist in relationship to all other phenomena. The feeling of alienation among so many people today has come about because they lack awareness of the interconnectedness of all things. We cannot separate ourselves from society or anything else. *This is like this because that is like that* summarizes the principle of interrelatedness. To water plants and experience compassion and interconnectedness is a wonderful practice of meditation.

Recycling

In the garbage, I see a rose.
In the rose, I see the garbage.
Everything is in transformation.
Even permanence is impermanent.

Whenever we throw something away, whether in the garbage can, the compost, or the recycling, it can smell terrible. Rotting organic matter smells especially terrible. But it can also become rich compost for fertilizing the garden.

The fragrant rose and the stinking garbage are two sides of the same existence. Without one, the other cannot be. Everything is in transformation. The rose that wilts after six days will become a part of the garbage. After six months the garbage is transformed into a rose.

When we speak of impermanence, we understand that everything is in transformation. This becomes that, and that becomes this. Looking deeply, we can contemplate one thing and see everything else in it. We are not disturbed by change when we see the interconnectedness and continuity of all things. It is not that the life of any individual is permanent, but that life itself continues. When we identify ourselves with life and go beyond the boundaries of a separate identity, we shall be able to see permanence in the impermanent, or the rose in the garbage.

With so many problems facing the world, it is not easy to have hope for the future. What we need, says Joan Halifax, is wise, realistic hope that sees all the suffering but trusts that the arc of history bends toward goodness. We are lost without hope, but it must be wise hope.

TEACHING

How to Have Wise Hope[7]

Joan Halifax

A good part of my life has been spent relating to situations that might be deemed hopeless—as an anti-war activist, a Civil Rights worker, a caregiver of dying people. I have also volunteered with death-row inmates, served in medical clinics in remote areas of the Himalayas—where life is hard, food is scarce, and access to health care is nil—and worked in Kathmandu with Rohingya refugees who have no status anywhere.

You might ask, Why bother? Why hold out hope for ending war or injustice? Why have hope for people who are dying, or for refugees fleeing from genocide, or for solutions to climate change?

I have often been troubled by the notion of hope. But recently, in part because of the work of social critic Rebecca Solnit and her powerful book *Hope in the Dark*, I am opening to another view of hope—what I call wise hope.

Ordinary hope is based in desire, wanting an outcome that could well be different from what will actually happen. Not getting what we hoped for is usually experienced as some kind of misfortune. Someone who is hopeful in this way has an expectation that always hovers in the background, the shadow of fear that one's wishes will not be fulfilled. This ordinary hope is a subtle expression of fear and a form of suffering.

Wise hope is not seeing things unrealistically but rather seeing things as they are, including the truth of suffering—both its existence and our capacity to transform it. It's when we realize we don't know what will happen that this kind of hope comes alive; in that spaciousness of uncertainty is the very space we need to act.

Too often we become paralyzed by the belief that there is nothing to hope for—that our cancer diagnosis is a one-way street with no exit, that our political situation is beyond repair, that there is no way out of our climate crisis. It becomes easy to think that nothing makes sense anymore, or that we have no power and there's no reason to act.

I often say that there should be just two words over the door of our meditation center in Santa Fe: Show up! Yes, suffering is present. We cannot deny it. There are tens of millions of refugees in the world today and there is ongoing conflict in many countries. Climate change is turning forests into deserts. Economic injustice is driving people into greater and greater poverty. Racism and sexism remain rampant.

But wise hope doesn't mean denying these realities. It means facing them, addressing them, and remembering what else is present, like the shifts in our values that recognize and move us to address suffering right now. Wise hope invites us to see suffering, not flee it.

The late Czech statesman Václav Havel said, "Hope is definitely not the same thing as optimism. It is not the conviction that something will turn out well but the certainty that something makes sense, regardless of how it turns out." We can't know, but we can trust that there will be movement, there will be change. And that we will be part of it. We move forward in our day and get out the vote, or sit at the bedside of a dying patient, or teach that third-grade class.

Dostoyevsky said, "To live without hope is to cease to live." His words remind us that apathy is not a mindful path. We are called to live with possibility, knowing full well that impermanence prevails. So why not just show up?

Journeys on the Complete Path of Mindfulness: Ethics

What are the building blocks for an ethical life? I think intention is the most important thing. It is the most subtle part of human psychology and it drives our thoughts, emotions, and actions. My wish or intention ethically is to live my life in a way that harms no one and helps everyone.

It's also important that we have the ability to regulate our emotions, which in the old days used to be called self-control. This is where mindfulness comes in. It gives us the ability to see what we're experiencing in a very honest and thoroughgoing way and gives us a little space to choose how to behave. So a certain measure of nonjudgmental self-awareness is essential for ethical behavior.

—Christopher Germer

Being of service—that's the place where things open up for me, where my heart opens. There is an ethical line that I draw which is my understanding of being good and loving. It is caring not just about my own liberation, but caring about the liberation of everyone, of all beings, from the entanglements of the mind and heart. When I look at my ethical compass, I'm always redialing it so I know the work that I'm doing is wholesome work, that it's work for the benefit of those who are most in need.

—Noliwe Alexander

When I act ethically it creates happiness inside me. It's the joyful feeling I have when I do acts of generosity. And because of my mindfulness practice, I allow myself to feel and kind of revel in the joyful feeling. We often skip over those pleasant experiences, but I allow myself to take pleasure in being ethical and living a well-lived life.

Let's say you have an impulse to act unethically. Bring your mindfulness to it in the moment and see how that is affecting you. Is there a lot of remorse or guilt? Bring your mindfulness there. Check in with yourself. What is the result when you act? Use your awareness to lean more deeply into how to act more ethically and what is the direct result of it. As opposed to somebody on high saying you should do something this way, you find out for yourself.

—Diana Winston

If we look at ethical practices at the deepest level,
I would say their core is non-harming.

Knowing what non-harming feels like goes hand in hand with cultivating mindfulness more deeply. Because when my mind is caught up in patterns, reactivity, and mental activity generally, there's less awareness of the heart and my interconnection with others. But when my mind is more still, I can touch into a deeper kind of interconnected compassion that guides me in my actions and tells me what I need to do and don't need to do.

So the quieting of mental activity through mindfulness creates a more refined awareness of our heart and mind, and of whether our behaviors reflect an ethics of non-harming, which comes out of feeling our interconnection with others.

—Lisa Ernst

What I've seen as being the most valuable "ethic" is a kind of continual practice of gratitude—gratitude toward whatever is coming up in this life, gratitude for the person who's in front of me, gratitude for the intensity of my challenges and the relief when they pass, gratitude for everything. Having that outlook makes me humble, and humility makes me receptive to people. Then compassion comes all on its own.

That completely changes everything. Now there are no enemies, just learning experiences. The world is giving you another opportunity to get over yourself, an opportunity to make contact with some human being who's really here. Then the right course of action arises. You're much more likely to see clearly what the situation is, because there is no "you" entangled in the middle of it, and you can act in a way that's more ethical and helpful and leads to less suffering.

—Jeff Warren

7

COMMUNITY

The Healing Power of Connection

So far in this book I have not quoted the Buddha. Even though he was the world's first and greatest mindfulness teacher, I haven't wanted to give the impression that mindfulness is in any way inherently or exclusively Buddhist. Nor have I wanted to reinforce the misperception that the mainstream mindfulness movement is some sort of backdoor attempt to introduce Buddhism into American society. But the Buddha said something that is so relevant to the topic of community and connection—and so surprising—that I have to quote it.

The story goes like this: One day, one of the Buddha's students asked him, "Is friendship half of the spiritual path?"

"No," the Buddha said, "it is the *whole* of the spiritual path."[1]

There are so many things that the Buddha could have said are the whole of the spiritual path—enlightenment, meditation, wisdom, compassion, to name a few. But instead he said it was friendship.

That was almost three thousand years ago, and we have to guess what the Buddha really meant. Here's what I think. I don't think he was talking about friendship in the narrow sense, even spiritual friendship.

I think he was talking about human connection in the deepest and most universal sense. He was talking about all the real and heartfelt ways we are friends with each other—as lovers, spouses, parents, children, colleagues, acquaintances, people we share interests and identities with, fellow citizens, and simply as humans. I think the Buddha was saying that the whole path is found in community and our connections to others.

As Sartre famously wrote, "Hell is other people." So is heaven. Nothing is more important to our lives than the quality of our relationships and connections to other people. The fruit of our human journey is to experience the goodness of loving, heartfelt community.

Our whole life is lived in community. Communities go from very small to embracing the entire universe. A marriage is a community. A family is a community. So is a workplace, a team, a club, a neighborhood. Anytime people who share interests or heritage or identity get together, they form a community. Nations are communities, humanity is a community, the Earth's ecosystem is a community. We're each a community too—of billions of cells in our body and many different voices, impulses, and thoughts in our minds.

To say that human connection is the whole of the path doesn't just mean that's where we find the greatest reward and deepest meaning. It means the whole path plays out in our relationships with each other. This is where we choose who we want to be and how we want to act. It is why we practice and try to develop ourselves. It is how we manifest the fruits of our practice, or lack thereof, in the happiness we create or the suffering we cause. This is as true for a secular path like mindfulness as it is for any spiritual path.

That's why community and connection is the final of the five keys of the Complete Path of Mindfulness. It is the culmination of the path, as it is of life itself. It is where our mindfulness practice bears fruit in a better life for ourselves, for those around us, and for the world.

The good news is that Complete Mindfulness offers us an effective, practical path to more caring, fulfilling, and enjoyable connection with others. This is where mindfulness meditation, insight, compassion, and ethics come together to create communities where people love, learn, and grow together, supporting one another on life's journey.

The Gift of Your Presence

We might think that the path to good human connection begins with ethics or compassion. Those are of course key to creating good communities, but in fact the most important work comes right at the beginning of our path—with our practice of mindfulness meditation.

At its simplest, mindfulness is the practice of being present, and there is nothing more important to our relationships with others than being present with them. As Thich Nhat Hanh says, "Being truly here is very important—being here for yourself, and for the one you love. How can you love if you are not here? A fundamental condition for love is your own presence. In order to love, you must be here. That is certain."[2]

What do people really want from us? What can we really give them? There's nothing wrong with help, advice, or comfort, of course, but the most important thing we can give people is our full presence and attention. When people say, "I'm here for you," it means "I am present with you now in body and mind. I am fully here for you." Nothing shows others our love and respect more than our willingness to be present with them. With our presence we are offering them our heart and mind.

Spending "quality time" with someone is another cliché, but what it really means is being fully present with them. Whether it's a child, partner, parent, colleague, or friend, think what a difference it makes when you are giving them the quality time of your full presence. Conversely, can you really help someone—can you really show your love for them—if you're only half present, distracted by your own thoughts and storylines? You can feel the difference, and so can they.

It's the stable mind you develop in your mindfulness meditation that allows you to give the gift of your full presence. Then you can use the other keys to benefit your relationships. Your insight shows your deep interconnection with others. Your empathy helps you understand what they are going through in life and what they really need. Because of your love and compassion, you are committed to bringing them happiness and lessening their suffering. Your ethics help you do that skillfully and effectively.

As Dr. Robert Waldinger writes in the following teaching, research shows that what makes people happiest—what really makes life worth living—are good connections to others. Friendship in the broadest sense—warmth, connection, and community—is the source of true happiness, goodness, and love. It is the whole of the Complete Path of Mindfulness, as it is of life.

In the practices and teachings that follow, you will learn helpful ways to create deeper connections and healthy, loving communities. From sharing a hug with someone to experiencing the infinite community that is the universe, you can offer your mindfulness and love and say, "I am here for you."

Practices and Teachings

TEACHING

What Really Makes Us Happy[3]

Dr. Robert Waldinger

Science now confirms what philosophers, poets, and lovers have known for millennia—that our connection to other human beings is both an essential truth of our existence and a pillar of happiness, health, and longevity.

In the Harvard Study of Adult Development, of which I am the director, we have studied thousands of lives over more than eighty-five years. In this unique longitudinal study of people over the course of their lives, we have watched the choices people make and how those choices affect their happiness, health, and well-being. We find that the people who are more connected to others—to family, to friends, to communities, and even to strangers—are happier and healthier, and that those with warmer relationships live longer than those who are more isolated. Human connection and community are essential to a life that feels happy, meaningful, healthy, and complete.

Our connections to others protect our brains as well as our bodies. Compared to people with fewer connections, those of us who are more socially active experience cognitive decline later, if we experience it at all, and that decline proceeds at a slower pace. Many other studies reveal the same findings, so that the power of human connection in building a good life is now an accepted scientific fact.

We know from experience and scientific investigation that relationships buffer us from some of the most challenging situations that life brings to all of us, including serious illness, lack of resources, and disappointments in our personal and work lives. Along with helping us through difficult times, relationships provide stimulation, novelty, and pleasure in myriad forms throughout life.

Yet our practical, everyday minds—so useful when fixing a leaky faucet or cooking a meal—are not built to show us the truth of our interconnectedness with all things. Built to help us survive and reproduce, our minds show us a world made up of birds and rocks and billions of people who appear to be separate and autonomous. We see a universe of beings striving for survival and competing against each other for what is good and desirable.

Seeing beyond the illusion of separateness is a slog. It takes time and effort. When we practice mindfulness, we wonder again and again, "Who is sitting here? Who is having these thoughts? Who is feeling this knee pain?"

When we ask these questions, we cannot find any separate, abiding self having these experiences. The boundaries between the self and the world gradually soften, and the sense of connection to others feels more alive. Glimpses of the truth of interconnection inspire us to connect with others, to care for others. Compassion—truly "feeling with" others—arises naturally. Mindfulness, wisdom, compassion, and community are intimately connected and naturally support each other.

A key is our motivation, the reason why we practice. Mindfulness, self-compassion, and similar practices have become staples of the multibillion-dollar wellness industry. We are promised that they are ways to improve this thing we call the self, helping us with depression, anxiety, low self-esteem, and a host of other personal afflictions.

While many of these claims for healing have merit, the focus on "I, me, and mine" runs the risk of leaving us marooned in what David Foster Wallace labeled our "tiny skull-sized kingdoms"—in the small, struggling, separate self that causes us so much unhappiness. When we undertake it as a self-improvement project, even mindfulness may foster a kind of splendid isolation that actually damages our health and shortens our lives.

Our minds not only delude us about our separateness; they also lie to us about whether we treat each other with kindness. The surprise is that we underestimate how kind people really are.

In every generation, people lament that the world is going to hell—that moral standards are declining, that we are meaner to each other than people were in the past. This makes us more wary of others and makes us feel more separate. (The media taps into these fears and reinforces them as a way to capture and hold our attention.) But in fact, as a research paper entitled "The Illusion of Moral Decline" shows, this perception is not true. Looking back over seventy-five years, the study shows that every generation has had the same complaint that morality was declining in our society. And yet when asked, "Have you been treated kindly by others recently?"

people over those same seventy-five years answered yes with the same frequency from one generation to the next.

The world *appears* to us to be less moral, less kind, but in fact our basic level of goodness has not changed. To help us anticipate danger and improve our chances of survival, our minds show us the world in a way that overemphasizes the bad at the expense of the good. This is the so-called negativity bias. And by comparison with a seemingly dangerous present, we remember the past as more positive than it actually was. (Hence, the wish to return to an idealized past that in fact never existed.)

Where does all this leave us? As we look deeply into the causes of unhappiness, we see that much of our suffering is optional, coming from minds that evolved to help us survive but not to make us happy. These minds paint the picture of a world in which we are separate, isolated, and competing for resources with other beings who are less kind than they used to be and are not to be trusted.

Seeing beyond this distorted perception to the truth of interconnectedness fosters a sense of well-being that is an antidote to the poison of delusive separateness. Human connection is a remedy for unhappiness that we can rely on. Through sustained mindful awareness, our essential connection to everyone and everything moves out of the shadows and becomes more visible, more real, and a source of comfort and joy.

Too often in this society our greetings are rote and superficial—a quick "Hi, how are ya?" gets the rote response, "Fine, thanks." How much better would it be if we could truly connect with people when we meet them, showing that we see and are present for them, and they for us. Stephen Murphy-Shigematsu recommends we try the South African practice of heartfelt greeting called *Sawubona*.

PRACTICE

I See You, I Am Here: The Secret to Heartfelt Communication[4]

Stephen Murphy-Shigematsu

Today we are more isolated than ever, and at the same time even more aware of our longing for connection and community. Many of us are reflecting on how much we value our human connections and how little we do to cultivate them, to express appreciation for others, and to feel grateful for what they do for us every day of our lives. We are realizing how much our existence depends on others.

Even as we long for more connection and feeling of community, we are locked into rituals and habits in which we encounter each other in our daily lives without really connecting. When we say "Hello," or even "How are you?" we do it as a routine, without meaning, and hope we simply get a similarly standard response. We rarely look into each other's eyes. We feel and act as if we are too busy to stop, engage with, and get to know the people with whom we interact.

By contrast, *Sawubona*, which is a common greeting in parts of South Africa, generates a transformative experience of truly seeing and being seen.

Truly seeing others is a basic form of respect, as revealed in the word's Latin origin, *respicere*, which means simply "to see clearly."

When we see, we respect. When we really see another, we see their humanity—our common humanity—and we sense our mutual vulnerability. When we really see people, we can no longer treat them indifferently or inhumanely. We see who they are and feel compassion. Real seeing brings light and inspires and empowers both seer and seen.

To enable us to enhance our connections through gentle rituals, I started a practice of seeing others based on the Zulu word *Sawubona*. It means "I see you," and the response is, "I see you too," or "I am here." I practice this in my meetings with others in my work, at home, and in daily life.

When I teach, I ask people to move around the room acknowledging each person they encounter with the greeting "I see you." The other person responds, "I am here," and then returns the greeting "I see you," receiving in turn the response "I am here." Eyes meet for a brief moment before parting and moving on to the next person.

Sawubona honors the mystery that we are here together in this moment. When people experience *Sawubona* as a group, they are astounded at their feelings of connection, which go quickly and dramatically beyond the boundaries they construct between themselves and others. They feel warmth generated inside them and in the atmosphere of the space. They feel seen, respected, and valued. At the end, their faces hurt from smiling so much.

Words alone don't solve deep-seated problems, but if in saying words we really open our hearts and see the other person, we will realize that, as one person observed after doing this practice, there are no enemies.

Words provide ritual for that to happen, but the key is what each of us is doing spiritually in that moment—being mindful, noticing others, acknowledging their existence, even without words. We can greet and treat people in a way that communicates the feeling of *Sawubona*, generating a mundane yet transformative experience of seeing and being seen. We bring ourselves into encounters with hearts open to the possibilities of what might happen.

Our need for connecting has never been greater. *Sawubona* consciousness leads to peaceful, nonviolent communication and can be done in formal or informal situations, with individuals or in groups. You can even do it at home, as a conscious ritual that can transform your family. When we are seen, we feel good—we know that we exist. So we know that it is good to do for others too. Let's find *Sawubona* moments in life.

Who doesn't need a hug? Giving a hug, getting a hug—it's one of the best ways to show and receive love. This simple and universal gesture is made even deeper and more satisfying when done with insight and presence. After you greet each other with *Sawubona*, you could do this hugging meditation developed by Thich Nhat Hanh to create the deep sense of connection that truly brings happiness.

PRACTICE

Hugging Meditation[5]

Thich Nhat Hanh

It's a pleasure to hug someone we love. But don't think it's something easy. Maybe we want to hug the other person but they aren't available—they're caught up in their anger, worries, or projects. Hugging is a deep practice and both people need to be completely present to do it correctly. That's why it's not always easy. So, we have to learn how.

Hugging meditation is a chance to practice our awareness of impermanence. Each time we hug, we know it may be the last time. Our deep awareness of the impermanent nature of things inspires us to be very mindful, and we naturally hug each other in a deep, authentic way, appreciating each other completely. This can be a good meditation to practice when you are angry with each other.

Close your eyes and practice breathing in and out to bring your insight of impermanence to life. Visualize yourself and your loved one three hundred years from now. Where will you be? In that moment, you know the only meaningful thing to do is to open your arms and hug the other person.

This is a two-step practice.

Step One

The first thing to do is to make yourself available. Breathe in and out, and come back to the present moment, so you are really there.

Then go to the person you want to hug and bow to them. If they have practiced mindfulness, then they will do their best to abandon the things that are possessing them and make themselves available to you. They will smile and bow, and you will know that they are available. Now hugging is possible.

Stand facing each other with your palms joined, breathing in and out three times. You can say silently:

Breathing in, I know that life is precious in this moment.

Breathing out, I cherish this moment of life.

Step Two

Take the person in your arms. While hugging, breathe consciously and hug with all your body, spirit, and heart. While you hold the other person, they become real, and you also become real. You can say silently something like this:

Breathing in, my loved one is in my arms. Breathing out, I am so happy.

Breathing in, they are alive. Breathing out, it is so precious to be alive together.

Breathing in, it is so wonderful to have them in my arms. Breathing out, I am very happy.

You may then release the other person and bow to each other to show thanks.

Marriage is one of our closest connections with another person, but in spite of that—or because of it—it's not easy. I suspect more marriages would last if people went into them with realistic expectations, as opposed to the romantic gauze marriage is often wrapped in. Based on her own nineteen years of marriage, Susan Piver suggests five commitments we can make every day that keep love alive amid the realities of being human and the uncertainties of life. They're a good foundation for a successful real-world marriage.

TEACHING

The Truth About Marriage Vows: Five Promises You Can Actually Keep[6]

Susan Piver

Next month, my partner and I celebrate our nineteenth wedding anniversary. *Nineteen years.* How the hell did that happen?!

As we get ready to celebrate nearly two decades of wedded bliss (and also of wedded hell, confusion, joy, and mystery), I've been thinking about our wedding day and the vows we made to each other. What do these vows mean, all these years later? Did we honor them? Do they bear any resemblance to what we imagined when we gazed into each other's eyes and said, "I do"?

The short answer is yes. Also, definitely no.

When we began to talk about getting married, we covered lots of topics: who would perform the ceremony, who to invite, what to wear, whether or not we could convince our favorite Cajun band to learn "Hava Nagilah." (We did. Shout out to Steve Riley and the Mamou Playboys.)

We spent time reading various liturgies and talking about what we liked and disliked at other people's weddings. As we read the words thousands and millions of other couples had spoken to each other, I became increasingly uncomfortable. Most of them ended with the words "I do." I do . . . what? Marriage is a commitment to love, have sex, and try to stay together with this one person, right?

Well, maybe, but I couldn't promise any of these things. I knew I couldn't say "I do" to love—feelings change and keep changing. I couldn't say yes to wanting to have sex with him for the rest of my life. Desire is unpredictable. And ask him to commit to me? Which me? I couldn't commit to remaining the same me.

Let's just be honest here. There is no way that you can know how your relationship is going to turn out, regardless of how carefully you prepare, how clear you are about your needs and expectations, and how intently you listen to your partner's wishes. Yet somehow when we commit to another person, we make and require promises. *I will always love you. I promise to cherish you. Nothing will ever come between us.*

There is no way such promises can be kept. Why? Because we are human beings on planet Earth.

Sometimes you will love each other and sometimes you will fume with rage.

Sometimes you will cherish your partner and sometimes you will wish they would, shall we say, disappear.

And something will come between you every single day: work, family, ambitions, depressions, confusions, and different ideas about everything from how much money is enough to the "right" way to load the dishwasher.

On our wedding day, we made beautiful vows to each other: to be generous, patient, kind, and caring. We meant these words and continue our attempts to honor them. However, when I look back, I see that in addition to these beautiful vows, there were vows we were also making, whether we knew it or not.

1. **I VOW NOT TO KNOW**

   To enter a relationship for the long term (whatever that might mean) is to say yes to the unfolding, impenetrable arc of uncertainty.

   I had thought that finding love was an end point, that some kind of search was over and I would find home. We would leap over the threshold together into whatever we imagined our ideal cottage to be. But really we stepped through a crazy looking glass. No matter how hard we tried, how crazy in love we were, or how skillfully we planned our life together, there was complete uncertainty about what the connection would feel like from day to day.

   I could give all the love I had (with great joy) and get back a blank stare. I could wake up as my crankiest, most sullen, and narcissistic self, roll over, and greet the face of unconditional acceptance. Or not. It's like the weather. You could read the signs and guess about atmospheric conditions, but really any type of front could blow through on any given day—and, like listening to a meteorologist explain why it's going to rain, I think, Who cares *why?* I just want to know what to wear today.

   We can't actually promise each other anything. The relationship never stabilizes, ever. This is the way it works. I have no idea why. The real skill is in how you ride the waves.

2. **I VOW TO BE HAPPY AND SAD**

It seems that I committed to a lifetime of delight and sadness, inseparable from each other. Every time I look into my dear one's eyes and feel how deeply we're connected, that moment disappears and I have to watch it do so. It's excruciating. It's much easier to do this with my thoughts on a meditation cushion than with the feeling I get from his breath on my shoulder as I fall asleep. But now I get that I have to repeat this until the end of my life, and that somehow this is love's road.

Each time my love expands by a molecule, it grows a molecule of sorrow. The more I love, the edgier it all feels and the more courage is required. Where you get this courage, I really don't know. Surprisingly, it just seems to be there. And if you're looking for a crucible in which to heat compassion, this is a really good one. Someone once told me that compassion is the ability to hold love and pain together in the same moment. So at least we're learning something, which is what I tell myself.

3. **I VOW TO BE IRRITATED AND IRRITATING**

I wish I had known that when you live with someone, there is continuous, mind-blowing irritation. (Actually I did know this, but I had forgotten.)

Weirdly, this irritation serves a purpose. It beckons me time and again out of myself. Often the irritation arises when I decide to replace my actual partner with a projection of a partner. He always figures out a way to tell me how unlike my projection he really is, which gives me yet another opportunity to choose between him and who I sort of hoped he would be. No matter how many times I prompt my husband with the correct lines, he does not get into character. This irritates me. I have to throw away the script and just begin to improvise. You're playing you and I'm playing me. Go.

4. **I VOW TO BUILD A HOME WHERE LOVE WANTS TO LIVE**

I didn't really understand that true love, deep love, does not arise, abide, or dissolve in connection with any particular feeling. It has almost nothing to do with feeling. (Nor is it an action, a commitment to stay, or the intention to be nice, honest, or whatever else I might have thought I was supposed to do in a relationship.)

Love has become the container in which we live. Through time and riding mysterious waves of passion, aggression, and ignorance (and boredom), I think we began to live within love itself. At least I did. Each time I opened up, dropped the script, extended myself, accepted what was being offered to me, stepped beyond my comfort zone to embrace him, the structure was reinforced. I no longer have any idea if I love my husband or not. I can't imagine what the feelings I have for him are called. I've even given up trying to give love to him or to our relationship. Our relationship is what gives us love, not the other way around.

5. **I VOW TO LET GO**

And finally, of course, we're saying "I do" to good-bye. This bond will end. "Hello" can only mean "goodbye," one way or another. Some relationships are just mistakes. Or people grow and change. Relationships crater and nobody knows why. And if all else fails, we will certainly part at death.

Saul Bellow once called this acknowledgment "the black backing on the mirror that allows us to see anything at all," and isn't that just the key to the whole thing? The deeper our connection becomes, the more I know the reality of its ending and the more passionately I'm able to feel his touch. I know this even when I hate him (and he can really be an asshole—I'm not kidding) and when I love him so much that I plead for the opportunity to be married for all our lifetimes.

And here's something else I've learned about a relationship: Okay, so it's not what you think it's going to be, the feelings are always changing, and you're going to have to say goodbye someday. But when you find your love, there is something inside that simply and inexplicably says hello to him. Yes to him. Of course to him. Certainly. Obviously it's you. There is no choice. I do.

When my daughter was young, she told me her teacher had defined sex as "the closest two people can get." I thought that was a pretty good answer (and was happy I didn't have to get into the actual details). If being present is the key to love, it is also the key to making love. Sex therapist Cheryl Fraser says mindfulness can be the cure for routine or uninspired sex and suggests how we can use it to heat up our sex lives. Trigger warning (in the good sense): Her story is pretty hot and may trigger thoughts of pleasurable things.

PRACTICE

Mindful Sex Is the Best Sex[7]

Cheryl Fraser

It's our second date. We talk animatedly over Darjeeling and scones. I'm struggling to focus on his words, distracted by his ocean-blue eyes and wondering what our first kiss will feel like. Suddenly he leans across the table and kisses me slowly and very, very well. The traffic noise disappears. My body quivers with energy. All that exists is this moment, these lips, and focused, intense, erotic pleasure.

Fast-forward ten years.

We are making love. It's . . . okay. We go through the routine—I touch him here, he strokes me there. I'm remembering the time we had hot sex on the ferry on our way to a meditation retreat, and he's probably making his grocery list.

We are having mindless sex.

Can you relate? Has your sex life lost the passion and pleasure you had in the beginning? When I ask couples this, the answer is almost always yes.

The research findings on sexual satisfaction in long-term couples are dismal. Up to 30 percent of long-term couples—pretty much regardless of gender or orientation—make love six or fewer times a year. Or not at all.

Those who do still make love regularly report diminished pleasure and intensity. A typical couple in my online passion program reports, "Honestly? These days sex is boring."

Are you willing to settle for nonexistent or mediocre, mindless sex?

I'm not.

As a psychologist, sex therapist, and mindfulness teacher, I've deeply explored how meditation can improve our sexual lives. I even wrote a book about it.

The reason sex with the same person over time can seem boring is not because your partner is suddenly unattractive or unskilled. He, she, or they are still as fascinating as they were on your second date. It's your mind that's bored and that makes lovemaking uninspired and repetitive. In other words, the problem is in your head, not your bed.

To reignite passion, take mindfulness off the meditation cushion and practice it between the sheets. Regular sex is often the antithesis of mindful. We shove the present moment aside in a rush to the finale, escape into sexual fantasy, and focus on what we get rather than what we give.

Mindful sex involves deliberately bringing focus and curiosity to your sensual life with your partner. Practicing mindfulness in bed can enhance your pleasure in many ways. When the mind is concentrated, the sensory experience of the object of mindfulness—be that the breath or the ripples preceding orgasm—feels more intense. Sex is simply better.

The pace of mindful sex also enhances sexual and emotional connection. Surveys indicate the average sexual encounter lasts only seven minutes—and that is from wink to snore. By slowing down, you can tantalize and tease, exploring every bit of skin. What's more, when you're truly in the moment, it's like time stops and you witness your beloved for the precious being they are. Your heart opens to love and compassion. I call this falling in love with the one you're already with.

What follows are three tips for practicing mindful sex.

Touch with Mindfulness and Curiosity

Mindfulness is the special sauce for an intensely pleasurable sexual experience. Don't believe me? Close your eyes and gently, slowly stroke your inner wrist with your fingertips. Pay close attention to the sensations.

What is your direct experience of this simple touch?

I've asked thousands of meditation students and couples to do this, and what they say is, "It felt very intense," or "It was erotic, a turn-on."

Imagine bringing that same attention to the sensation of your lover teasing their tongue up your inner thigh.

I invite you to lay with your lover and take turns giving and receiving sensual touch. Focus your attention on the direct experience without clinging or expectations. And bring curiosity along for the ride. After all, we each have an entire body wired for sense pleasure.

Yet most sexual encounters are what I call "nipple nipple crotch goodnight." That's not mindful; it's mindless. Instead of limiting your touch to a few typical areas, try licking the back of your partner's knees or trailing your long hair along their lower spine.

Slow Down and Let Go

Regular sex tends to be goal-oriented (orgasm or bust), and it tends to race to climax in a linear path. Slow sex allows you to focus on the path itself. By making love without making orgasm the goal, you will naturally find yourself bringing more variety to the experience you are co-creating. You may kiss for longer, explore bodies more creatively, or switch sexual positions. There's so much eroticism in this moment as you linger on the sensations of mouth on nipple, of fingernails grazing skin.

Reality Beats Fantasy, So Be Here Now

What do you think about when you're making love? Perhaps like many people, instead of being fully here with your beloved, you're lost in the distraction of fantasized sex with someone else (or planning your Caribbean vacation).

If you want transcendent sex with your partner, increase your concentration. One beautiful practice is to remain conscious and present as you approach orgasm. Rather than zoning out on your own pleasure, stay connected with your partner's eyes and breath. As sensations of orgasm move through you, imagine sharing this energy with them. In the same way, receive their orgasm when they share it with you. This can intensify your pleasure and your emotional connection.

Be here now, with this lover, with this breath. Then linger together in the afterglow, bodies and minds entwined. Nowhere to go, nothing to be. Just this. The sense of your separate self may dissolve as you move from me to we to emptiness.

Ultimately, as with every other experience, great sex is all in your head. Quite simply, mindfulness can make you a better lover, and one who uncovers more pleasure and open-hearted love.

Given this, I decide to re-create that astounding tea-shop kiss. I take a shower and watch the challenges of the day swirl down the drain. I meditate as I soap my skin. Then I beckon my mate to bed. I slow down, I show up, I take delight in the shape of his lips and the gleam in his ocean-blue eyes. I see him as new and exciting, for in this present moment everything is new. Then I lean across the pillow and kiss him slowly and very, very well. And our bodies quiver, together.

Good parenting is one way we create the kind of future we want—for our children and for the world. It's how we break the cycle of suffering by not passing on the trauma we may have experienced in our own childhood. Karen Maezen Miller, the author of *Momma Zen*, has these tips for mindful parenting, but they're good rules for any time in life.

PRACTICE

Eight Practical Guidelines for Mindful Parenting[8]

Karen Maezen Miller

1. **PRACTICE IN PLAIN SIGHT**

   Place your meditation cushion in a conspicuous place in your home, such as on your bedroom floor. As you pass by, let it invite you to practice meditation daily. Even five minutes in the morning or night can turn your life around.

2. **LIVE BY ROUTINE**

   Take the needless guesswork out of meals and bedtimes. Let everyone relax into the predictable flow of a healthy and secure life.

3. **TURN OFF THE ENGINES**

   Discipline TV and computer usage and reduce artificial distraction, escapism, and stimulation. This begins with you.

4. **ELEVATE THE SMALL**

   And overlook the large. Want to change the world? Forget the philosophical lessons. Instruct your child in how to brush their teeth, and then do it, together, twice a day.

5. **GIVE MORE ATTENTION**

   And less of everything else. Devote one hour a day to giving undistracted attention to your children. Not in activities driven by your agenda, but according to their terms. Undivided attention is the most concrete expression of love you can give.

6. **TAKE A BREAK**

   Before you break in two. Designate a chair in your home as a "quiet chair," where you can retreat to decelerate conflicts. Or walk around the block and see how quickly your own two feet can stamp out the fire on your head.

7. **BE THE FIRST TO APOLOGIZE**

   Practice the miracle of atonement and instantly restore household harmony. By your doing it, your children will learn how.

8. **BE THE LAST TO KNOW**

   Refrain from making judgments and foregone conclusions about your children. Watch their lives unfold, and be surprised. The show is marvelous, and yours is the best seat in the house.

Stereotyping people on the basis of their identity is one of the biggest blocks to developing a real sense of human community, whether it's in our neighborhood, our workplace, or society as a whole. No matter how enlightened or progressive we think we are, we may be subtly and unconsciously stereotyping people who are different from us. Here's a mindfulness practice we can do to bring unconscious bias into awareness so we relate to people fully and authentically.

PRACTICE

Four Ways to Overcome Unconscious Bias[9]

Matthew Freeman

At a recent retreat I facilitated focused on social change, a diverse group of people gathered, from company and foundation executives to grassroots activists and public-housing residents. Their goal? To confront their own biases, form relationships across differences, and start to rebuild trust in their community. In our politically polarized society, the authentic conversations they had about race, religious differences, and our country's often painful history were rare, courageous, and transformative.

Efforts like these exist alongside mounting evidence that in just about every facet of life—from education and health to housing and criminal justice—we are all acting in unconsciously biased ways. But there is a solution to this problem: learning to overcome bias against people through deliberate effort.

Here are some of the steps we recommend as a good way to begin fighting bias in yourself. As hard as it can feel to confront your unconscious biases, with motivation and effort these simple steps can set you down that path.

1. **PAY ATTENTION TO HOW YOUR BIAS SHAPES YOUR ENVIRONMENT** Eliminating the impact of bias in your life requires you to acknowledge that it exists in the first place. Acknowledging that you have unconscious bias is not admitting a moral failing—this is part of the human condition.

   Start a campaign of self-awareness, paying attention to the subtle ways in which bias may be impacting your behavior. Ask yourself: Are there people at work I always ask for advice, and others I ignore? Who is part of my friend group and who might be missing?

   You can also take an inventory of who you trust. Just off the top of your head, name the top few people you would call if you received bad news or great news. How are those people similar to or different from you? Most of us trust others who are similar to us in significant ways.

   Lastly, take an inventory of the media you are consuming, including news, books, music, TV shows, and movies. Are their perspectives basically similar to yours? Are the characters or authors telling stories that represent a different context from your own?

   Once we acknowledge our bias and begin to pay attention to how it impacts us, we will be ready to do the work to overcome it.

2. **EXPOSE YOURSELF TO COUNTER-STEREOTYPICAL IMAGES** One of the most powerful ways to combat unconscious bias is to diversify the stories we encounter, so that we can connect with the humanity of people who may look and sound different

to us. This means watching movies, reading books, or attending performances that target groups we are less familiar with.

It can also mean purposefully seeking inspiration from moral exemplars of different ethnicities, races, genders, and abilities. Studies have shown that being exposed to counter-stereotypical images and stories of people from other groups leads to less implicit bias.

3. REACH OUT ACROSS DIFFERENCE

We can also seek ways to connect with people who are different from us in our everyday lives, whether at work or in our personal life. That means keeping your eyes open and looking for opportunities rather than waiting for them to fall into your lap.

For example, when you go to a work or social event, don't simply scan the crowd for people you already know; look for people you don't know—who might seem different from you—and see if you can strike up a conversation. Simple contact can be a powerful way to combat bias.

I took this step in my own life by joining an African-American church. As the only white person there, I initially felt awkward, unaware of social norms, and unfamiliar with the style of worship. Over time, however, I formed deep and meaningful relationships that have lasted over a decade, long after I stopped attending that church. The proactive step of seeking to make myself a minority in an everyday part of my life paid off through helping me take off my cultural blinders and form relationships with people I would have never met otherwise.

4. ASK, DON'T ASSUME. LISTEN, DON'T JUDGE

Once you expand your comfort zone through building new relationships and consuming different media, it becomes easier to include more people in your own circles of trust. Research has shown that cross-group friendships can make a big difference in reducing prejudice and bias.

But how to create that trust? By learning to ask rather than assume, and to listen rather than judge. In this way, we can stop the disconnection that may arise through misunderstanding.

In psychologist Beverly Tatum's excellent book on racial-identity development, *Why Are All the Black Kids Sitting Together in the Cafeteria?*, she writes about how a typical racial disconnect happens between grade-school friends at a very young age:

Imagine an African-American student has a negative interaction with a teacher, which she perceives as racially motivated. She shares this with her lifelong white friend, whose immediate response is, "That teacher is great; I'm sure she isn't racist!" That is the moment, according to Tatum, when self-segregation begins and kids start to look for others who can understand and discuss their experiences.

The antidote to this disconnection is authentic listening and learning to ask meaningful questions. Your friend's interpretation of her negative experience may not be correct—perhaps the teacher wasn't being racist or sexist. But if your first reaction is to tell her she's wrong before you even listen to her, you are driving a wedge between you.

To authentically connect with people across differences, you must suspend your own judgment long enough to actually hear their experiences. Ask open-ended questions and seek to understand rather than to challenge or convince.

As hard as it can feel to confront your unconscious biases, with motivation and effort these simple steps can set you down that path. And building authentic relationships across differences is an essential part of your journey.

The next step for the mindfulness movement is to become a real community. While millions of people today practice mindfulness on their own, there are few places they can meet, practice together, and inspire each other, either online or in real life. It is as a true national community that the mindfulness movement will become complete. Here are some ways you can help build it.

TEACHING

Start Your Own Mindfulness Group[10]

Tara Brach

Mindfulness meditation groups are a wonderful way of connecting with others to share and deepen your meditation practice. These groups come in many shapes and sizes and provide community, accountability, and a supportive space to connect with others while steadying and enriching your practice.

Meditation groups frequently start off with a handful of interested friends meeting in one person's home (or alternating homes) to practice. As attendance increases—or even from the very beginning—groups might meet in a room or hall in a church, library, or other building. Online groups can provide much-needed support and connection for those who have limited access to "in-person" resources due to geography, health, or scheduling limitations.

There is no required minimum number of participants. Groups have functioned successfully for years with only two or three members. Some people prefer the intimacy of a small group while others feel more supported by the stronger collective energy of larger groups.

The size of the group may depend upon whether you choose to have an open- or closed-group format. In an open group, drop-ins are encouraged and new members are welcome at any time. Closed groups typically set a number of spaces that feels comfortable and stop adding new members once that limit has been reached. They then will add new members from time to time as space opens up.

This is an important choice and will affect the makeup of your group. Open groups tend to be larger and are often in a state of flux, providing ongoing opportunities to meet new people and make new connections. Smaller closed groups allow members to bond and get to know each other over time. Which of these you choose will be unique to your group and what feels best to your members.

Similarly, there is no one "right" schedule. The frequency and length of each meeting will largely depend upon the activities planned for the group. You might meet weekly, every two weeks or even once a month, depending on the desires of the participants. Meetings might be an hour or may stretch out over an entire evening if your group gathers to share a meal or listen to a talk and engage in mindful discussion afterward. Online groups will need to consider time zones in setting a meeting schedule.

Groups often find it helpful to establish basic guidelines regarding the purpose of the meetings and, from time to time, review and revise them as needed. Basic guidelines provide a structure for the group meetings and help orient new members as they join an existing group. These might include a description of the group format, time and frequency of meetings, whether the group will be open or closed, and the group's primary sources of inspiration or direction (if any).

Your group's time together may consist of any number of activities. It could be as bare-bones as a simple sitting meditation—guided, silent, or some of each—and a friendly greeting before starting or re-entering your daily life. Some groups like to include a reading, guided meditation, talk (live or recorded), or more in-depth sharing time. Others might be drawn to walking meditation or enjoying a meal together in mindfulness. Some groups develop around applying mindfulness to a common interest or theme, e.g., addiction, parenting, mental health professionals, etc.

One popular format for many groups is to begin with a guided or silent sitting meditation, followed by a short check-in from each member and open time for sharing joys, difficulties, and questions about their meditation practice and how it is working (or not) in their daily lives. The group then closes with a short sitting or loving-kindness meditation as a way to foster a greater sense of connection to each other and to the world.

The sharing period gives participants the opportunity to listen deeply to one another while also paying attention to what arises in themselves. Some groups like to choose specific topics to focus the sharing (such as forgiveness, mindfulness at work, dealing with conflict, or working with anxiety), while others prefer a more open-ended discussion format. The confidentiality of the group creates a safe and supportive refuge where each individual is nourished as they share freely from real lives and hearts.

Organizing a meditation group is incredibly rewarding and, like anything else in life, can be quite challenging. All groups are likely to go through rough patches and have growing pains from time to time. Each meeting is a learning experience and it is important for facilitators to be open to feedback from other members and willing to make adjustments as the group forms and settles. The effort will be well worth it.

Journeys on the Complete Path of Mindfulness: Community and Connection

When you meet somebody else who practices mindfulness, you're probably going to be appropriately more trusting of them. You're going to be more open with them about your inner world and trust them to hold it. In a challenging world where it's hard to know who to trust, especially online, it's really nice to have a sense that along with mindfulness may come a greater commitment to ethics. There are no guarantees, of course, but a mindfulness practice could be a probability marker of a moral dimension that you can lean on in other people. That can give us a sense of greater security through being in mindfulness community. Of course, no community is perfect, even our own!

—Rick Hanson

Meditating and developing myself in a vacuum would never have worked for me. The minute I started my meditation practice, I stepped into a community of mindfulness practitioners. Instantly. That was core. I couldn't even separate those things out because that is where I was able to begin to see interconnection in a real-time way. Opening my heart to others in community, I could work with the hurt and vulnerability we all share. Opening my heart and connecting and really touching into all of the places that I had been hurt or that I felt vulnerable, I could work with others in something that we shared. That gave me a foundation of support to hang in there despite the challenges. Without community, it never would have happened for me. I don't think I could ever have done it in isolation.

—Lisa Ernst

I have so much respect for the power of community, either to facilitate inner peace or to disturb inner peace. So it's really important that we decide, when we have a choice, what communities we're going to be in. The kind of community I look for are people whose core values are love and compassion. If these are their core values, it doesn't matter to me what their background is. Those are the people who help me to grow in the way that I would like to grow, which is to grow in love and compassion.

That's the joy side but then there's the challenging side. We are in a global community with people we may not want to be with who cause us suffering, and who we cause to suffer. We must learn to be with others who have different opinions, desires, cultural backgrounds, and views. This teaches us the qualities of humility and compassion that extend beyond our own little circle.

—Christopher Germer

When I first did a meditation retreat for people of color, it felt like home. It felt like I didn't have to look over my shoulder and that I wasn't observed as being different. The same thing happened in the LGBTQIA-plus retreats.

When I am among my own communities, I no longer have to be vigilant. You are able to access the heart at that moment, you're no longer closed, you're no longer constricted. It's like, ah, there's a way in which the breath becomes accessible.

It's feeling that the community can come together. We can heal together. We can practice together. We can actually do this transformational work of working toward liberation together. That doesn't say we can't do it within the dominant culture, but there is something really rich about doing it with folks that you have an affinity with.

—Noliwe Alexander

Connection is absolutely essential. Whether that's with your partner, a group of friends, or the universe as a whole, we feel at home when we're connected. What does that mean? We feel like we're in our true nature, who we really are, which is one with other people or with everything. That's where true happiness comes from.

—Kristin Neff

8

PRACTICES FOR MINDFUL LIVING

Mindfulness is about real life—your life, my life, our lives together. It's about how to make life good, happy, and meaningful every day.

Like life, mindfulness practice has infinite variations. Yes, there are some basics. You start by resting mindfully in the present and using the power of your insight to understand yourself and this reality you're experiencing. With that foundation, you can develop all the things that make life good, like love, compassion, ethics, and connection to others. If there is any sort of belief required, it is only the belief in your human goodness and the goodness of this world. But in the end, that's not even a belief—it's something you experience.

From that basic framework, you can then do a whole range of helpful practices, each specifically designed to bring mindfulness to a different aspect of your life. You are limited only by your own insight and creativity in creating helpful ways to benefit from mindfulness.

In this chapter you'll learn different mindfulness practices that will enhance your daily life. I marvel at the people who created and teach us these practices—their deep insight, their grasp of human psychology, their realism, their ability to develop step-by-step techniques that really work. In a world full of fatuous remedies to the problems of life, these practices for mindful living stand out for their effectiveness and common sense.

Mindfulness is a complete path in two senses. Mindfulness is complete in its depth, addressing the realities of life at their most profound. It is also complete in its breadth, because anything we do can be done mindfully.

Mindfulness is both profound and practical, and these are inseparable. For something to be practical—to really work—it must be based in profound truths about the nature of reality, why we suffer, and how we can really lead the life we want. And if something is truly profound, it will be practical and help our lives.

In these practices for mindful living, and the many more that are possible, you will experience the unity of the profound and the practical that is the Complete Path of Mindfulness. May they help you make life—with all its challenges and ups and downs—happy, meaningful, and mindful every day.

Practices

Being in nature is one of the best ways to get out of your thinking mind. On the other hand, you have to get out of your thinking mind to really be in nature, and mindfulness can help. Here's a practice to connect you to the sights, sounds, and smells of nature so you can step out of your thoughts and enjoy all of the benefits of nature to your mental and physical well-being.

PRACTICE

Nature: Arriving Practice[1]

Mark Coleman

Arriving in a particular place, mindfully aware and attuned, is one of the simplest and yet most important ways to enter into relationship with nature. It is a way of sensitively orienting to the environment you find yourself in. It allows us to let go of our busy, thinking mind and mental preoccupations and instead arrive in our senses in the moment.

On my Awake in the Wild nature programs, when I bring people to a particular place to meditate—perhaps in a forest, along an ocean bluff, or in a shady canyon in the desert—I share this process of "arriving" as a way to begin to help people orient to the particularities of place.

Once you arrive at a place outdoors that you would like to spend time or meditate in, find somewhere you can sit or rest comfortably for ten to fifteen minutes. Prior to meditating or trying to be mindful, invite a quality of relaxation and rest at ease sitting on the earth.

Then open up your senses fully to begin the process of "arriving." Notice what immediately allures your attention. Look around and take in the variety of life here. You may be pulled to the array of colors around you, or to gaze at the tree canopy or at the clouds. Perhaps the intimacy with life on the ground catches your attention.

Notice the sounds of this place, the soundscape of the forest, the insects, frogs, or birdsong. You may notice the ebb and flow of sounds, particularly as winds blow through the landscape. Maybe you are captivated by the sound of silence and how that touches a sense of stillness within you.

Sometimes you may simply feel all the sensory impressions as you sit in this landscape—the softness or hardness of the ground, the breeze blowing against your skin, the warmth or coolness of the air, the sunlight against your body.

Occasionally you may sense the fragrances that are here, perhaps the rich smells of the forest after rainfall or the sweet aroma of blossoming flowers in spring, or you may notice the salty air with each in-breath as you sit by the ocean.

One of the things that can captivate our attention is the dynamism of a place. You may be drawn to the movement of leaves in the trees, the changing patterns on the surface of water, the cumulus clouds mushrooming in the sky, or the way dappled light moves through the forest.

What is key to all these sense impressions is to notice how effortlessly you are brought into the present moment without any effort or strain. Nature spontaneously allures our curiosity to its effervescent, rich, changing forms.

This natural quality of knowing brings forth an important point—that being outdoors allows a more relaxed, natural quality of attention. Mindfulness practice outdoors, when attuned to our sensory experience, can be effortless and peaceful and happens almost by itself.

So as you continue to sit here in this place, let your attention continue to be drawn to whatever catches your interest. See how easy it is to reside in the present moment. Observe how this simple act of arriving allows you to enter into a particular landscape, to become familiar with it. Notice how it deepens your sense of connection with life around you.

Each time you move to a different place outdoors, be sure to begin by doing this practice of "arriving" even if only for a few moments. Doing so will help you attune more intimately to wherever you are.

Mindfulness of a simple act like drinking a cup of tea can be about more than just being present. As a practice it can give you deep insight into your own nature, the nature of tea, and the act of drinking. With each sip you can experience the reality of interbeing.

PRACTICE

How to Drink a Mindful Cup of Tea[2]

Joseph Emet

Here is a homemade *koan* for drinking tea: *Who is enjoying this tea?*

Ask yourself this question with each sip. When you encounter that person, let them go. You need a break from their story now and then. Otherwise your tea break will not really be a break at all.

Constantly rehearsing the story of our roles, obligations, and commitments wears us down. Yes, we may be mothers, doctors, servers, or office workers, but at the core, we are more than these things. We are "breath-breathing humans," as the Sufi poet Rumi said. Whatever your story, you are more than that story. Get in touch—and stay in touch—with the breath-breathing human you are as you enjoy your tea.

"Just this," remind yourself with each sip. "Just this." Sit and breathe like a flower in a meadow, enjoying the sun.

If you have ever watched one of Thich Nhat Hanh's talks, you have probably witnessed elements of tea meditation. Halfway through a talk, Thich Nhat Hanh will pause and pour himself a cup of tea. Then, as several hundred listeners watch his every move, he will slowly raise the cup to his lips and enjoy a few unhurried sips. He sometimes holds the cup with both hands as if to illustrate that his whole attention is on it.

Thich Nhat Hanh truly takes a break when he drinks his tea. He is not using the time to prepare his next topic. Paradoxically, taking a true break is more effective than using the time to think of your next move. As you disengage even momentarily from your surface mind, you access deeper layers of your self to include in your discourse or journey. That allows you to talk, move, and act more authentically as a whole person.

Thich Nhat Hanh can do this in the presence of hundreds. See if you can do it when you are having tea with someone (or alone, for that matter). Here's a five-step practice you can do once your tea is ready.

1. **PAUSE**

   Take a few moments to sit with your cup of tea before you start drinking it. You want this time to be a meditation break as well as a tea break. Even if you meditated that morning, by 3 p.m. it's a dim memory. With a few conscious breaths now, you can reconnect with that meditative space.

2. **TOUCH THE INTERBEING NATURE OF THE TEA**

   See the soil, rain, and sun that went into creating this drink, and the women and men whose hands harvested, prepared, packaged, shipped, and sold it. "The entire universe can be seen in a flower," Thich Nhat Hanh wrote in *Love Letter to the Earth*. This vision is rewarding in itself, and is good training for seeing everything with the same eyes, including the person sitting in front of you.

3. **TOUCH YOUR OWN INTERBEING NATURE**

   Your stress, happiness, and unhappiness are made up of your opinions and attitudes. In turn, your state of mind affects how others feel around you. Let go of your opinions and attitudes. Feel your stress dissolve. Feel it float away. Feel it drop to the ground.

4. **ENJOY THE FIRST SIPS**
   "To be here and now and enjoy the present moment is our most important task," says Thich Nhat Hanh in *Being Peace*. Let the aroma of the tea fill the space of your mind until there is no room for thoughts. Let the thinking mind become a tea-enjoying mind.

5. **RELAX AND EXPAND YOUR VISION**
   Be silent for the first few sips. Notice how expanding the context of your vision puts your momentary concerns and problems in perspective. When you are relaxed, you are more creative and see more possibilities in each situation. See this moment as an important and productive part of your day. If you can step outside the box for a few moments now, you will return to your task with a fresh mind.

Breaks for meditation throughout the day act as pressure valves for emptying your mind and finding freedom. So you can apply these steps to other activities in your daily life, such as eating dinner, washing dishes, or even riding the bus. They are all great opportunities to practice stillness in motion, our natural condition on the spinning Earth.

Since self-acceptance is the first step on the path to healing, one of the goals of mindfulness practice is to accept and experience difficult feelings and traumas you may deny or numb yourself to. But for many of us it is just as hard to accept happiness and joy, to enjoy the goodness in ourselves and the pleasure in our lives. The good news is that the same mindfulness techniques you use to face the difficulties of life can also help you open your heart to life's happiness and joy. Allyson Pimentel teaches a practice to savor the great joy of parenting, but you can use it to open yourself to the joy of anything. Happiness and joy are right here. Take them.

PRACTICE

Savor the Joy[3]

Allyson Pimentel

Being a parent in these uneasy times is like taking a master class in life's ten thousand joys and ten thousand sorrows. The path of parenting contains moments of tremendous joy, pride, and possibility, plus moments of heartbreak, fear, and confusion.

As our children grow up in a world with so much beauty and so much devastation, our task becomes ever-more complex. As my mother-in-law often says, "Small children, small problems; big children, big problems." With all the problems we parents hold and help our children through—from colic to broken bones to broken hearts to feelings of disconnection and alienation—we can lose sight of the pleasure present on the path of parenting.

Pleasure is often easiest to access when our children are small and we feel deeply connected with them, delighting in their first sounds, smiles, or steps. Pleasure may be harder to access as our children grow into teens, when their neurological curriculum demands that they defy, differentiate, and turn away from us toward their own future.

It can be harder still when we contemplate the challenges of the societal, political, and ecological future we are leaving our children to inherit. We may recognize with deep discomfort that our children are becoming more comfortable staring at their screens than making eye contact, more at ease in the virtual world than they are in the natural one, unsafe even in their schools. So, what can we do when, as Wendell Berry wonders in his poem "The Peace of Wild Things," "despair for the world grows in me and I wake in the night at the least sound in fear of what my life and my children's lives may be"?

One thing we can do is to savor the pleasure and joy in parenting. Savoring is enjoying and appreciating a pleasant thing completely, especially by dwelling or lingering on it. It can be a vital nourishment and fortification on the path of parenting. Research in the field of positive psychology suggests that appreciation of life's pleasures builds happiness. It can prolong positive emotions and buffer against negative ones.

Savoring requires presence. It relies on the senses, and it can be deepened with practice. Mindfulness is a powerful precursor to savoring. Mindfulness expands our capacity to hold all that parenting requires of us. It helps us meet the pain and the pleasure with openness and kindness. The practice of savoring specifically invites us to use the powers of attention we cultivate through mindfulness more pointedly—to aim it at the pleasure and joy present in our lives and in our children's lives.

Savoring pleasure is not to be confused with grasping after it or needing it—it is simply being with it as fully as possible. One of the beauties of savoring is that it comes so very naturally. Noticing what feels good just . . . feels good.

Staying with what feels good—breathing into it, inviting it to be fully felt, seen, and known—can be more of a challenge. So here are two practices—an informal one you can use throughout your day and a more formal practice you can do as part of your mindfulness meditation—to help you stay with all that is joyful and pleasurable in parenting (and anywhere else in your life).

Savor the Present Moment

When you notice a pleasurable or joyful moment that has arisen naturally between you and your child, stay with it, notice it, name it, and breathe into it.

Engage your sensory processes. If you catch a whiff of your newborn's smell, or the smell of the scrambled eggs your newly self-sufficient middle schooler has just made, keep smelling. Linger for a moment. Breathe it in. Notice what's happening in your body, mind, and heart. Is it relaxation? Gratitude? Feelings of love or appreciation?

Take a moment to marvel at this smell. Or this smile, this loving glance, this funny joke, this life skill your child is developing, this feeling of joy in the togetherness you're sharing—whatever it may be, marvel at it.

You could also name it: "Ah, this is what love feels like. This is tenderness." You can do this as many times a day as you notice something that makes you feel good. The beauty of this practice is that the more you notice pleasure and joy, the more pleasure and joy you will notice.

Savoring Meditation

You can also devote time to savoring in your formal meditation practice. It can be a stand-alone practice or something you do at the beginning or end of a period of mindfulness meditation.

To do this, call to mind an image, memory, or moment that you wish to savor. It could be a time in the past when your child was especially happy or thriving, or an imagined beautiful moment in the future.

Lovingly hold an image in your mind of them in their joy, success, safety, achievement, flow, health, alignment.

Notice the details; luxuriate in them. Feel what this pleasure feels like in your body and being. Breathe into and through the sensations as if to aerate them, giving them more space to be felt and to expand.

Let your mind wander over the good, the pleasurable, the joyful. As best you can, incline your mind toward pleasure. As in the informal practice of savoring, you can add a phrase to deepen the experience, such as, "This feels so good. This is what happiness feels like."

Whether you practice savoring informally or formally, you can enhance the experience by sharing it. You can reflect together with your child about beautiful moments or positive experiences and help them cultivate their own ability to savor what is good in their lives. You can model your process for them by inviting them to participate and share in your joy. Because savoring is inherently connecting, it can serve as one antidote to the disconnections and distortions of modern life.

Expressing gratitude can also deepen the experience of savoring, as if you are sprinkling thanksgiving onto whatever dish you're savoring to boost its flavor. Yet even as you savor and give thanks, you may notice some resistance, pain, or discomfort. You can acknowledge and accept that pain and pleasure exist alongside one another, and that's the way it is. That's life. The mind's negativity bias has its purpose—its awareness of suffering is designed to protect you—but you can gently remind yourself that right now, in this moment, you are privileging pleasure. You are joining with joy. You are delighting in delight. You are savoring parenting.

Mindfulness develops the kind of direct experience, unmediated by concepts and thoughts, that unleashes your inner creativity. Conversely, art is itself a type of mindfulness practice, putting you in touch with your deepest self and the world around you. This practice, combining two different forms of artistic expression, shows why mindfulness and creativity work so well together.

PRACTICE

Creativity: The Art of the Moment[4]

Rachel Rose

My eyes are closed, my breath warm and sufficient. I feel connected and ready for the next moment. I softly open my eyes, reach for my paintbrush, and slosh blue paint across my page. And there it is—fear. My teeth clench, and I think how silly I was to even think I could paint.

I often tell myself that, but today is different. Today, because of my mindfulness practice, I notice this pernicious story as it begins to take shape. So instead of giving in to fear and self-doubt, I pause, place my hand on my heart, and choose a compassionate approach.

I tell myself that I am courageous—that making a mark on the page is the way I practice making my mark in this world. With this act of love, my creative process unfolds, a dance of marks, awareness, and compassion. This is the practice of creative mindfulness. It's both a gateway to the present moment and a chance to choose a new perspective on life.

In my work, I help people practice mindful creativity. We use art-making, writing, movement, and music to enter the present moment and cultivate a new perspective on our experiences. Like yoga, mindful walking, or following the breath in traditional meditation, mindful creativity is another pathway to awareness in which we observe the present moment with intention and without judgment.

The best way to understand creative mindfulness is to experience it. In that spirit, I invite you to create a small abstract painting and poem as a mindfulness practice. This invitation doesn't require skill or previous experience. You just need a willingness to meet the process with curiosity and intention.

In this exercise, you will intentionally engage in a creative act as a place to witness your thoughts, feelings, ideas, judgments, and stories. Your attention will be on your deepest impulses, which will guide you toward specific colors, marks, shapes, and lines you will make. By trusting these impulses and being a curious observer of your process, you can discover new awareness about yourself and your inner world. Here is how to practice mindful creativity:

1. **PREPARE YOUR SUPPLIES.**
   Simple supplies are best. All you need is a piece of paper, painter's tape or masking tape, a journal or paper for writing, and two different color media, such as crayons and pastels or paint and markers. Tape your paper down, making a thick border along the edges of your page. This will keep your paper from moving and create a white space around the perimeter of your piece.

2. **ARRIVE IN THE MOMENT.**
   Spend a few moments centering and arriving in the moment. You can do this with some practice at the end of your regular meditation session. Or you can simply spend a few minutes with your breath and body, observing your thoughts, feelings, and perceptions in whatever way feels comfortable for you.

3. **SET YOUR INTENTION.**
   Once you feel present and relaxed, begin by setting an intention or asking a question. For example, you may intend to pay particular attention to your body while you create, or explore the feelings that come up for you. Or you may want to ask a specific question, such as, "What can I learn about my stress today?" or "What's preventing me from being more curious in my life?" Your intention or question will act as an anchor for your process. You can formalize it by writing it out in your journal or writing paper.

4. **MAKE MARKS.**

   Looking at your color media, check in with your impulses and select the colors you want to use with each medium. When the feeling to move arises from within you, select your first color medium and, with impulse as your guide, make a few marks, shapes, and/or lines on the page. Repeat this process with the remaining colors. If you choose a wet medium like paint, you may want to observe it drying naturally, or you can speed up the process with a hairdryer or by putting it in the sun.

5. **NOTICE AND NOTATE.**

   As you make your marks, notice the thoughts, feelings, ideas, judgments, and stories that come up for you. Are you feeling uncomfortable as you try something new? Are you tempted to judge this creation as good, bad, ugly, or pretty? Are there any emotions, memories, or thoughts that have come up?

   Each time you notice something, pause and take note of it or write it out on your paper. Pay attention to these experiences with gentle curiosity for as long as you need, and then return to your creation when you are ready.

6. **WRITE A POEM.**

   When your art is dry, carefully peel off the masking tape. Notice how revealing the white space on the edges changes your experience of the piece. Take a few moments to observe your creation with fresh eyes and from various perspectives.

   Return to your intention or question, and when you're ready, move to writing. With a trusting and open approach, write a quick three-line poem about your piece. Let this be an opportunity to write without skill or craft. The point is to express through words the sentiment and feelings that are coming up for you.

Look at your art and poem together. Give them a title and write it down.

7. **CLOSE.**

Then, with your art and poem nearby, place your hand on your heart, close your eyes, and return to a place of stillness. Offer gratitude to the process and to yourself for showing up. In the hours and days that follow your experience of mindful creativity, ponder the following questions to help deepen your practice:

When you consider the image and the poem, what thoughts, feelings, or emotions come up for you? What's the bigger meaning or purpose of this process for you, your life, and your mindfulness process in general? How might you continue to build upon this creative mindfulness exercise and welcome creative expression into other areas of your life?

Criticizing yourself, trying to meet society's expectations about your body, obsessively trying to fill some inner void—there's little in life that brings up more issues than food. Mindful eating is a proven way to improve your relationship with food and let go of all the stories and baggage that come along with it. Physician Jan Chozen Bays, a leading teacher of mindful eating, helps you quiet three troublesome inner voices with a lot to say—none of it helpful—about how you eat.

PRACTICE

Mindful Eating: Quiet the Three Inner Voices[5]

Jan Chozen Bays

When our relationship to eating and food is out of balance, it is easy to be overcome with negative emotions. We may feel aversion to the sight of our body in the mirror, jealousy toward people who can eat "anything they want," or anger toward ourselves for our inability to end our struggle with food and eating. What can we do to counteract these unhappy feelings?

When our mind is full of the voices of conflicting thoughts and emotions, it is hard to do anything in a deliberate and straightforward way. . . . Meditation helps to settle and quiet the mind, to create some space around the inner voices. We can begin to sort them out, to hear what individual voices are trying to tell us.

When we do this inner listening we may discover a trio of voices that can take over our lives and make us miserable. . . . When this trio—the inner perfectionist, pusher, and critic—get a grip on any area of your life, they have the power to destroy it. They can undermine your trust in yourself and in others. They can make you stop doing something you love to do. They will suck the life out of your life. . . .

The Inner Perfectionist

The job of the inner perfectionist is to look around for examples of perfection so it can tell you what you should aim for. If you are aiming to be more compassionate, the inner perfectionist might point out Mother Teresa or the Dalai Lama as your role models. If your goal is to become more intelligent, then it will direct your attention to Albert Einstein or Stephen Hawking.

An inner perfectionist that is concerned with the body looks at magazines or movies or people passing on the street and says, "You see that skinny but impossibly large-breasted lady (or that bulked-up hulk of a man)? That's perfection, that's what I want you to aim for."

The Inner Pusher

The inner pusher's job is to tell you what to do in order to achieve perfection and then to push you to do it. The inner pusher loves to make lists, long lists of things to do. . . . The inner pusher is aware of which paragon of beauty or virtue the inner perfectionist has chosen and will tell you what you have to do to become like them.

The Inner Critic

The last of this powerful trio is the inner critic. Its job is to criticize. That's all it does. Whatever comes into its field of vision is fair game for attack by the critic. It is never satisfied, because, as a human being, you will always be imperfect, unable to meet the standards set up by the perfectionist. You will never be as compassionate as Mother Teresa, as intelligent as Einstein, or have a body like the magazine models. . . .

With voices like these on the inside, who needs enemies on the outside? With inner voices like these, it's a miracle that people can make any improvements in their lives.

An essential aspect of mindfulness is to see through these voices, to not be caught or fooled by them. When you start to practice mindfulness, you notice that there's almost constant chatter going on in your mind—this is true for everyone. Even longtime meditators experience this chatter; they have learned how to quickly quiet it down. The mind is constantly producing thoughts. That's what it does. But we don't have to believe our minds all the time. . . .

Practice: Mindfulness of the Inner Critic

Listen for the voice of the inner critic commenting on food, eating habits, weight, and appearance. Listen within your own mind, but also listen as others talk. Be aware of these types of inner-critic comments on TV or radio shows. Comedians often speak disparagingly about themselves—notice the voice of the inner critic in what they say.

If you are working with a group, ask others to tell you when they hear you speaking through the inner critic about yourself. An example is, "I'm hopeless at doing these exercises."

Money is another thing people get weird about. Our conflicted attitudes toward money can cause a lot of problems—how often family conflict revolves around money—and a lot of our neurotic beliefs about money are passed down from our parents. Financial advisor Spencer Sherman brings our psychological issues about money into the open and teaches us how we can use mindfulness to free ourselves from old learned patterns. Because money may not bring happiness, but it can certainly bring unhappiness.

PRACTICE

Unlearn Your Money Beliefs[6]

Spencer Sherman

Beliefs are powerful and it's our job as mindfulness practitioners to loosen their grip on us. If we agree that everything is impermanent, then are we ready to see the impermanence of our own beliefs about money and soften our clinging to them?

You may believe that you don't have enough money, that the stock market can't be trusted, that you're not competent with money, that rich people are happier, or that you'll feel secure when your financial situation improves. The clinging is compounded when you aren't even aware of your beliefs. I didn't know, for example, that I valued money more than my life—until I risked my life to retrieve my files from a burning building.

Our allegiance to our money beliefs can lead us to invest impulsively, avoid addressing our finances, become stingy with ourselves and other people, blindly rely on the advice of others, or focus our energies on acquiring shiny objects that fall short of our expectations.

In short, when we cling to beliefs about money, we suffer what Buddhism calls the three poisons: greed/fear, aversion/avoidance, and delusion/ignorance. But it doesn't have to be this way. Money beliefs, even lifelong, are as impermanent as any other thought or belief. If we loosen their grip on us just a little, we will find our innate money wisdom becomes accessible, we will be more likely to discern sensible financial opportunities, and we will feel a lot more at ease.

When it comes to money, our conditioning has been so strong and so long-lasting that we often aren't even aware of it. So the first step is being open to the possibility that you are deluded about money. Being successful with your finances becomes much less challenging when you gain awareness of the conditioning that blocks your common sense.

The question is, why do we have so many delusions about money? The reason is that our beliefs about money were formed when we were young children, and those deeply rooted childhood beliefs often override what we learn later as adults.

For example, as adults we might embrace the idea that more money doesn't necessarily make us happier. But we find that our money actions and reactions are more aligned with the opposite view—that money will make us happy—which was planted in our minds when we were young.

Even the most advanced meditators often remain on autopilot about their money behaviors. Our deeply implanted habits can butt up against our adult wisdom, and we find ourselves more grasping and more aversive than we'd like. This disconnect only exacerbates our sense of confusion about money.

What further complicates the domain of money is that there's almost no environment in which we feel safe telling anyone about our real money issues and fears. Money is such a taboo subject that we don't know how other people experience it and we can't share our own experiences. We also don't have the training to investigate and speak about money issues in conscious, intentional, and mature ways. We tend to either disengage about money or be very reactive to it.

This inability to nonjudgmentally recognize and examine our money beliefs keeps our conditioning in place. Think about a money decision you made, maybe an impulsive decision you made that didn't turn out well. Can you trace what belief you were clinging to that supported that action? As we examine our financial history, awareness starts to loosen up the grip our money beliefs have on us. Here's a step-by-step practice to help you do that.

Practice: Surface Your Money Beliefs

As you calm your mind and body, bring to mind a money challenge you've had or an emotion that's related with money. Become very aware of the physical sensations that arise as you do this—how your breathing changes, how the speed and quality of your thoughts change. Commit to just sensing what you feel without leaping to any insights or commentary.

Now ask yourself: What's the belief that supports this money challenge or emotion? Spend the next few minutes befriending the younger version of yourself who learned this belief. Offer compassion to this young person for adopting and clinging to such a fixed belief.

Finally, ask yourself two questions. First, would this money challenge or emotion change if you had learned the opposite belief? Sit in silence without reaching for any answers. Now ask yourself: Who am I without this belief? After a few minutes, allow your awareness to widen and open. Consciously let go of your beliefs. Let go of identifying with these beliefs. Let go of clinging.

We return now to the roots of the mindfulness movement—to health. While there are some proven ways that mindfulness can help our physical health, it is most useful in helping us deal mentally with health problems when they happen. One issue is that we often need other people's help when we're sick, and this is difficult to face if we have always taken pride in being self-sufficient and in charge. The nursing professor Susan Bauer-Wu has this advice about how to ask for and accept the help we may need at a difficult time.

PRACTICE

Health: How to Accept the Help You Need[7]

Susan Bauer-Wu

Asking for and accepting help from others can be one of the greatest challenges for people living with a serious illness. Basic everyday activities that you have done for yourself for as long as you can remember, like driving, cooking, and taking a shower, may now be difficult and necessitate assistance from family, friends, and professionals.

This can be especially hard for people who have an independent spirit or those who enjoy taking care of others. Also, our society values a do-it-yourself attitude. A natural tendency is to resist help as long as possible or to deny that you ever need it. Accepting help may feel like a sign of weakness, dependence, or giving in to the illness. However, accepting help is actually a wise and essential step toward caring for yourself and an entry to opening up to love and care from others. . . .

Freely receiving others' help demonstrates a sense of acceptance of what is happening. There are softness and spaciousness in the experience of gracefully receiving and accepting assistance that translate into a lighter mood, more relaxed body, connection with others, and general ease in living. This also provides an opportunity for loved ones to reciprocate and express gratitude for the love and care you have provided to them over the years. It helps them to feel good about themselves and allows them to see that they can make a positive difference in your life. You may sense their satisfaction when they assist you. They feel helpful rather than helpless.

A friend of mine reflected on her dear friend Mary Ellen, who, while living with a serious and debilitating illness, was an amazing teacher in how to gracefully receive care. Mary Ellen had a deep sense of knowing that we human beings are enlivened when we extend care and kindness to others. For their monthly women's circle that met at different homes, Mary Ellen proactively called ahead of time to find out the most accessible entrance. With weaker legs, she set gentle and clear directions for her friends to assist her in settling into a seat, letting them know exactly where to stand, extend a hand, and how to help. Throughout, Mary Ellen maintained a radiant smile and a humble heart, overflowing with gratitude for all who were present.

Accepting and receiving help doesn't mean that you need to completely lose your independence. You can have others help you and you can still do things yourself; they are not mutually exclusive. You and your loved ones can also do things together. The goal is for you to be aware of and discern what you can reasonably do yourself and what you actually need assistance with. Regular mindfulness practice helps with discernment. It facilitates tuning in to your body, seeing more clearly, and making sound decisions as they relate to your self-care. . . .

Practice: Receiving and Accepting Help

- Settle your body and gently close your eyes or maintain a soft gaze. With kindness, settle your mind by bringing attention to the sensations of breathing or to another neutral sensation that may be more comfortable for you. Simply rest in stillness and with awareness for a few moments.
- Think about a situation when you needed something, and you didn't ask for help but wished that you had. Consider what prevented you from asking for assistance. What held you back? Be aware of how you feel right now as you bring this to mind.
- Bring to mind a situation when you declined others' offers to help you when deep down you knew you needed it. Who offered to help and what were the circumstances? What held you back from accepting the help? Do you feel unsettled or satisfied in how you handled this? Notice how you feel as you consider this.
- Bring to mind a situation when you may have asked for help. Whom did you ask? What were the circumstances? How did they respond to your request? How did you feel afterward? How do you feel right now as you remember this? If no such situation comes to mind, that's okay too.
- Bring to mind someone whom you love and care about and who loves and cares about you. With this person in mind, imagine them offering to assist you with something you need.

Recognize the good intentions behind the offer. Sense how you feel as you gently open to this person's kindness and generosity. Imagine yourself graciously accepting this offer. Notice how you feel right now as you bring this to mind.

- With this same person in mind, someone whom you love and care about and who loves and cares about you, imagine asking them for help with something you need. Remember that this is someone whom you trust and who wants to help you. Allow yourself to open up to this person's caring. Imagine asking them for help in such a way that conveys your sincere gratitude. Notice how you feel in this moment as you consider this.

There is a New Age trope—in fact a simplistic version of a teaching by the Buddha—that "pain is unavoidable but suffering is optional." This is a bit disingenuous, because of course physical pain causes suffering. What it really means is that we can avoid the extra suffering caused by how we handle our pain. The Buddha called this "the second arrow" that causes more suffering after we are hit by the first arrow. As you remember, the very first use of mindfulness in a secular context was Jon Kabat-Zinn's program of Mindfulness-Based Stress Reduction to help people in chronic pain. Those pioneering patients found that the calm and insight of mindfulness practice helped them suffer less from their pain, and we too can benefit from teachings like these when we face the unavoidable.

PRACTICE

Mindfulness for When You're in Pain[8]

Peter Fernando

When we experience pain in the body, to begin with, it is important to establish an attitude of wisdom that will be sustainable.

The first thing to remember is that we're not trying to get rid of pain. This isn't an attempt to destroy, get rid of, or cut pain out of existence. Although this may be challenging, particularly if the experience of pain is intense, there is a great wisdom in this approach. When we enter into the practice with an open heart, we taste for ourselves how it actually works.

That in the mind that is setting pain up as an enemy and seeks to push it away actually increases the sense of pain being painful. It generates the sense that pain is unacceptable and can't be included in awareness. In contrast, what we are trying to feel into is an awareness that can be inclusive, sensitive, and awake, without holding to a sense that pain is "wrong." Through this the quality of pain begins to be felt as more amorphous, mysterious, and less stuck.

As we have seen already, the first step is to look at the relationship we have to pain in this very moment. So take a moment now to notice what perceptions, mind states, or attitudes are arising in relation to the felt experience of painful sensation. Shine the light of your curious awareness into this aspect of your inner experience.

It could be a sense of "I wish this would go away." Or maybe it's an underlying current of irritation and anger, such as "I hate this." Sometimes what we find is fear riffing on particular constructs of the future in the mind's eye. Try to taste these flavors of heart energy with no judgment. Trust in a radical, stripped-down awareness, free from commenting, measuring, or judging these states as "spiritual" or "unspiritual." Instead, just feel the whole sense of what is arising in this moment. Give yourself a few moments to do that right now.

Now see if you can expand awareness to touch the pain as well as the mind state. Notice that the mind state—the energy of heart and emotion—is not the pain. The pain itself is just so. The fear, anger, worry, or dislike is something that the heart is doing in this moment. We may not be doing it consciously—we may also be experiencing the results of habitual intentionality from the past—but it is something that can be either amplified or relaxed through choices we make in the present moment.

Allow attention to gently come into the hub of this activity of mind with a steady, open presence. Feel how it moves and flows. Inquire for yourself with the question "What function does this serve?" Ask this without harshness or judgment. It is an invitation for you to inquire directly into the mind state from a place of innocent inquiry. Don't assume anything. This is the only way intuitive wisdom can arise. Put the book down now, and spend a few moments with this inquiry.

Now shifting your attention slightly, see if you can get a sense of how that mind state affects the way the pain is received in awareness. You can even consciously amplify the thoughts of anger or fear to really sense what they do to the experience of painful sensation. Can you notice how they heighten the intensity of pain; how they make it seem like it is the whole of our conscious experience? They focus on it, amplify it, and make it seem huge.

In contrast, feel what it is like to trust that in yourself which can relax that contracted mind state, even to some degree. Relax the scenarios in the mind, the edges of tightness, and come back into a really simple presence. Return to a place of not-knowing in yourself. Sense into the possibility of being available to the very experience of the body right now. Feel into an open, receptive, porous awareness that includes the feelings of discomfort or pain that are here.

The trick with this approach is not to try to bring about a particular outcome but rather to relate to the mind and body in an experimental way. Notice what causes what in the present moment. It is like a science experiment in the context of the open, loving heart.

However, the general principle is that the simpler, the more open, the more innocent we can be with the experience of discomfort or pain, the more the sensations themselves can flow through awareness. They are allowed to be themselves. In doing this there is often an experience of discharging or releasing around the psychological pain that often accompanies them.

Attending in this way, a quality of compassion may begin to emerge. In the presence of physical pain, this can be felt as a silent but pervasive quality of heart. Can you feel that sense in yourself right now? It is compassion for the very pain of having a body that hurts. What is it like to fully feel the unpleasant and get that sense of "Yeah. This hurts"? Allow yourself to meet that hurting with the energy of compassion. Allow that compassion to suffuse your whole sense of yourself as you attend to it in this way. Take some time now to explore this possibility.

Compassion is a deeper quality than self-blame, hatred, or fear. It is the connection to what is most deeply human in the heart—your unobstructed human sensitivity. Allow this heart feeling of compassion to flow through the bodily system. Imagine it drenching the cells—up from the feet and circling through all the areas of the body as it is sensed in your awareness right now. Allow the whole sense of your body to be pervaded with this tender feeling of caring. Give yourself full permission to hold the difficult, the broken, in this vulnerable way. You can let yourself relax all the agendas, doubts, and inner violence. Be here in your own quiet, compassionate presence. This is great work you are doing. Trust that.

Through this process, the physical pain may not go away, but you have the opportunity to feel into a sense of freedom. While you may not be free of the sensations, can you feel the possibility of relaxing out of the core sense of affliction around the physical experience? Take a moment to seed awareness with this possibility.

What is it like to attune to freedom of heart in this moment? Can you sense the cooling, refreshing quality that comes about when your awareness is focused on this deep longing for release rather than caught in contracted judgments or reactions about the pain that is here? This freedom of heart isn't the freedom to control or to always make life as we want it, however. It is the here-and-now release from the sense that this moment is "wrong." Trust in an innocent, open kind of attention as you sit or lie here. Soften the edges of inner division. There is no need to divide yourself from yourself.

Keep inclining toward a relaxation on the cellular level. You can keep finding a refuge in nonreactivity and noncomplication. Allow awareness to encompass the body with as little need to fix, understand, or make a story out of it as possible. Expand and soften your attention so that it becomes a resonant field of knowing. Incline your heart toward relaxation and ease.

A good night's sleep sets us up for a good day, but for people with chronic sleep problems—about a third of us—night is a time of stress and struggle that leads to a tired and lifeless day. There are no easy solutions to sleep problems—drugs have all kinds of negative repercussions, and intentionally trying to quiet your mind may only activate it. Instead, you could relax, let go, and ground yourself using these mindfulness-based ways to get to sleep.

PRACTICE

Five Ways to Help You Get to Sleep[9]

Joseph Emet

Consider the comfort of your bed. Are you enjoying it, or are you mentally somewhere else, stressing about something that happened during the day or might happen tomorrow? Mindfulness practices promote being in the here and now over being in the past or the future—being in your senses over being in your thoughts. In helping you to be present, mindfulness meditation can cultivate feelings of contentment, peace, and happiness. When it's time to go to bed, these feelings translate into a relaxed attitude and better sleep.

Clarity about the difference between meditation and rumination is important for an optimal sleep routine. Meditation is intentional; the intention can be to let go of thoughts instead of following them, or a resolve to focus on the breath.

In contrast, rumination happens spontaneously. Studies show that we spend 30 to 50 percent of our mental activity in thoughts that are neither related to what we're doing nor to our surroundings. This can be a problem at bedtime as the body has trouble telling thoughts from reality. Thus, if your thoughts are replaying an argument you had earlier in the day, then your heart rate, blood pressure, and level of stress hormones will match those feelings instead of feelings that will foster a peaceful drift into sleep. Meditation can help you go to sleep, whereas rumination can keep you awake.

Although I didn't start meditating in order to sleep better, a good night's sleep has been one of the unexpected gifts of meditation. I use the two essential practices of focusing on the breath and letting go of thoughts every night. My personal challenge has been going back to sleep after waking up at night—a problem that affects up to 35 percent of us. Now when I wake up, I sit on the edge of the bed and do a period of meditation. After a short time, my mind is peaceful, and I'm ready to fall back to sleep.

If you find meditation challenging, try the following steps. Do each step for three breaths.

1. **FOCUS ON YOUR BREATH.**

   Breathe slowly and deeply from the diaphragm, concentrating on the sensations of breathing.

   Always breathe through your nose. The nose makes important contributions to your health. Glands in the sinuses produce nitric oxide, which helps dilate the blood vessels and improve circulation. The nose humidifies and filters the air.

   Is one nostril blocked? Lie on the other side. This unblocks it within a few minutes. Are both nostrils blocked? Cup your hand at the faucet and fill your nose with cold water for a few seconds. A blocked nose isn't necessarily due to mucus, so blowing your nose may not always fix it. Sometimes the cause is the erectile tissue inside the nose. Nasal blockage and mouth-breathing contribute to snoring, which in turn may interfere with sleep.

2. **DO A BODY SCAN.**

   A body scan is systematic. You start at one end, say the feet, and work your way up—focusing on different parts of the body, noticing any tension, and letting it go. Some yoga teachers offer a shortened version of a body scan at the end of a class. That was my first introduction to it, and I'd sometimes notice fellow yoga practitioners falling asleep in class while doing it.

   Whether on the yoga mat or in bed, a body scan is effective as a relaxation technique.

   When I lead a group through a body scan, I start by asking people to feel if one foot is colder than the other, and I ask them to notice the pressure they feel on the buttocks from sitting.

(We are usually sitting in a meditation class.) Then we work our way up. When we come to the neck, I note that the head is ten pounds heavier for each inch it's leaning forward. I notice a few people straightening up as I say that. Coming to the facial muscles, I usually quote Thich Nhat Hanh: "Sometimes I smile because I'm happy, and sometimes I'm happy because I smile." I also remind people of the old adage: "The face is the mirror of the mind."

A body scan is a good practice for body awareness and relaxation. Focusing on the body works as an antidote to being in our thoughts, for the body is always here now, whereas thoughts can be anywhere, anytime. We need that grounding at bedtime.

3. **CONDUCT A SCAN OF YOUR EMOTIONS.**

Notice with compassion what's on your mind. The psychological term "negativity bias" refers to our tendency to think more about negative things and to accord them more importance. This creates anxiety rather than happiness, and discontent rather than contentment. Both can interfere with sleep.

The first step in overcoming the negativity bias is being aware of it. Then with a smile, urge your mind to notice that the glass it sees as half empty is also half full. We tend to take what we have for granted, and this gets in the way of contentment. Reach for contentment. Look at all the things you take for granted and appreciate life's blessings.

4. **FOCUS ON WHAT YOU WANT.**

Thinking doesn't stop when we go to bed. There's no "off" button. Forceful directions, such as saying to yourself, "I will stop thinking," don't work.

Give yourself positive directions instead. An obvious example of this is what happens when you say, "I will not think of a pink elephant." You think of a pink elephant! But think of a blue elephant instead, and the pink elephant disappears. Thus, "I will not think of that argument I had with my spouse," is likely to be counterproductive. It's better to say to yourself, "I will focus on my breath."

5. **LET GO.**

The goal of doing your best is more realistic than the goal of being perfect. Keep in mind that we control our intentions and our actions, but not the results of our actions. With hindsight, we may see what we should have done; however, that knowledge wasn't available during the moment we acted.

"I've done my best today; may all people be happy and well" is a soothing evening prayer. It celebrates a compassionate heart while tacitly acknowledging its limits.

If your mind serves you self-bashing thoughts at night, turn them toward self-appreciation. Focus on your motives and your efforts—the things that you do control.

Our culture says, "If at first, you don't succeed, try harder." Such messages are valuable in certain areas. For example, if we try harder, we can run faster, at least to a certain extent. But in areas where we don't have conscious control, trying harder doesn't work at all; it's often counterproductive. Instead of helping, the extra effort gets in the way. Sleep is one of those areas.

Striving or worrying about sleep only makes it more difficult to attain. Just focus on your breathing. Let go of everything else.

Once you've cycled through these five steps, extend the meditation period by continuing with conscious breathing, or try repeating the steps from the beginning.

If you don't fall asleep after a reasonable time of meditating, get out of bed. Put yourself to work doing something that needs to be done. Do this with a positive mindset, considering the extra time as a gift. Use up your energy. You'll check off an item or two from your to-do list, and you may feel more inclined to sleep afterward.

Finally, be aware that pairing meditation with certain lifestyle choices is particularly effective for nurturing healthy sleep patterns. Our lifestyle, including our caffeine consumption and the amount of exercise we do, has a bearing on how well we sleep.

Caffeine doesn't affect everyone the same way. For some people, it can stay in the blood for more than nine hours. It turns out that 40 percent of us are fast caffeine metabolizers; 15 percent of us are particularly slow at it; and the rest fall somewhere in between. If you know someone who drinks cup after cup and then sleeps peacefully, don't try to imitate them. It may not work for you. A good way to find out how coffee affects your sleep is to go without it or only drink the decaffeinated stuff for a week.

Studies show that regular exercise correlates with better sleep. These days, over half of all work is done while sitting at a desk, so this makes intentionally finding ways to exercise all the more necessary. Bike to work if you can, find a gym close by, or run. Do what you need to do to get a daily dose of exercise. You'll appreciate it at bedtime.

Sweet dreams, my friends!

Adolescence is a famously difficult phase of life. Your teenager is struggling to find a new, independent identity in the face of all kinds of social and personal pressures. As a parent you don't know what to do when hormones, emotions, and reactivity rage and family life becomes chaotic. You only want to help, but too often you only seem to be making things worse.

But with all its challenges, says psychotherapist Daniel Ahearn, adolescence can be a rich time of deeper connection between you and your teenager. He has five tips based on mindfulness practice and attachment theory to help your teenager feel heard, trusted, and securely loved and navigate a good path forward in life.

PRACTICE

How to Parent Teens with Presence[10]

Daniel Ahearn

Parenting a teenager is like walking a tightrope—balancing love and limits, guidance and space. It's a time of shedding the child and meeting the emerging adult.

As teens develop, they're swept up in hormonal changes and external pressures that can radically influence their behavior. And today's adolescents face tremendous pressures: academic stress, social expectations, societal and ecological challenges, and an avalanche of digital information to process. No wonder many feel overwhelmed. In their struggle to find their way in the world, they may rebel, withdraw, or act out.

But it's not all bad news. This intense growth phase offers an opportunity for deeper connection. One of the wonders of parenting teens is witnessing their evolution into independent, thoughtful individuals. This phase calls for a shift in our parenting approach and perspective. It's a time to let our children spread their wings. Instead of trying to control our teens, the invitation is to offer them guidance. The focus is on connection, not correction.

In my work as a psychotherapist with teens and their families, I often see heartbreak emerge when people parent from wishful thinking instead of what's actually happening. Parents get lost in the labor of parenting and miss the wonder of it. They treat their teens like younger children and chase after certain "good" behaviors from them.

When teens act out, we often react to what they did instead of listening for what they need. This creates a cycle of misunderstanding and disconnection. But when we stay curious and collaborative, teens feel safe enough to show us their full selves—messy parts included. That's where real growth happens. It's empowering to help a teen learn from mistakes and trust that they can figure out the next step.

Of course, this is the ideal, and maybe it's not always possible. Life is busy. Maybe we're working, trying to catch up on sleep, consuming parenting advice, meditating, exercising—just trying to stay afloat. In all of this, we can sometimes forget that we're people raising other people. Often, we're parenting from our own unhealed past rather than from a place of being truly awake and settled.

Clear, authentic communication is the lifeline of connection. Without it, we feel unseen, unheard, and alone. As a therapist, one of the most common things I hear is, "I just don't feel like they see or hear me." Parents and teens alike admit to feeling needy—and ashamed of that neediness. Something's off.

John Bowlby, the pioneer of attachment psychology, put it simply: "We are only as needy as our unmet needs." So how do we foster skillful communication and meet those needs?

Fortunately, both mindfulness and attachment psychology offer powerful frameworks. Their insights converge in a way that can guide deep connection and healing—what we might call *attachment repair*.

In attachment psychology, the developmental goal that we aspire to is a deeply experienced security that brings a sense of freedom to explore the world while anchored in safe and loving relationships.

In contemporary attachment psychology, there are five primary dimensions that are known to promote security and can guide parenting through all phases and periods of development. These can also be viewed through a mindfulness lens.

1. **AWARENESS AND SAFETY.**
   Both mindfulness and attachment theory emphasize awareness as key to connection. Awareness means noticing what we're truly responding to, without being swept away. Safety is the bedrock for growth. Mindful presence—listening without judgment and being emotionally available—builds trust. To be a secure base for your teen, you must feel safe in yourself. That doesn't mean being perfect. It means being responsive instead of reactive. Teens are wired to test and seek reactions. Our job is to respond from safe and grounded awareness. This means understanding our feelings without being overwhelmed by them.

2. **ATTUNEMENT.**
   Attunement is focused attention—the interest and ability to accurately tune in and really see your teen's experience. It begins early in life but can deepen at any stage. Adolescence is a critical time for shifting unhelpful patterns. Being attuned means meeting your teen's perspective with curiosity, not criticism. You might get it wrong, but try again. Build this skill together. That's how trust grows.

3. **SOOTHING.**
   Soothing, or helping your teen feel safe and secure, can include sharing your own vulnerability, especially in the context of attuned recognition of your teen's distress. Compassion is the deep wish to be with another's suffering, and bringing this compassionate presence to your teen can be profoundly comforting. When a parent calmly communicates, "I get that you're hurting,

and I'm here," the teen's nervous system begins to settle. The journey becomes collaborative, not one-sided. Authenticity and intimacy in these conversations create a stable foundation for communication.

4. **EXPRESSED DELIGHT.**

   Expressed delight is the visible joy of seeing your child. My friend calls it "the unmistakable joy." It's about celebrating the child's being, not just their actions or achievements. Let your face light up when they enter the room. This joy fosters a deep sense of security and love.

5. **EXPLORATION.**

   Exploration is essential to adolescence. It's how teens discover who they are. Our role shifts from *protecting* them from the world to *guiding* them through it. Healthy relationships and strong communication support this exploration. Adolescence is when you see the echoes of early parenting—what worked and what didn't. There can be both joy and sorrow in that recognition. Mindfulness practice gives us tools to meet this moment with presence, not regret, and model a secure base—a dependable relationship from which a child can venture out and return for support and regulation.

Secure attachment isn't about getting it right all the time. It's about being present enough to repair when we get it wrong. The teen years offer a second chance—not just for your child, but for you. Communication grounded in awareness becomes a shared practice of discovery.

And when your teen grows into an adult who comes back—not just out of obligation, but with stories, insight, and delight—that will be the reward for being present now.

In a slogan deeply rooted in mindfulness, "First thought, best thought" was how the poet Allen Ginsberg described the writing process. When you open yourself to what arises spontaneously in your mind, without planning or strategizing, your writing is free, direct, and full of self-discovery. Like meditation, it is a way to get to know yourself.

PRACTICE

Let It Flow: Mindful Journaling[11]

James C. Hopkins

Journaling helps us open to our immediate or recent experience. The main idea behind journaling is usually about capturing the moment—just "getting it down on paper." Revision comes later, but journaling itself is nonjudgmental and observational. In this way, journaling is like meditation.

Meditation is the practice of simply sitting and becoming familiar with your mind—watching thoughts as they come and go, allowing the mind to settle, and becoming familiar with that state. In meditation, you observe thoughts arising, without naming them, without liking them or disliking them. Breathing is happening. Sound is happening. You're observing your mind.

Journaling is also a way of becoming familiar with the mind. Your pen is moving, and you're capturing details, impressions, passing thoughts, and observations as they occur. But you're not yet shaping your feelings and thoughts; you're just familiarizing yourself with them.

Mindful journaling and mindfulness meditation are both practices and habits that must be cultivated. What follows are five tried-and-true tips for mindful journaling.

1. **MAXIMIZE YOUR INTENTIONALITY.**

   If you're starting a journaling practice at home, set aside a dedicated time and place. If possible, sit in a favorite chair or at a special desk, maybe one not used for activities like working online.

   Don't try to journal for hours. Just do it for five to ten minutes. Then take a break. Try not to get distracted, and when you are distracted, come back to the journaling, just as you come back to the breath when you're distracted in meditation.

   Remind yourself: "I am doing this. I'm taking it seriously." Hold on to details, but not tightly. Be open to revision, but later.

2. **USE A POEM TO START.**

   Maybe your morning journaling practice takes off just by putting your pen to paper. But maybe it doesn't always come easily, and you need a way to kick-start the process. Consider opening up a book of poetry and reading a poem. It just might inspire you.

   Laurie Wagner is a popular writing teacher and coach in the San Francisco area, as well as the author of seven books. Wagner begins her online poetry classes by reading a poem. "The poem is like micro-dosing," she says, "an elixir. Because it's short, it's not lobbing anything at you. The poem can take you into a world very quickly. When we hear the poem we don't ask, 'What does this mean?' but rather 'Where does it take me?'"

   When journaling, starting with a poem spins you around and plays with you. It reminds you that we're all able to experience a world beyond concept. The poem points us to that world, and for a moment, we're present in its nonconceptual beauty.

3. **WHEN YOU GET STUCK.**

Journaling is about expressing and exploring, not using the destination-oriented critical mind. In journaling, we're willing to host everything that comes through, without eliminating things because they "don't fit." But sometimes, we get stuck in the middle of that process, and when we do, there are phrases that can help us get back into the flow.

Here are some phrases to facilitate exploration:

What I really want to tell you is . . .
If you really knew me . . .
What I forgot to say is . . .
I don't want to talk about it, but . . .

These jump-off lines aren't intended to start us over again; rather, they help us go deeper and access our own material. These lines keep us open, driving us back into the process. Feel free to come up with your own go-to phrases.

4. **NO JUDGMENT.**

When best-selling author Eric Weiner tries to meditate, he reports feeling very judgmental. He thinks, "I can't do this meditation—shit! I'm thinking again!" As Weiner puts it, "That's the judging mind, and it gets in the way of meditation."

It's the same with journaling. You need to bypass thoughts like "I can't write," or "That detail doesn't matter." Later, when you go back to revise, says Weiner, "then the critical faculties of the mind come in, and you are judging. In the first stage, however, just kill your internal editor."

With mindful journaling, we're trying to get out of our own way and remain in the flow of awareness without any judgment, to get to ourselves. We're trying to reach something that's still us, but more essentially us. That's what journaling is about.

5. **FULLY ENGAGED, WITHOUT ATTACHMENT.**
With journaling, you're letting go and trying to be honest with yourself. You're excavating the mind. You're letting things move through you. Later, you may edit and modify in order to make a point or advance your opinions. But before that happens, at its best, both the mind and the writing are in sync. You're not detached when writing; you're fully engaged, but you're nonattached to the outcome.

   Jeff Greenwald, a best-selling author and photographer, says, "All aspects of writing call for mindfulness because you always want to be in the moment. It's like riding a motorcycle. You're completely focused when you're in that moment."

   Integrating mindfulness practice and creativity of any kind seems always to be a good idea, but the merging of mindfulness and journaling is an especially potent mixture. It gives access to a whole conscious universe that includes instinct and intuition. What comes out of the practice of mindful journaling is powerful and surprising, fresh yet familiar.

NOTES

2. MINDFULNESS IN THE MODERN WORLD

1. Thich Nhat Hanh, *The Pocket Thich Nhat Hanh*, ed. Melvin McLeod (Shambhala Publications, 2017), 5.
2. Thich Nhat Hanh, *The Pocket Thich Nhat Hanh*, 3–4.
3. Thich Nhat Hanh, *The Pocket Thich Nhat Hanh*, 7.
4. Thich Nhat Hanh, *The Pocket Thich Nhat Hanh*, 7.
5. Thich Nhat Hanh, *The Pocket Thich Nhat Hanh*, 15.
6. Thich Nhat Hanh, *Your True Home: The Everyday Wisdom of Thich Nhat Hanh*, ed. Melvin McLeod (Shambhala Publications, 2011), 296.
7. Thich Nhat Hanh, *The Pocket Thich Nhat Hanh*, 11–12.
8. Thich Nhat Hanh, *The Pocket Thich Nhat Hanh*, 10.
9. Thich Nhat Hanh, *Reconciliation: Healing the Inner Child* (Parallax Press, 2010). This excerpt is from an adaptation published by Lionsroar.com, "Thich Nhat Hanh on How to Heal Your Inner Child," August 4, 2025, www.lionsroar.com/healing-the-child-within.
10. Jon Kabat-Zinn, "Jon Kabat-Zinn Brings Mindfulness to Life," in conversation with Melvin McLeod, 2024, *Lion's Roar*, https://promo.lionsroar.com/jon-kabat-zinn-free-video-series/.
11. Kabat-Zinn, "Jon Kabat-Zinn Brings Mindfulness to Life."
12. Kabat-Zinn, "Jon Kabat-Zinn Brings Mindfulness to Life."
13. Kabat-Zinn, "Jon Kabat-Zinn Brings Mindfulness to Life."
14. Adapted from Jon Kabat-Zinn, *Mindfulness for All* (Balance, 2019), ix–xi.

3. MINDFULNESS MEDITATION

1. "What Is Mindfulness?" *Greater Good Magazine*, https://greatergood.berkeley.edu/topic/mindfulness/definition.
2. Thich Nhat Hanh, *The Pocket Thich Nhat Hanh*, ed. Melvin McLeod (Shambhala Publications, 2017), 6.
3. Leslie Booker, "How to Practice Walking Meditation," *Lion's Roar*, June 11, 2024, www.lionsroar.com/how-to-practice-walking-meditation.
4. Christopher Germer, "Affectionate Breathing," https://chrisgermer.com/wp-content/uploads/2020/11/Affectionate-Breathing_2017.pdf.
5. Jon Kabat-Zinn, "How Mindfulness Gives Us Our Life Back," from *Meditation Is Not What You Think* (Balance, 2018), x–xi and xii–xiii.
6. Greater Good Science Center, "Body Scan Meditation," https://ggia.berkeley.edu/practice/body_scan_meditation. Adaptation published by Lionsroar.com, www.lionsroar.com/body-scan-meditation-stress-relief/.
7. Pema Chödrön, "Take Three Conscious Breaths," *Lion's Roar*, April 2, 2017, www.lionsroar.com/take-three-conscious-breaths/.
8. Leslie Davis, "Three Questions for Coming Back to Now," *Lion's Roar*, November 17, 2024, www.lionsroar.com/three-questions-for-coming-back-to-now.
9. Diana Winston, "How to Meditate Every Day—Even If You Would Rather Be Thrown into a Shark-Infested Ocean," *Lion's Roar*, January 19, 2018, www.lionsroar.com/sit-every-day-advice-plus-ten-suggestions-for-having-a-regular-daily-practice-even-if-you-would-rather-be-thrown-into-a-shark-infested-ocean/.

4. INSIGHT

1. Shauna Shapiro, "Mindfulness Meditation: Train Your Mind to Change Your Life," in "5 Keys to Complete Mindfulness," *Lion's Roar*, July 5, 2024, www.lionsroar.com/5-keys-to-complete-mindfulness/.
2. Shapiro, "Mindfulness Meditation."
3. Gullu Singh, "Insight: The Power of Seeing Reality Clearly," in "5 Keys to Complete Mindfulness," *Lion's Roar*, July 5, 2024, www.lionsroar.com/5-keys-to-complete-mindfulness/.
4. Rick Hanson, "The Liberating Light of Insight," *Lion's Roar*, June 1, 2025, www.lionsroar.com/the-liberating-light-of-insight/.
5. Trudy Goodman, "Get to the Root of Your Patterns," *Lion's Roar*, September 14, 2020, www.lionsroar.com/get-to-the-root-of-your-patterns/.

6. Diana Winston, "3 Ways to Uncover Your Natural Awareness," *Lion's Roar*, February 20, 2025, www.lionsroar.com/uncover-your-natural-awareness/.

5. LOVE AND COMPASSION

1. Kristin Neff, "A Self-Compassion Meditation to Be Kind to Yourself," *Lion's Roar*, September 3, 2025, www.lionsroar.com/self-compassion-meditation-be-kind-to-yourself/.
2. Christopher Germer, "Loving-Kindness for Ourselves," https://chrisgermer.com/wp-content/uploads/2020/11/LK-for-Ourselves_2017.pdf.
3. Lisa Ernst, "How to Love Yourself," *Lion's Roar*, February 21, 2025, www.lionsroar.com/how-to-love-yourself/.
4. Tara Brach, "RAIN: Recognize, Allow, Investigate, Nurture," www.tarabrach.com/rain/.
5. Diana Winston, "The Power of Mindfulness," *Lion's Roar*, March 16, 2025, www.lionsroar.com/mindfulness-the-power-of-awareness/.
6. Melvin Escobar, "How to Practice Mindful Breathing for Anxiety," *Lion's Roar*, November 26, 2024, www.lionsroar.com/how-to-practice-mindful-breathing-for-anxiety/.
7. Cyndi Lee, "Take Refuge in Your Body," *Lion's Roar*, August 13, 2021, www.lionsroar.com/take-refuge-in-your-body/.
8. Sister Chan Khong, "How to Practice Deep Relaxation," *Lion's Roar*, April 25, 2025, www.lionsroar.com/how-to-practice-deep-relaxation/.
9. Arisika Razak, "Loving-Kindness Meditation for All Beings and All Bodies," *Lion's Roar*, April 3, 2024, www.lionsroar.com/loving-kindness-meditation-for-all-beings-all-bodies/.
10. Christopher Germer, "Loving-Kindness for a Loved One," https://chrisgermer.com/wp-content/uploads/2020/11/Loving-Kindness-for-a-Loved-One.pdf.
11. Sharon Salzberg, *Lovingkindness: The Revolutionary Art of Happiness* (Shambhala, 2020), 19–20, 25–26.
12. Judy Lief, "The Power of Tonglen," *Lion's Roar*, August 8, 2023, www.lionsroar.com/the-power-of-tonglen/.
13. Pema Chödrön, "Tonglen: Bad In, Good Out," *Lion's Roar*, October 2, 2017, www.lionsroar.com/tonglen-bad-in-good-out-september-2010/.
14. Joan Halifax, "Help When Your Heart Breaks," *Lion's Roar*, September 24, 2022, www.lionsroar.com/help-when-your-heart-breaks/.

15. Karen Armstrong, "The Charter for Compassion," https://charterforcompassion.org/sign-the-charter.html.

6. ETHICS

1. Dan Zigmond, "Meditation Is a Political Act," *Lion's Roar*, May 31, 2022, www.lionsroar.com/meditation-is-a-political-act/.
2. Thich Nhat Hanh, *Mindfulness Survival Kit: Five Essential Practices* (Parallax, 2013).
3. Gil Fronsdal, "Mindful Speaking," www.insightmeditationcenter.org/books-articles/mindful-speaking/.
4. Rhonda V. Magee, "Ethics: Living Our Values," *Lion's Roar*, July 5, 2024, www.lionsroar.com/5-keys-to-complete-mindfulness/.
5. Daniel Goleman, "How to Be a Force for Good," *Lion's Roar*, July 8, 2020, www.lionsroar.com/how-to-be-a-force-for-good/.
6. Thich Nhat Hanh, *The World We Have: A Buddhist Approach to Peace and Ecology* (Parallax, 2008).
7. Joan Halifax, "Yes, We Can Have Hope," *Lion's Roar*, www.lionsroar.com/yes-we-can-have-hope/.

7. COMMUNITY

1. *Upaḍḍhasutta*, Saṁyutta Nikāya, 45.2.
2. Thich Nhat Hanh, *The Pocket Thich Nhat Hanh*, ed. Melvin McLeod (Shambhala Publications, 2017), 14.
3. Robert Waldinger, "Community: The Healing Power of Connection," *Lion's Roar*, July 5, 2024, www.lionsroar.com/5-keys-to-complete-mindfulness/.
4. Stephen Murphy-Shigematsu, "I See You, I Am Here: The Secret to Heartfelt Communication," *Lion's Roar*, June 2, 2021, www.lionsroar.com/i-see-you-i-am-here-the-secret-to-heartfelt-communication/.
5. Thich Nhat Hanh, "Thich Nhat Hanh's Hugging Meditation," *Lion's Roar*, June 27, 2024, www.lionsroar.com/how-to-practice-hugging-meditation/.
6. Susan Piver, "The Truth About Marriage Vows: Five Promises You Can Keep," *Medium*, May 30, 2017, https://medium.com/@spiver/the-truth-about-marriage-vows-the-five-promises-that-are-really-needed-f9b6f3ba1123.
7. Cheryl Fraser, "How to Have Mindful Sex," *Lion's Roar*, June 13, 2025, www.lionsroar.com/how-to-have-mindful-sex/.

8. Karen Maezen Miller, "8 Practical Guidelines for Mindful Parenting," *Lion's Roar*, June 15, 2024, www.lionsroar.com/karen-millers-8-practical-guidelines-for-mindful-parents/.
9. Matthew Freeman, adapted from *Overcoming Bias: Building Authentic Relationships Across Differences* (Berrett-Koehler, 2016), https://greatergood.berkeley.edu/article/item/how_to_build_relationships_across_difference.
10. Tara Brach, "How to Start a Mindfulness Meditation Group," https://www.tarabrach.com/starting-meditation-group/.

8. PRACTICES FOR MINDFUL LIVING

1. Mark Coleman, *A Field Guide to Nature Meditation: 52 Mindfulness Practices for Joy, Wisdom, and Wonder* (Awake in the Wild, 2022), 23–25.
2. Joseph Emet, "How to Drink a Mindful Cup of Tea," *Lion's Roar*, May 19, 2024, www.lionsroar.com/drinking-a-mindful-cup-of-tea/.
3. Allyson Pimentel, "Savor the Joy," *Lion's Roar*, July 26, 2022, www.lionsroar.com/savor-the-joy/.
4. Rachel Rose, "The Art of Mindfulness," *Lion's Roar*, March 28, 2024, www.lionsroar.com/the-art-of-mindfulness/.
5. Jan Chozen Bays, *Mindful Eating* (Shambhala, 2017), 125, 126–27, 128, 129, 131.
6. Spencer Sherman, "What Were You Taught About Money?" *Lion's Roar*, May 31, 2022, www.lionsroar.com/what-were-you-taught-about-money/.
7. Susan Bauer-Wu, *Leaves Falling Gently* (Shambhala, 2025), 113, 115–16, 118–19.
8. Peter Fernando, *Finding Freedom from Illness* (Shambhala, 2016), 177–81.
9. Joseph Emet, "What to Do When You Can't Sleep," *Lion's Roar*, May 24, 2024, www.lionsroar.com/what-to-do-when-you-cant-sleep/.
10. Daniel Ahearn, "Parenting Teens with Presence," *Lion's Roar*, July 31, 2025, www.lionsroar.com/parenting-teens-with-presence/.
11. James C. Hopkins, "5 Tips for Mindful Journaling," *Lion's Roar*, January 12, 2025, www.lionsroar.com/5-tips-for-mindful-journaling/.

CONTRIBUTORS

Daniel Ahearn is a Los Angeles–based psychotherapist specializing in attachment repair through Integrative Attachment Therapy.

Noliwe Alexander is the cofounder and executive director of Deep Time Liberation, which offers retreats using meditation, storytelling, and culturally specific journeys to help people of the African diaspora heal from intergenerational and ancestral trauma.

Karen Armstrong is one of the great religious thinkers of our time. Her work focuses on values such as compassion and the Golden Rule that are shared by the world's religions. She is the founder of the Charter for Compassion.

Susan Bauer-Wu, PhD, RN, is a clinician, researcher, mindfulness teacher, and global leader in contemplative science and health care. She is the author of *A Future We Can Love* and *Leaves Falling Gently.*

Jan Chozen Bays, MD, is a mindful-eating educator and pediatrician specializing in work with abused children. She is the author of *Mindful Eating* and *Mindful Medicine.*

Leslie Booker is a meditation teacher, writer, and engaged spirituality leader. She was named one of the twelve most influential women in the mindfulness movement by *Mindful* magazine.

Tara Brach, PhD, is a psychologist and one of America's leading mindfulness teachers. With Jack Kornfield she cofounded the Mindfulness Teacher Training Program and is the author of such books as *Radical Acceptance*, *True Refuge*, and *Radical Compassion.*

Clair Brown, PhD, is professor of economics emerita at the University of California, Berkeley. She led the development of a measure of economic performance based on the quality of life called the Genuine Progress Index and is deeply involved in climate justice work.

Pema Chödrön is a Buddhist nun and one of America's most loved spiritual teachers. She is the author of such classics as *When Things Fall Apart*, *The Wisdom of No Escape*, and *The Places That Scare You.*

Mark Coleman is the creator of Awake in the Wild Nature Meditation, which he teaches in online and in-person programs. He is the author of *Awake in the Wild* and *A Field Guide to Nature Meditation.*

Leslie J. Davis is a poet and writer. She is a member of Thich Nhat Hanh's Order of Interbeing and founded Dharma Mamas, a community for mindful mothers.

Joseph Emet is the author of *Sleep Better with Mindfulness Meditation* and *A Basket of Plums: Songs for the Practice of Mindfulness Meditation. Finding the Blue Sky* is a memoir of his journey toward well-being and happiness through mindfulness.

Lisa Ernst is a meditation teacher, artist, and founder of One Dharma Nashville.

Melvin Escobar is a psychotherapist, yoga instructor, and core teacher at East Bay Meditation Center in Oakland, California.

Peter Fernando is cofounder of Original Nature Meditation Centre in Wellington, New Zealand. A longtime sufferer of chronic pain and health problems, he's been helping people deal with chronic pain since 2009.

Cheryl Fraser, PhD, is a psychologist and sex therapist. She is the author of *Buddha's Bedroom: The Mindful Loving Path to Sexual Passion and Lifelong Intimacy* and host of the *Sex, Love & Elephants* podcast.

Matthew Freeman is an internationally recognized consultant on diversity, equity, and inclusion issues. He is the author of *Overcoming Bias: Building Authentic Relationships Across Differences.*

Gil Fronsdal, PhD, is the founder and primary teacher of the Insight Meditation Center in Redwood City, California. He is the author of *The Issue at Hand: Essays on Buddhist Mindfulness Practice.*

Christopher Germer, PhD, is a clinical psychologist and leading expert on self-compassion. In 2010 he developed the Mindful Self-Compassion Program in partnership with Kristin Neff, which has been taught to more than a quarter of a million people worldwide. He is the author of *The Mindful Self-Compassion Workbook.*

Daniel Goleman, PhD, is a psychologist, science journalist, and the best-selling author of *Emotional Intelligence.*

Trudy Goodman, PhD, is a psychologist and a leading teacher in the Insight Meditation tradition. She is the founder of InsightLA.

Joan Halifax, PhD, is an anthropologist, activist, and leader in end-of-life care. She is the founder of Upaya Zen Center and author of *Standing at the Edge* and *In a Moment, In a Breath: 55 Meditations to Cultivate a Courageous Heart.*

Rick Hanson, PhD, is a psychologist, an expert on positive neuroplasticity, and founder of the Global Compassion Initiative. He is the best-selling author of *Hardwiring Happiness*, *Making Great Relationships*, and *Mother Nurture*, and the founder of the Wellspring Institute for Neuroscience and Contemplative Wisdom.

James C. Hopkins lives in Kathmandu and is the director of Himalayan Writers' Workshop, an organization that creates writing journeys in Nepal and Bhutan for writers from around the world. He is the author of seven books of poetry.

Jon Kabat-Zinn, PhD, is the creator of the Mindfulness-Based Stress Reduction program and the acknowledged founder of the mainstream mindfulness movement. He is a professor emeritus at the University of Massachusetts Medical School, where he founded the Center for Mindfulness in Medicine, Health Care, and Society. He has written such foundational books of the mindfulness movement as *Full Catastrophe Living*, *Wherever You Go, There You Are*, and *Coming to Our Senses.*

Sister Chan Khong was Thich Nhat Hanh's closest collaborator and today is an Elder nun of the Plum Village International monastic community. Her books include *Beginning Anew*, *Deep Relaxation*, and her autobiography, *Learning to Love.*

Cyndi Lee is the creator of OM Yoga, which combines the practices of vinyasa yoga, mindfulness, and compassion. One of the most influential yoga teachers in the United States, she is the author of *Yoga Body, Buddha Mind*; *May I Be Happy*; and *OM Yoga: A Guide to Daily Practice*. She is an ordained Buddhist chaplain.

Judy Lief is a teacher of Buddhism and mindfulness and a leader in the contemplative approach to death and dying. She is the author of *Making Friends with Death* and has edited many books by her Buddhist teacher, the late Chögyam Trungpa Rinpoche.

Rhonda V. Magee is one of America's leading mindfulness teachers. She is the author of *The Inner Work of Racial Justice* and professor emeritus at the University of San Francisco, where she is the founding director of the Center for Contemplative Law and Ethics. She teaches online and internationally and is the founder of the Mount Iris Meditation Community (mountiris.com), which is dedicated to the practice of soul-hearted mindfulness.

Karen Maezen Miller is an American Zen teacher whose writing focuses on mindfulness in daily life. She is the author of *Hand Wash Cold: Care Instructions for an Ordinary Life* and *Momma Zen*.

Stephen Murphy-Shigematsu, PhD, is an American-Japanese psychologist whose work draws on mindfulness, Asian wisdom, and science. His book *From Mindfulness to Heartfulness: Transforming Self and Society with Compassion* elucidates eight principles of heartful living combining mindfulness, compassion, and responsibility.

Kristin Neff, PhD, is one of the world's leading experts on the practice and benefit of self-compassion. She is the author of *Self-Compassion: The Proven Power of Being Kind to Yourself* and *Fierce Self-Compassion: How Women Can Harness Kindness to Speak Up, Claim Their Power, and Thrive*. With Christopher Germer she developed the Mindful Self-Compassion program.

Thich Nhat Hanh (1926–2022) was one of the great spiritual teachers of our time. Zen master, peace activist, and poet, he founded the Engaged Buddhism movement and was known as the "father of mindfulness" for his presentation of mindfulness to a global audience. Among his many books are such classics as *The Miracle of Mindfulness*, *You Are Here: Discovering the Magic of the Present Moment*, and *Call Me by My True Names: The Collected Poems of Thich Nhat Hanh*.

Allyson Pimentel, PhD, is a psychologist who works at the intersection of mindfulness practice, mental health, and healing. She is co-director of Mindful USC at the University of Southern California.

Susan Piver is a meditation teacher, relationship expert, and founder of the Open Heart Project. Among her books are *The Hard Questions* and *The Wisdom of a Broken Heart.*

Arisika Razak is professor emerita at the California Institute of Integral Studies in San Francisco. She has been an inner-city midwife for more than two decades and has led embodied healing workshops for more than thirty-five years. She teaches at the East Bay Meditation Center.

Rachel Rose is an arts educator, contemplative artist, and writer. She is the founder of the Mindful Art Circle, an online community practicing mindfulness through the arts.

Sharon Salzberg is a renowned teacher of mindfulness, loving-kindness, and Insight Meditation. As a cofounder of the Insight Meditation Society and a best-selling author, she has played a pioneering role in mainstreaming meditation and inspiring a generation of mindfulness teachers and practitioners. She is the author of thirteen books, including the classics *Real Happiness* and *Lovingkindness.*

Spencer Sherman is a meditation teacher and successful financial advisor who offers a mindfulness-based approach to help people break free of money anxiety and take conscious control of their financial decisions. He is the author of *The Cure for Money Madness* and teaches online courses and in-person retreats.

Gullu Singh is an authorized MBSR teacher and offers seminars, classes, and workshops on mindfulness for individuals and organizations. A lawyer, he has taught mindfulness workshops to bar associations, law firms, and other legal groups.

Robert Waldinger, MD, is a psychiatrist, Zen teacher, and director of the famed Harvard Study of Adult Development. Based on the study's findings, he wrote the bestseller *The Good Life: Lessons from the World's Longest Scientific Study of Happiness.*

Jeff Warren is a meditation teacher and coauthor of *Meditation for Fidgety Skeptics*. Drawing on his own experience, he teaches how meditation can—and cannot—help people with mental-health challenges. He writes and teaches at the Substack Home Base with Jeff Warren.

Diana Winston is one of America's most influential mindfulness experts. She is the director of UCLA Mindful, the mindfulness education center of UCLA Health. At UCLA's Mindfulness Awareness Research Center, she developed the evidence-based Mindfulness Awareness Practices (MAPS) curriculum and trained more than five hundred mindfulness teachers from around the world. She is the author of *The Little Book of Being: Practices and Guidance for Discovering Your Natural Awareness* and is a founding board member of the International Mindfulness Teachers Association.

CREDITS

As you will see below, many of the practices and teachings in this book were first published in *Lion's Roar* magazine and on Lionsroar.com. For a comprehensive selection of excellent articles about mindfulness and mindful living, including many practices and in-depth teachings, go to Lionsroar.com/mindfulness.

"Healing the Wounded Child Within Us." Adapted from *Reconciliation: Healing the Inner Child* (2010), by Thich Nhat Hanh, with permission from Parallax Press, Berkeley, California. www.parallax.org.

"Mindfulness for All." From *Mindfulness for All*, by Jon Kabat-Zinn, copyright © 2019. Reprinted by permission of Balance, an imprint of Hachette Book Group, Inc.

"Walking Meditation," by Leslie Booker. Reprinted by permission of the author and the Lion's Roar Foundation. www.lionsroar.com.

"Affectionate Breathing," by Christopher Germer. Reprinted by permission of the author.

"How Mindfulness Gives Us Our Life Back." From *Meditation Is Not What You Think*, by Jon Kabat-Zinn, copyright © 2018. Reprinted by permission of Balance, an imprint of Hachette Book Group, Inc.

"Mindful Body Scan." With permission of Greater Good Science Center. This practice originally appeared on Greater Good in Action, Greater Good Science Center at UC Berkeley's online collection of research-based practices for a happier, more meaningful life. Adaptation published by Lionsroar.com, www.lionsroar.com/body-scan-meditation-stress-relief/.

"Take Three Conscious Breaths," by Pema Chödrön. Reprinted by permission of the author and the Lion's Roar Foundation. www.lionsroar.com.

"Three Questions for Coming Back to Now," by Leslie Davis. Reprinted by permission of the Lion's Roar Foundation. www.lionsroar.com.

"Ten Tips for Having a Daily Practice (Even if You Would Rather Be Thrown into a Shark-Infested Ocean)," by Diana Winston. Reprinted by permission of the author and the Lion's Roar Foundation. www.lionsroar.com.

"Discover the Basic Nature of All Experiences," by Rick Hanson. Reprinted by permission of the author and the Lion's Roar Foundation. www.lionsroar.com.

"How Insight Frees You from Habitual Patterns," by Trudy Goodman. Reprinted by permission of the author and the Lion's Roar Foundation. www.lionsroar.com.

"Experience Your Natural Awareness," by Diana Winston. Reprinted by permission of the author and the Lion's Roar Foundation. www.lionsroar.com.

"Mindful Self-Compassion," by Kristin Neff. Reprinted by permission of the author and the Lion's Roar Foundation. www.lionsroar.com.

"Kind Words," by Christopher Germer. Reprinted by permission of the author.

"Give Yourself Loving-Kindness," by Lisa Ernst. Reprinted by permission of the author and the Lion's Roar Foundation. www.lionsroar.com.

"RAIN: Recognize, Allow, Investigate, Nurture," by Tara Brach. Reprinted by permission of the author.

"Free Yourself from Guilt, Shame, and Self-Criticism," by Diana Winston. Reprinted by permission of the author and the Lion's Roar Foundation. www.lionsroar.com.

"Mindful Breathing to Calm Anxiety," by Melvin Escobar. Reprinted by permission of the author and the Lion's Roar Foundation. www.lionsroar.com.

"Grounding Touch," by Cyndi Lee. Reprinted by permission of the author and the Lion's Roar Foundation. www.lionsroar.com.

"Deep Relaxation," by Sister Chan Khong. Reprinted by permission of the author and the Lion's Roar Foundation. www.lionsroar.com.

"Loving-Kindness (*Metta*) Meditation," by Arisika Razak. Reprinted by permission of the author and the Lion's Roar Foundation. www.lionsroar.com.

"Loving-Kindness for a Loved One," by Christopher Germer. Reprinted by permission of the author.

"Healing Separateness." From *Lovingkindness: The Revolutionary Art of Happiness*, by Sharon Salzberg, copyright © 1995, 2020 by Sharon Salzberg. Reprinted by arrangement with Shambhala Publications, Inc., Boulder, CO. www.shambhala.com.

"Sending Out and Taking In (*Tonglen*)," by Judy Lief. Reprinted by permission of the author and the Lion's Roar Foundation. www.lionsroar.com.

"The Ultimate Alchemy," by Pema Chödrön. Reprinted by permission of the author and the Lion's Roar Foundation. www.lionsroar.com.

"GRACE: Help When Your Heart Breaks," by Joan Halifax. Reprinted by permission of the author and the Lion's Roar Foundation. www.lionsroar.com.

"The Five Mindfulness Trainings." From the *Mindfulness Survival Kit: Five Essential Practices* (2013), by Thich Nhat Hanh, with permission from Parallax Press, Berkeley, California. www.parallax.org.

"Mindful Speaking," by Gil Fronsdal. Reprinted by permission of the author.

"How Diversity Transforms Your Ethics—and Your Mindfulness," by Rhonda V. Magee. Reprinted by permission of the author and the Lion's Roar Foundation. www.lionsroar.com.

"6 Ways to Be a Force for Good," by Daniel Goleman. Reprinted by permission of the author and the Lion's Roar Foundation. www.lionsroar.com.

"Earth Gathas: Recitations for a Sustainable Life." Adapted from *The World We Have: A Buddhist Approach to Peace and Ecology*, by Thich Nhat Hanh, copyright © 2008 by Unified Buddhist Church. With permission from Parallax Press.

"How to Have Wise Hope," by Joan Halifax. Reprinted by permission of the author and the Lion's Roar Foundation. www.lionsroar.com.

"What Really Makes Us Happy," by Dr. Robert Waldinger. Reprinted by permission of the author and the Lion's Roar Foundation. www.lionsroar.com.

"I See You, I Am Here: The Secret to Heartfelt Communication," by Stephen Murphy-Shigematsu. Reprinted by permission of the author and the Lion's Roar Foundation. www.lionsroar.com.

"Hugging Meditation," by Thich Nhat Hanh. Reprinted by permission of Parallax Press and the Lion's Roar Foundation. www.lionsroar.com.

"The Truth About Marriage Vows: Five Promises You Can Actually Keep," by Susan Piver. Reprinted by permission of the author.

"Mindful Sex Is the Best Sex," by Cheryl Fraser. Reprinted by permission of the author and the Lion's Roar Foundation. www.lionsroar.com.

"8 Practical Guidelines for Mindful Parenting," by Karen Maezen Miller. Reprinted by permission of the author and the Lion's Roar Foundation. www.lionsroar .com.

"4 Ways to Overcome Unconscious Bias." Adapted from *Overcoming Bias: Building Authentic Relationships Across Differences,* by Tiffany Jana and Matthew Freeman. With permission from Berrett-Koehler Publishers, copyright © 2016. ISBN 1626567255.

"Start Your Own Mindfulness Group," by Tara Brach. Reprinted by permission of the author.

"Arriving Practice." From *A Field Guide to Nature Meditation: 52 Mindfulness Practices for Joy, Wisdom, and Wonder*, by Mark Coleman. Reprinted with permission of Awake in the Wild.

"How to Drink a Mindful Cup of Tea," by Joseph Emet. Reprinted by permission of the author and the Lion's Roar Foundation. www.lionsroar.com.

"Savor the Joy," by Allyson Pimentel. Reprinted by permission of the author and the Lion's Roar Foundation. www.lionsroar.com.

"Creativity: The Art of This Moment," by Rachel Rose. Reprinted by permission of the author and the Lion's Roar Foundation. www.lionsroar.com.

"Quiet the Three Inner Voices." From *Mindful Eating*, by Jan Chozen Bays, MD, copyright © 2009, 2017 by Jan Chozen Bays. Reprinted by arrangement with Shambhala Publications, Inc., Boulder, CO. www.shambhala.com.

"Unlearn Your Old Money Beliefs," by Spencer Sherman. Reprinted by permission of the author and the Lion's Roar Foundation. www.lionsroar.com.

"How to Accept the Help You Need." From *Leaves Falling Gently*, by Susan Bauer-Wu. Copyright © 2011, 2025 by Susan Bauer-Wu. Reprinted by arrangement with Shambhala Publications, Inc., Boulder, CO. www.shambhala.com

"Mindfulness for When You're in Pain." From *Finding Freedom from Illness*, by Peter Fernando. Copyright © 2016 by Peter Fernando. Reprinted by arrangement with Shambhala Publications, Inc., Boulder, CO. www.shambhala.com.

"5 Ways to Help You Get to Sleep," by Joseph Emet. Reprinted by permission of the author and the Lion's Roar Foundation. www.lionsroar.com.

"How to Parent Teens with Presence," by Daniel Ahearn. Reprinted by permission of the author and the Lion's Roar Foundation. www.lionsroar.com.

"Let It Flow: Mindful Journaling," by James C. Hopkins. Reprinted by permission of the author and the Lion's Roar Foundation. www.lionsroar.com.

ABOUT THE AUTHOR

I didn't grow up in a spiritual family—if we had any religion, it was skiing—and since it was the 1950s, we had never heard of meditation or mindfulness.

As a typical baby boomer, I explored New Age spirituality and Eastern religion in college, aided by various substances that showed me reality wasn't necessarily what I thought it was. Returning to my native Montreal, I began a career in journalism. Then one day, sitting in front of a bank of police radios at the old *Montreal Star* newspaper, where I was a junior police reporter, I opened a book about Buddhism I had casually bought. I felt an instant and deep connection to it, and I remain a dedicated Buddhist to this day.

In the following years I alternated between a successful career as a journalist at the Canadian Broadcasting Corporation and doing weird things like spending a year alone in a cabin in the woods and backpacking around India looking for a Buddhist teacher. My colleagues were baffled but indulgent. I won a national journalism award for a television series exposing a fraudulent Buddhist guru and became a network correspondent for CBC Television.

In 1992 the spiritual and professional sides of my life came together when I was named editor in chief of the small Buddhist newspaper that would eventually become Lion's Roar, the largest Buddhist media organization in the English language. I edited several books, including three books of teachings by Thich Nhat Hanh, the Best Buddhist Writing series, and *Mindful Politics: A Buddhist Guide to Making the World a Better Place.*

While I remained a committed Buddhist, something happened in 2009 that opened my eyes to the great potential of secular, or mainstream, mindfulness. That year Jon Kabat-Zinn visited our offices and talked about his project to present the proven benefits of mindfulness in a modern, scientific framework whose appeal would not be limited to those attracted to an Eastern religion like Buddhism, or necessarily to religion at all.

Since then I have been committed to the great transformative potential of the secular mindfulness path, which I believe is a new and authentic contemplative tradition brilliantly conceived for the modern world. It is my hope that this book, and the Complete Path of Mindfulness it presents, will contribute to the advance of this historic movement. As Jon Kabat-Zinn says, "Mindfulness for all!" There is nothing the world needs more.

There is little that is original in this book. It has all been said before by great teachers of our time, and indeed throughout history. This book is inspired by three figures in particular—Jon Kabat-Zinn, Thich Nhat Hanh, and the Dalai Lama—who have transcended the limits of any one tradition and offered the universal benefits of mindfulness, compassion, and interbeing to all humanity. I am deeply grateful to them for their world-changing wisdom.

I would like to thank my many friends and colleagues over the years at Lion's Roar, where I am now an editor at large. In particular I want to thank Andrea Miller, Rod Meade Sperry, Ben Moore, Beth Wallace, Dan Scott, Lilly Greenblatt, Molly DeShong, Andy Karr, Barry Boyce, and the late Cindy Littlefair. Together we have worked to spread the benefits of meditation, wisdom, and compassion in the modern world. It has been a joy to share this cause with everyone at Lion's Roar.

I would like to recognize the many fine mindfulness teachers and leaders who have generously contributed their meditation instructions and teachings to this book. In their wisdom we see the great strength of today's mindfulness movement.

I would also like to thank everyone at Shambhala Publications, who have been a pleasure to work with, and the Hemera Foundation for their support of this book.

Finally, my heart belongs to my partner, Pam, and our daughter, Pearl. Thank you for the love and goodness you bring into my life, and into the world.